Bisexuality, Religion and Sp

This book brings together the work of an international team of experts investigating the intersection of bisexuality, religion and spirituality. Drawing from disciplines such as sociology, psychology, theology, religious studies and literary studies, it critically examines, both theoretically and empirically, the lived experiences of bisexual people of diverse religious faiths and spiritualities, in the context of the UK, Canada, Lebanon, Turkey, Australia and the USA. As an important and insightful exploration of an under-researched and often misunderstood minority, this book will appeal to scholars across the social sciences with interests in sexuality, religion, spirituality and identity.

Andrew Kam-Tuck Yip is Professor of Sociology at the University of Nottingham, UK. His recent books include *Sexual Identities: A Multi-faith Exploration of Young Adults* (with Sarah-Jane Page), *Cosmopolitan Dharma: Race, Sexuality, and Gender in British Buddhism* (with Sharon Smith and Sally Munt), *Understanding Young Buddhists: Living out Ethical Journeys* (with Sarah-Jane Page), *Critical Pedagogy, Sexuality Education, and Young People* (with Fida Sanjakdar) and *Intersecting Sexuality and Religion: Sociological Perspectives* (with Sarah-Jane Page). He is currently writing, with Carl Ridler, a book provisionally entitled *Intersecting and Contested Identities: Gay and Bisexual Arab Men in Everyday Life.*

Alex Toft is a Research Fellow in the Nottingham Centre for Children, Young People and Families at Nottingham Trent University. His research focuses upon sexuality, gender, disability, spirituality and identity. His publications include *Young, Disabled and LGBT+: Voices, Identities and Intersections* (with Anita Franklin), and he has published in journals such as *Sexualities* and *Journal of LGBT Youth.* He has worked on projects funded by organisations such as the NSPCC and the Fundamental Rights Agency (EU), and recently received British Academy funding to conduct research exploring the negotiation of identity in the lives of young disabled LGBT+ people.

Routledge Studies in the Sociology of Religion

A platform for the latest scholarly research in the sociology of religion, this series welcomes both theoretical and empirical studies that pay close attention to religion in social context. It publishes work that explores the ways in which religions adapt or react to social change and how spirituality lends meaning to people's lives and shapes individual, collective and national identities.

Sacred Marriages
A Discourse Analysis
David Mullins

A Visual Approach to the Study of Religious Orders
Zooming in on Monasteries
Edited by Marcin Jewdokimow and Thomas Quartier

Bisexuality, Religion and Spirituality
Critical Perspectives
Edited by Andrew Kam-Tuck Yip and Alex Toft

For more information about this series, please visit: https://www.routledge.com/Routledge-Studies-in-the-Sociology-of-Religion/book-series/RRSR

Bisexuality, Religion and Spirituality

Critical Perspectives

Edited by
Andrew Kam-Tuck Yip and Alex Toft

Routledge
Taylor & Francis Group
LONDON AND NEW YORK

First published 2020 by Routledge

2 Park Square, Milton Park, Abingdon, Oxon OX14 4RN
605 Third Avenue, New York, NY 10017

Routledge is an imprint of the Taylor & Francis Group, an informa business

First issued in paperback 2021

British Library Cataloguing-in-Publication Data
A catalogue record for this book is available from the British Library

Library of Congress Cataloging-in-Publication Data
Names: Yip, Andrew K. T., 1963- editor. | Toft, Alex, editor.
Title: Bisexuality, religion and spirituality : critical perspectives / edited by Andrew Kam-Tuck Yip and Alex Toft.
Description: Abingdon, Oxon ; New York, NY : Routledge, 2020. |
Series: Routledge studies in the sociology of religion |
Includes bibliographical references and index.
Identifiers: LCCN 2019048488 (print) | LCCN 2019048489 (ebook) |
ISBN 9780367030209 (hardback) | ISBN 9780429019913 (ebook)
Subjects: LCSH: Bisexuality--Religious aspects. |
Bisexuals--Religious life. | Spiritual life.
Classification: LCC BL65.H64 B57 2020 (print) | LCC BL65.H64 (ebook) |
DDC 200.86/63dc23
LC record available at https://lccn.loc.gov/2019048488
LC ebook record available at https://lccn.loc.gov/2019048489

ISBN: 978-0-367-03020-9 (hbk)
ISBN: 978-1-03-217458-7 (pbk)
DOI: 10.4324/9780429019913

Typeset in Times New Roman
by Taylor & Francis Books

Contents

Contributors

Andrew Kam-Tuck Yip [Editor] is Professor of Sociology at the University of Nottingham, UK. His recent books include *Sexual Identities: A Multi-faith Exploration of Young Adults* (2013, with Sarah-Jane Page), *Cosmopolitan Dharma: Race, Sexuality, and Gender in British Buddhism* (2016, with Sharon Smith and Sally Munt), *Understanding Young Buddhists: Living out Ethical Journeys* (2017, with Sarah-Jane Page), *Critical Pedagogy, Sexuality Education, and Young People* (2018, with Fida Sanjakdar) and *Intersecting Sexuality and Religion: Sociological Perspectives* (2020, with Sarah-Jane Page). He is currently writing, with Carl Ridler, a book provisionally entitled *Intersecting and Contested Identities: Gay and Bisexual Arab Men in Everyday Life.*

Alex Toft [Editor] is a Research Fellow in the Nottingham Centre for Children, Young People and Families at Nottingham Trent University. His research focuses upon sexuality, gender, disability, spirituality and identity. His publications include *Young, Disabled and LGBT+: Voices, Identities and Intersections* (2020, with Anita Franklin), and he has published in journals such as *Sexualities* and *Journal of LGBT Youth*. He has worked on projects funded by organisations such as the NSPCC and the Fundamental Rights Agency (EU), and recently received British Academy funding to conduct research exploring the negotiation of identity in the lives of young disabled LGBT+ people.

Shayan Asadi is a BA (Specialized Honours) in Psychology graduate from York University in Canada. He is currently assisting with health research in advance of applying to Clinical Psychology graduate programmes in the near future. He is passionate about researching risk factors for depression, anxiety and suicidality in LGBTQ+ populations.

Douglas Ezzy is Professor of Sociology at the University of Tasmania, Australia. His research is driven by a fascination with how people make meaningful and dignified lives. He is lead investigator on the Australian Research Council Discovery project "Religious Diversity in Australia" and a co-Chief Investigator on a Canadian SSHRC Partnership Grant led by Professor Lori Beaman to examine "Understanding Nonreligion in a

Complex Future". His books include *LGBT Christians* (2017, with Bronwyn Fielder), *Reinventing Church* (2016, with Helen and James Collins), *Sex, Death and Witchcraft* (2014), *Teenage Witches* (2007, with Helen Berger) and *Qualitative Analysis* (2002).

Bronwyn Fielder is a postdoctoral researcher at the University of Tasmania, Australia. Her research focuses on the reproduction of inequalities in society and ways in which these inequalities can be addressed. Her book *Lesbian, Gay, Bisexual and Transgendered Christians: Queer Christians, Authentic Selves* (co-authored with Douglas Ezzy) was published in 2018. She is currently working with a team of researchers on a project funded by the Tasmanian government investigating the experience of LGBT+ individuals in the workplace.

Anita Franklin is a Professor of Childhood Studies at the University of Portsmouth, UK. Her research focuses predominantly on disabled children and young people and their experiences of decision-making, education, health and social care provision, child protection, and issues of inequality and inclusion. She has developed methodologies to support disabled young researchers to be co-leaders in academic studies. Publications include *Young, Disabled and LGBT+: Voices, Identities and Intersections* (2020, with Alex Toft), and she has published in journals including *Sexualities, Journal of Children's Services, Children and Youth Services Review* and *Child and Family Social Work*.

Chris Greenough is Senior Lecturer in Theology and Religion at Edge Hill University, UK. His research focuses on the intersections between gender, sexuality and religion, especially in queer theory and queer studies. His recent books include *Undoing Theology: Life Stories from Non-normative Christians* (2018) and *Queer Theologies: The Basics* (2019). He has also published book chapters and journal articles on queer methods in the study of religion.

Rusi Jaspal is Pro Vice-Chancellor (Research) and Professor of Psychology & Sexual Health at De Montfort University, Leicester, UK and Adjunct Professor at Abo Akademi University, Turku, Finland. He is a Chartered Psychologist and a Fellow of the British Psychological Society. He is the author of *Enhancing Sexual Health, Self-Identity & Wellbeing among Men Who Have Sex with Men: A Guide for Practitioners* (2018) and *The Social Psychology of Gay Men* (2019), and co-editor with Dame Glynis Breakwell of *Identity Process Theory: Identity, Social Action and Social Change* (2014).

Ismaël Maatouk is a dermatologist in Clemenceau Medical Centre in Beirut-Lebanon with a research focus on sexually transmitted infections and sexual health. He is an honorary research fellow at De Montfort University, Leicester, UK. His clinical, educational and research interests are at the interface of sexual health, sexually transmitted diseases and identity. He has lectured at multiple local and international conferences about his research findings concerning sexual health in Lebanon and the Middle East.

Sarah-Jane Page is Senior Lecturer and sociologist of religion based at Aston University, Birmingham, UK. Her research is centred upon the relationship between religion, gender and sexuality, utilising feminist approaches. She has worked on projects examining youth sexualities, clergy motherhood in the Church of England, clergy husbands, qualitative attitudes to gender and sexuality issues, anti-abortion activism and Roman Catholic attitudes to abortion. She has co-published two monographs – *Religious and Sexual Identities* (2013) and *Understanding Young Buddhists* (2017) – both co-authored with Prof. Andrew Yip. She has also published widely in various edited collections and academic journals.

Margaret Robinson is a bisexual and two-spirit scholar from Eskikewa'kik, Nova Scotia, Canada and a member of the Lennox Island First Nation. She conducts community-based research with sexual and gender minority communities and with Indigenous peoples. She has published in *Signs: A Journal of Women in Culture & Society, Journal of Homosexuality, Psychology of Sexual Orientation and Gender Diversity* and *Journal of Bisexuality*. She is Assistant Professor in the Department of Sociology & Social Anthropology at Dalhousie University, and an Affiliate Scientist with the Institute for Mental Health Policy Research at the Centre for Addiction & Mental Health in Toronto, Canada.

Carol A. Shepherd is a Sociology Lecturer at Andover College and Visiting Research Fellow at the University of Winchester, UK. She is also Secretary of the European Forum of LGBT Christian Groups (Amsterdam). Her publications include the monograph *Bisexuality in the Western Christian Church* (2018) and the autobiographical work *119 My Life as a Bisexual Christian* (2016). She is currently working on a pastoral guide to bisexuality, *Bi: The Way*, and has a chapter forthcoming in *Bisexuality in Europe* (2020), edited by Emiel Maliepaard and Renate Baumgartner.

Heather Shipley is Project Manager for the *Nonreligion in a Complex Future* SSHRC Partnership Grant, led by Lori Beaman (University of Ottawa, Canada). Her research focuses on the construction, management and regulation of religion, gender, sexuality and sexual orientation as identity categories in media, legal and public discourse. Her publications include *Identities Under Construction: Religion, Gender and Sexuality among Youth in Canada* (2020, with Pamela Dickey Young), "Sites of Resistance: LGBTQI+ Experiences at Trinity Western University", *Canadian Journal of Law and Society* (2019) and *Young People and the Diversity of (Non)Religious Identities in International Perspective* (2019, co-edited with Elisabeth Arweck).

Cheryl Stobie is an Associate Professor of English Studies at the University of KwaZulu-Natal, South Africa. She has published widely in the area of fictional and autobiographical representations of LGBTQ sexuality in South/African and other texts, both written and visual. Her monograph *Somewhere in the Double Rainbow: Representations of Bisexuality in Post-Apartheid Novels* (2007) and over 30 peer-reviewed articles, chapters in books and other work focus on various representations of queer, mainly bisexuality. She is one of the editors of *Current Writing: Text and Reception in Southern Africa*. Her most recent project focuses on representations of precarity in South/African literature.

Pamela Dickey Young is Professor, School of Religion, Queen's University, Kingston, Canada. Her research concerns the intersections of religion, sex, gender and public policy. Her publications include *Identities Under Construction: Religion, Gender and Sexuality Among Youth in Canada* (2020, with Heather Shipley), *Religion, Sex and Politics: Christian Churches and Same-Sex Marriage in Canada* (2012), *Women and Religious Traditions*, 3rd edition (2015, edited with Leona Anderson), "Informal Sex Education: Forces that Shape Youth Identities and Practices", in *Critical Pedagogy, Sexuality Education and Young People*, edited by Andrew Yip and Fida Sanjakdar (2018).

1 Bisexuality, religion and spirituality

Instigating a dialogue

Alex Toft and Andrew Kam-Tuck Yip

Introduction

The purpose of this volume is to instigate a dialogue; a much-needed dialogue. Yes, we need to talk about bisexuality; more specifically, bisexuality as a lived experience and an identity in religious and spiritual spaces. Indisputably, the last three decades have witnessed the proliferation of literature on non-normative sexualities, which is a highly encouraging development. However, bisexuality is very often an appendage in this dialogue that, in reality, privileges homosexuality. Research that examines bisexuality in its own right is a minority endeavour. This scarcity is even more evident and striking in research specifically on bisexuality in relation to religion and spirituality. For example, the 20-year-old *Journal of Bisexuality*, which has been playing a pivotal role in bisexuality scholarship, rarely publishes articles on this topic, reflecting the acute paucity of research in this area.

Against this backdrop, we decided to turn the spotlight on bisexuality, religion and spirituality by inviting an international team of scholars with expertise in different disciplines – sociology, psychology, theology, religious studies and literary studies – to offer their critical perspectives. Across ten contributions, the authors examine this topic theoretically and empirically within the context of the UK, Canada, Lebanon, Turkey, Australia and the USA. Not surprisingly, the vast majority of the research in this area – as with that pertaining to homosexuality, religion and spirituality – concentrates on Christianity. This is reflected in this volume too, but there are also contributions that bring Sufism, Buddhism, Islam, Paganism, Judaism and non-religion into the conversation.

In the remainder of this chapter, we shall discuss briefly two themes that unify the key concerns of the contributions in this volume: *bisexuality and its discontents* and *mixing bisexuality with religion and spirituality: muddling the waters?* It is not our intention to offer an exhaustive literature review on these two themes. The contributions in this volume collectively have done a remarkable job in this respect. They all offer a critical engagement with extant literature, aided ably by the lived experiences, texts and cultures they study. Our aim here is to highlight some key texts and issues. After that, we shall introduce the contributions, followed by some concluding remarks, reflecting on the research journey ahead.

Bisexuality and its discontents

As we have asserted above, research that examines bisexuality in its own right is a minority endeavour (for a comprehensive review, see e.g. Anderson and McCormack, 2016; Barker et al., 2012; Klesse, 2018; Monro, 2015; Monro, Hines and Osborne, 2017). One principal theme of this corpus of research literature is the pervasiveness of prejudice against – and, indeed, fear of (i.e. biphobia) – bisexuality and bisexual people in heterosexual as well as lesbian and gay communities. All the contributions in this volume echo this theme. This scenario is perpetuated by a deep-rooted misunderstanding of bisexuality as a distinct human sexuality, in our culture which is so fundamentally constituted by monosexism as well as gender and sexual binarism. We have argued elsewhere (Toft and Yip, 2018) that monosexism is an interweaving and interlocking system of meanings and practices which stipulates that an individual's sexual self-identification must exclusively and consistently position on one identity, namely 'heterosexual' or 'homosexual'. This construction of human sexuality perpetuates the hegemony of the hetero/homo dichotomy, and an individual's position on either side of the binary. Consequently, bisexual people's emotional attachment and erotic attraction to both genders de-stabilises and disrupts the gender specificity and exclusivity that monosexism obstinately demands. That is deeply troubling and intimidating to many people, which explains the circulation and reinscription of stereotypes about bisexual people as being 'confused', 'undecided' or 'going through a phase' in terms of their sexual identity development. In terms of relationship formation, bisexual people have been routinely and suspiciously perceived as 'promiscuous', 'hypersexed', 'incapable of monogamy' and 'uncommitted to coupledom' (e.g. Klesse, 2007, 2018; Monro, 2015). Klesse rightly asserts that, 'Bisexuality has assumed a precarious position in western discourses on sexuality, continuously evoked as a core element of sexual knowledge and/or theory yet at the same time disavowed as a feature of a mature personality' (2018: 1361).

One phenomenon thrives vis-à-vis this stigmatising backdrop – bisexual erasure: the systematic invalidation of bisexuality and obliteration of the voices and visibility of bisexual people in everyday language and social relations. This erasure operates not only in heterosexual spaces, but also in lesbian and gay spaces (e.g. Gonzalez et al., 2017; Maliepaard, 2017; Van Alphen, 2019; Yoshino, 2000), eroding positive and accurate 'bisexual display' (Hartman, 2013; Hartman-Linck, 2014). Within this context, it is not surprising that research overwhelmingly reports that bisexuals, compared to their heterosexual and lesbian and gay counterparts, experience a lower level of sexual and mental health, and wellbeing (e.g. Flanders, 2016; Friedman et al., 2014). Chapters 9 to 11 of this volume speak to this theme, offering contrasting observations and findings.

Mixing bisexuality, religion and spirituality: muddling the waters?

As we have argued above – and so have several of the contributions in this volume – in spite of the expansion of research on religion and non-normative sexualities, bisexuality is conspicuously under-represented. Reflecting the current state of play, this under-representation is demonstrated in several extensive volumes on sexuality and religion such as Boisvert and Daniel-Hughes (2016), Hunt (2015), Hunt and Yip (2012) and Taylor and Snowdon (2014). Indeed, research in this field that exclusively examines bisexuality, religion and spirituality is few and far between, with notable exceptions such as recent works by Levy and Harr (2018), Robinson (2015), Shepherd (2018) and Toft (2012, 2014). In many ways, this is unsurprising. In the contestations of non-normative sexualities and religion, high-profile issues that capture public and research attention are same-sex marriage and gay men in leadership positions, as evidenced in the perennial debate that has been threatening to fracture the Anglican Communion with 85 million members globally (e.g. Brittain and McKinnon, 2018; McKinnon and Brittain, 2020). Nonetheless, this signifies the prominence of homosexuality in such a discourse, and the continued erasure of bisexuality within it.

We would also contend that, especially in religious spaces, this scenario is predicated on the erroneous assumption and expectation that bisexual people, compared to their lesbian and gay counterparts, have a 'choice', i.e. choosing heterosexuality (e.g. Lingwood, 2012; Shepherd, 2018). This evinces not only the power of heteronormativity, but also that of monosexism, as we have argued above and elsewhere (Toft and Yip, 2018). The potency of monosexism is strengthened by conterminous cultural ideologies such as 'compulsory coupledom' (Wilkinson, 2013) and compulsory monogamy (as a marker of commitment and faithfulness). In the popular – but erroneous – imagination, bisexuality is inherently antithetical to such cultural and religious ideals.

This is particularly axiomatic within Abrahamic religious spaces, leading to experiences of tension and conflict amongst bisexual religious actors (e.g. Levy and Harr, 2018; Shepherd, 2018). However, other religious and spiritual spaces such as Paganism and New Age seem to offer a more conducive and nurturing environment for the exploration and accommodation of ambiguity and fluidity that bisexuality imbues (e.g. Browne and Dinnie, 2010; Dinnie and Browne, 2011; Ezzy, 2014; Fielder and Ezzy, 2017; Robinson, 2003). Contributions in this volume certainly affirm this narrative. While bisexual erasure is evident within institutional Christianity, Islam and Judaism (see Chapters 2 to 7; Chapters 9 to 11), it is less so in Buddhism, Sufism, Paganism and non-religion (as a belief system), enabling bisexual individuals to accommodate their sexual and religious identities more harmoniously (see Chapters 2, 4, 5 and 8).

Overall, this underlines an important message: we must not homogenise religion, and we must recognise that the intersection between religion and (bi) sexuality generates multifarious rather than monolithic outcomes. Furthermore, it is also crucial to be mindful of intrareligious differences and interreligious similarities in our exploration of this complex intersection (e.g. Page and Shipley, forthcoming; Page and Yip, 2020; Yip, 2015; Young and Shipley, 2020).

Introducing the chapters

In our effort to offer a variety of critical perspectives on bisexuality, religion and spirituality, we deliberately solicited some contributors outside of our own field of sociology. Therefore, while Chapters 2 to 6 are primarily sociological in nature, there are also contributions from theology (Chapter 7), literary studies (Chapter 8) and psychology (Chapters 9 to 11). Using a variety of methodologies and from a variety of academic disciplines, the ten contributions explore the two themes we have highlighted above in diverse geographical and cultural contexts.

The book begins with sociological considerations. In Chapter 2, Heather Shipley and Pamela Dickey Young examine the identity constructions and negotiations of young bisexual adults in Canada. They explore the intersections of identities in order to best understand how bisexuality is constructed in relation to the young adults' other fluid identities. Importantly, the chapter compares the bisexual respondents to the rest of the non-bisexual sample in order to understand the differences and similarities in experience. The young adults consider bisexuality a poor identifier to accurately describe their lives, and this is resisted for a variety of reasons, including bisexuality's reliance upon binary gender categories and perceived negative stereotypes about bisexuality. However, bisexuality is ultimately used as an identifier for simplicity and for the benefit of others' understanding. The chapter shows that the respondents feel that young adulthood is a period in their lives in which identities are perhaps less restricted and they feel able to challenge gender and sexual boundaries within religious traditions.

In Chapter 3, Alex Toft and Anita Franklin focus upon the lives of young people, with an exploration into the intersection of youth, bisexuality, disability and Christianity in the life of one young person. The chapter represents a unique exploration of a number of contested identities, and sheds light on how such identities are negotiated. Using the life-story of Abigail, the chapter shows how she worked to fit her faith with her sexual identity, practising an individualism amongst a culture of discrimination bound up with misconceptions about her disability and her sexuality. Although her experiences of religious life have been largely negative, Abigail highlights the important role Christianity plays in her life. Abigail's story uncovers the prevailing ableism and heteronormativity which have denied her access to support, but most importantly the validation of her identity.

Andrew Kam-Tuck Yip and Sarah-Jane Page explore, in Chapter 4, how, as a minority within and minority, young bisexual adults experience bisexual erasure within some religious traditions (primarily Abrahamic) but much less so in others, such as Buddhism. The chapter examines the negotiations young people undertake in relation to their sexual, religious and social lives. It shows how sexual and religious identifications should not be understood in a monolithic fashion. The chapter maps stories of 'conflict and tension' and 'accommodation and adaptation' in order to capture the complexity of the young bisexual people's lives.

In Chapter 5, Douglas Ezzy and Bronwyn Fielder introduce Paganism into the dialogue, by examining the reasons why Christianity struggles to embrace bisexuality, compared to Paganism. Through the analytic lens of liminality, they argue that as Paganism focuses upon rituals, involving erotic, bisexual and hermaphroditic deities, it is able to embrace the ambiguity and complexity that encapsulates bisexuality. Christianity, however, with its emphasis on belief and sincerity, struggles to develop a constructive understanding of bisexuality. The chapter demonstrates that different religions and spiritualities create varied nature of the rituals and structure of liminality, and that significantly informs their responses to bisexuality.

Alex Toft, in Chapter 6, presents findings from a British mixed-method study exploring identity in the lives of bisexual Christians. The chapter attempts to bring together the key themes and findings in relation to the spiritual and sexual lives of the research participants, and suggests that it is most fruitful to explore the findings in terms of an intersectional approach in order to understand bisexual Christianity more fully. Toft suggests that the participants strenuously re-shape their religious lives, reflecting an individualisation of faith. He further argues that separating religious and sexual lives for analysis is over-simplification, as spirituality and bisexuality inform and interact with each other. The chapter ultimately encourages work which is mindful of this and embraces bisexual Christianity with its complexities and ambiguities.

Chris Greenough, in Chapter 7, presents the story of Sam, a Christian, gender-fluid bisexual person. The chapter uses sexual storytelling to explore bisexuality and how identity can be understood. Greenough asserts that queer theology can help us understand that sexuality and religious faith are not fixed. By embracing 'identification', recognising the processual, mutable, therefore unfinished nature of identity, we can understand that sexuality and faith are ongoing processes. Queer theology, he argues, is a way to pull plural identifications together whilst accepting such ambiguities. Using the theoretical and theological framework of Althaus-Reid in the analysis of Sam's story, Greenough shows how sexuality and faith are not fixed and rigid constructs.

In Chapter 8, Cheryl Stobie presents a queer feminist reading of Elif Shafak's celebrated novel *The Forty Rules of Love* (2010) in order to explore bisexuality and Sufism. Stobie contends that the novel – which interlaces the thirteenth-century narrative of Sufi companions Rumi and Shams (both married men) with a contemporary heterosexual love story – creates a productive platform to position the theoretical lens of bisexuality. The chapters posits that bisexuality and Sufism can be conceptualised as unorthodox, fluid and anti-binarist. The chapter argues that the novel successfully visualises a queer-friendly, mystical and emancipatory version of Islam that embraces for the socially marginalised.

Chapter 9 leads the volume to the consideration of psychological perspectives in the study of bisexuality, religion and spirituality. In this chapter, Ismaël Maatouk and Rusi Jaspal apply social representations theory and identity process theory to examine identity construction and wellbeing in the lives of bisexual Lebanese men. Although empirical work specifically on Lebanese bisexual men is currently non-existent, Maatouk and Jaspal have offered some invaluable hypotheses and insights on how dominant religious and cultural norms in Lebanon are bisexual-unfriendly, and there is a need to offer social support for bisexual men who often remain hidden because of fear.

In Chapter 10, Carol A. Shepherd examines depression and suicidality in bisexual Christians in the UK and the USA. Shepherd asserts that bisexual people experience a large degree of social stigma, resulting in both identity erasure and identity degradation, which is significantly detrimental to their health and wellbeing. This is evident in the sweeping erasure of bisexuality within pastoral practices and liturgical resources in Christian institutions. She cautions that the current situation is likely to continue on both sides of the Atlantic, where bisexuality is largely overshadowed by gay, lesbian and, increasingly, transgender issues.

Margaret Robinson and Shayan Asadi, in Chapter 11, draw upon data from a large-scale project in Ontario, Canada. The authors examine the impact of being religious and bisexual in relation to anxiety, depression and social support. Religiosity was not found to be a risk factor for the participants, as it did not impact upon mental health. This appears to disconfirm research which has highlighted the lack of support for religious bisexual people, and this negatively impacts upon their wellbeing. However, Robinson and Asadi suggest that such a finding is possibly a result of secularity or individualised faith which distances bisexual Christians from potentially anxiety-inducing situations.

Concluding remarks

In their extensive historiographical and textual study on the representation of bisexuality in sexuality studies in the UK and USA between 1970 and 2015, Monro, Hines and Osborne (2017) convincingly demonstrate the existence of bisexual erasure in social sciences. Their analysis reveals that, during the 45-year period, sexualities scholarship consistently overlooked and marginalised bisexuality. The contributing factors to this scenario includes 'the heterosexist nature of the literature, the impact of gay and lesbian-focused identity politics, and queer deconstructionism' (2017: 663). Appropriately, they call for the mainstreaming of bisexuality into this scholarship.

We join their call, and that of other scholars (e.g. Monro, 2015, 2018; Page and Shipley, forthcoming) for research that investigates the voices and lived experiences of bisexuals in their own right. The specific focus we place on bisexuality, religion and spirituality in this volume is one step towards that goal. As the contributions collectively attest, such research engenders insights that enrich our understanding of how dominant discourses such as monosexism, 'compulsory coupledom' and compulsory monogamy – often religiously legitimised – consolidate and perpetuate the misunderstanding, stigmatisation and erasure of bisexuality. This could generate tension and conflict which undermine the spiritual, sexual and mental health of religious and spiritual bisexual people. Nonetheless, as this volume has also demonstrated, religious and spiritual bisexual people, as sexual and religious actors, also creatively carve out bisexual-friendly meanings, theologies, practices and spaces that empower them to integrate their sexual and religious identities.

To go even further in this journey, we call for more research to interrogate, in a more nuanced way, the intersection between bisexuality and different types of belief systems. We would include in this non-religion and unbelief (e. g. Lee, 2015), not as an unproblematised 'Other' of religion, but as a belief system in its own right which is meaning-generating and influential of individuals' worldview and social positioning, including the management of their sexuality. In this endeavour, we also need to bring into the conversation more non-Christian perspectives and voices, including those that emanate from non-institutional spaces. Although many of their pieces do not aim to be academic in nature, *Blessed Bi Spirit* (Kolodny, 2000) and *Sexuality, Religion and the Sacred* (Hutchins and Williams, 2012) are much-needed anthologies that have performed this task outstandingly.

Equally, we should also pay attention to voices and identities that signify an amalgamation of diverse religious, spiritual and even secular sources, rather than discrete and exclusive labels and categories (e.g. Ursic, 2014). Young people, in their construction of ethical framework and navigation of everyday life, are particularly inclined to this formulation of hyphenated identities (e.g. Christian-Buddhist-Pagan, humanist-Muslim), as they place emphasis on the utility and functionality of such diverse sources rather than their theological essence and 'purity' (e.g. Madge, Hemming and Stenson, 2014; Page and Yip, 2017; Yip and Page, 2013; Young and Shipley, 2020). Yes, it is complex. But it is precisely in this complexity and 'messiness' that richness resides, waiting for perceptive scholars to induce its unfolding. Several of the contributions in this volume have addressed these issues. We need more.

As Udis-Kessler fittingly reminds us, experiences of bisexual people offer 'a model for life outside the boundaries of destructive hierarchical dualisms' (2000: 15). Dualisms or binaries of different kinds – for example, white/black, men/women, heterosexual/homosexual – assume the superiority of the former, and the inferiority of the latter. They force us to embrace an 'either–or' existence. They are, in essence, calamitous and insidious, limiting our consciousness and experience of the complexity, intricacy and multiplicity of humanity. We believe that, bisexuality – with its queering spirt of liminality and fluidity – can serve as a catalyst to liberate us from the shackles of sexual and gender binarism, and help us envision a world beyond binary that celebrates the kaleidoscope of humanity. It sounds like a dream. But who says we can't dare to dream?

References

Anderson, E. and McCormack, M. 2016. *The Changing Dynamics of Bisexual Men's Lives: Social Research Perspectives.* Basel: Springer.

Barker, M., Richards, C., Jones, R., Bowes-Cotton, H., Plowman, T., Yockney, J. and Morgan, M. 2012. *The Bisexual Report: Bisexual Inclusion in LGBT Equality and Diversity,* Milton Keynes: The Open University. [Online] Available at: http://oro.open.ac.uk/52881/1/The%20BisexualityReport%20Feb.2012_0.pdf [accessed 1 May 2019]

Barker, M., Yockney, J., Richards, C., Jones, R., Bowes-Catton, H. and Plowman, T., 2012. Guidelines for researching and writing about bisexuality. *Journal of Bisexuality,* 12(3), 376–392.

Boisvert, D.L. and Daniel-Hughes, C. 2016. *The Bloomsbury Reader in Religion, Sexuality and Gender.* London: Bloomsbury.

Brittain, C.C. and McKinnon, A. 2018. *Anglican Communion at a Crossroads: The Crises of a Global Church.* University Park: Penn State University Press.

Browne, K. and Dinnie, E. 2010. New Age spiritualities: Findhorn and the sexual self, in *Queer Spiritual Spaces: Sexuality and Sacred Places,* edited by K. Browne, S.R. Munt and A.K.T. Yip. Farnham: Ashgate, 169–198.

Dinnie, E. and Browne, K. 2011. Creating a sexual self in heteronormative space: Integrations and imperatives amongst spiritual seekers at the Findhorn Community. *Sociological Research Online,* 16(1). [Online] Available at: http://www.socresonline.org.uk/16/1/7.html [accessed 12 July 2019].

Ezzy, D. 2014. *Sex, Death and Witchcraft.* London: Bloomsbury.

Fielder, B. and Ezzy , D. 2017. *Lesbian, Gay, Bisexual and Transgender Christians: Queer Christians, Authentic Selves.* London: Bloomsbury.

Flanders, C.E. 2016. Bisexuality, social identity, and well-being: An exploratory study. *Sexualities,* 19(5/6), 497–516.

Friedman, M.R., Dodge, B., Schick, V., Herbenick, D., Hubach Randolph, D., Bowling, J., Goncalves, G., Krier, S. and Reece, M. 2014. From bias to bisexual health disparities: Attitudes toward bisexual men and women in the United States. *LGBT Health* 1(4), 309–318.

Gonzalez, K.A., Ramirez, J.L. and Galupo, M.P. 2017. "I was and still am": Narratives of bisexual marking in the# StillBisexual campaign. *Sexuality & Culture,* 21(2), 493–515.

Hartman, J.E. 2013. Creating a bisexual display: Making bisexuality visible. *Journal of Bisexuality,* 13(1), 39–62.

Hartman-Linck, J.E. 2014. Keeping bisexuality alive: Maintaining bisexual visibility in monogamous relationships. *Journal of Bisexuality,* 14(2), 177–193.

Hunt, S. 2015. *Religion and LGBTQ Sexualities: Critical Essays.* Farnham: Ashgate.

Hunt, S. and Yip, A. K. T. 2012. *The Ashgate Research Companion to Contemporary Religion and Sexuality.* Farnham: Ashgate.

Hutchins, L. and Williams, H. Sharif. 2012. *Sexuality, Religion and the Sacred: Bisexual, Pansexual and Polysexual Perspectives.* London: Routledge.

Klesse, C. 2007. *The Spectre of Promiscuity: Gay Male and Bisexual Non-monogamies and Polyamories.* Aldershot: Ashgate.

Klesse, C. 2018. Dancing on the waves or being washed away? Representations of bisexualities in Liquid Modernity. *Sexualities*, 21(8), 1360–1367.

Kolodny, D.R. 2000. *Blessed Bi Spirit: Bisexual People of Faith.* London: Continuum.

Lee, L. 2015. *Recognising the Non-religious: Reimagining the Secular.* Oxford: Oxford University Press.

Levy, D.L. and Harr, J. 2018. "I never felt like there was a place for me": Experiences of bisexual and pansexual individuals with a Christian upbringing. *Journal of Bisexuality*, 18(2): 186–205.

Lingwood, S. 2012. Bi Christian Unitarian: A theology of transgression, in *Sexuality, Religion and the Sacred: Bisexual, Pansexual and Polysexual Perspectives*, edited by L. Hutchins and H. Sharif Williams. London: Routledge, 45–53.

Madge, N., Hemming, P.J. and Stenson, K. 2014. *Youth on Religion: The Development, Negotiation and Impact of Faith and Non-faith Identity.* London: Routledge.

Maliepaard, E., 2017. Bisexuality in the Netherlands: Connecting bisexual passing, communities, and identities. *Journal of Bisexuality*, 17(3), 325–348.

McKinnon, A. and Brittain, C. 2020. Anglican Disputes over Sexuality in the Intersection of Global Power Relations: Accounts from African Church Leaders, in *Intersecting Religion and Sexuality: Critical Perspectives*, edited by S. Page and A. K.T. Yip. Leiden: Brill.

Monro, S. 2015. *Bisexuality: Identities, Politics, and Theories.* Basingstoke: Palgrave Macmillan.

Monro, S. 2018. Sexualities studies: The last 20 years. *Sexualities*, 21(8), 1229–1233.

Monro, S., Hines, S. and Osborne, A., 2017. Is bisexuality invisible? A review of sexualities scholarship 1970–2015. *The Sociological Review*, 65(4), 663–681.

Page, S. and Shipley, H. Forthcoming. *Religions and Sexualities: Theories, Themes and Methodologies.* Abingdon: Routledge.

Page, S. and Yip, A.K.T. 2017. *Understanding Young Buddhists: Living out Ethical Journeys.* Leiden: Brill.

Page, S. and Yip, A.K.T. 2020. *Intersecting Religion and Sexuality: Sociological Perspectives.* Leiden: Brill.

Robinson, M. 2003. Bisexual women and lesbians: What will keep us in our churches? *Making Waves: An Ecumenical Feminist Journal*, 3(2), 30–32.

Robinson, M. 2015. Bisexual people, in *The Oxford Handbook of Theology, Sexuality and Gender*, edited by A. Thatcher. Oxford: Oxford University Press, 640–656.

Shepherd, C.A. 2018. *Bisexuality and the Western Christian Church: The Damage of Silence.* London: Palgrave Macmillan

Taylor, Y. and Snowdon, R. 2014. *Queering Religion, Religious Queers.* New York: Routledge.

Toft, A. 2012. Bisexuality and Christianity: Negotiating disparate identities in church life, in *The Ashgate Research Companion to Contemporary Religion and Sexuality*, edited by S. Hunt and A.K.T. Yip. Farnham: Ashgate, 189–203.

Toft, A. 2014. Re-imagining bisexuality and Christianity: The negotiation of Christianity in the lives of bisexual women and men. *Sexualities*, 17(5–6), 546–564.

Toft, A. and Yip, A.K.T. 2018. Intimacy negotiated: The management of relationships and the construction of personal communities in the lives of bisexual women and men. *Sexualities*, 21(1–2), 233–250.

Udis-Kessler, A. 2000. The holy leper and the bisexual Christian, in *Blessed Bi Spirit: Bisexual People of Faith*, edited by D.R. Kolodny. London: Continuum, 11–16.

Ursic, E. 2014. Bi the way: Rethinking categories of religious identity. *The International Journal of Religion and Spirituality in Society*, 3(4). https://doi.org/10.18848/2154-8633/CGP/v03i04 [Accessed 2 August 2019]

Van Alphen, E.C.J. 2019. Erasing bisexual identity: The visibility and invisibility of bisexuality as a sexual identity in the Dutch homosexual movement, 1946–1972. *Journal of Homosexuality*, 64(2): 273–288

Wilkinson, E. 2013. Learning to love again: 'Broken families', citizenship and the state promotion of coupledom. *Geoforum*, 49, 206–213.

Yip, A.K.T. 2015. When religion meets sexuality: Two tales of intersection, in *Religion and Sexuality: Diversity and the Limits of Tolerance*, edited by P. Dickey Young, H. Shipley and T. Trothen. Vancouver: University of British Columbia Press, 119–140.

Yip, A.K.T. and Page, S. 2013. *Religious and Sexual Identities: A Multi-faith Exploration of Young Adults*. Farnham: Ashgate.

Yoshino, K. 2000. The epistemic contract of bisexual erasure. *Stanford Law Review*, 52(2): 353–461.

Young, P. Dickey and Shipley, H. 2020. *Identities under Construction: Religion, Gender and Sexuality among Youth in Canada*. Montreal: McGill-Queen's University Press.

2 Bisexuality, (non)religion and spirituality in Canadian young adults

Heather Shipley and Pamela Dickey Young

Introduction

At a time when cognizance of the landscape regarding religious diversity and religious difference is increasing, knowledge about the fluidity of (non)religious[1] and spiritual identities is still working to catch up. This is also the case for research and knowledge on bisexuality, let alone bisexuality, (non)religion and spiritual identities at the intersections.[2] Further analysis of the categories of (non)religion and spirituality is warranted, as we argue elsewhere (Shipley and Young, 2014; Young and Shipley, 2020) with particular attention to intersectionality, gender and sexuality.

This chapter explores the lived experiences and reflections of participants in the Religion, Gender and Sexuality among Youth in Canada (RGSY)[3] project who self-identified as bisexual with particular reference to the relationship of bisexual identity and (non)religious/spiritual identities. Comparing our bisexual respondents to the full cohort of RGSY respondents who do not identify as bisexual (i.e. those who identify as heterosexual, homosexual, gay, lesbian and so forth), we will consider the similarities and differences evidenced in our bisexual cohort and reflect on future directions in the study of bisexuality, (non)religion and spirituality.

Research on young people, religion and spirituality is rapidly expanding; the multiple ways that young people understand, negotiate and construct their (non)religion and spiritual identities lends itself to new ways of understanding the categories and identity development across intersecting identities (Beyer and Ramji, 2013; Gareau et al., 2018; Yip and Page, 2013, among others). As we consider the young people in this study who identify as bisexual in relation to the other young adults who do not identify as bisexual in the study, we will explore the ways this minority sexual identity can still be experienced as a disadvantage within a group of young adults whose openness to sexual diversity is quite pronounced (Shipley, 2019; Shipley and Young, 2017). The majority of participants in the RGSY project offer nuanced reflections on gender and sexual diversity, express acceptance towards a range of sexualities and sexual behaviours (as long as they are consensual), and are well versed in the queer and feminist literature that informs contemporary understanding of gender and sexual identity fluidity.

Non-heterosexual participants, including bisexual participants, in our study detail homophobic experiences, fear of reprisal for expressions of gender non-conformity and (for some) describe their sexuality as a source of stress in their lives. Although these experiences are not reflective of the overall attitude of participants in our research sample, they are experiences that non-heterosexual participants describe as occurring across a variety of sites – family, school, public spaces (Shipley and Young, 2017; Young and Shipley, 2020).

In our data we see that though our respondents overall express support for LGBTQI+ groups and individuals and a desire for religious organizations to become more accepting of gender and sexual diversity, the experience of harmful stereotypes of gender and sexual diversity are still pervasive, creating negative responses and further complexities in the negotiation and construction of identity. With this framework in mind, we explore the following questions: what are the constraints that young people see within the category of bisexuality; how does that connect to religious teachings and religious acceptance of sexual diversity; and does that subsequently influence their willingness (or resistance) to identify with the term?

Youth is a time to explore, question and construct identity (Collins-Mayo and Dandelion, 2010; Freitas, 2008; Smith and Smith, 2009). In general, participants in the RGSY project demonstrate that their relationship to (non)religious, gendered and sexual identities is fluid, shifting and negotiated – they inherit traditions and expectations from their families but do not feel bound by those beliefs or practices. (Non)religious and spiritual identities are deeply connected to their sense of self and are also seen as behavioural practices, for example connected to family; to attending church when home at Christmas but identifying as non-religious and otherwise not engaging in religious practices; to picking and choosing from different ideological and spiritual teachings to build a spiritual-but-not-religious identity that conforms with contemporary society; to wishing that their atheist identity would garner the same respect that religious identities garner; and so on. Identities are complex and nuanced, they are under construction and are negotiated in relation to familial ties, personal experience and their 'imagined futures' (Page et al., 2012).

For bisexual participants, these understandings are further impacted by their sexual identity. As bisexuality is a category that is less understood, often overlooked, and frequently seen to be 'confused' rather than defined (Carillo and Hoffman, 2018; Toft, 2012), bisexual participants in this study describe the complexity of the process of understanding their own sexuality and reflect on how that relates to their religious, nonreligious and spiritual identities.

In this chapter we will canvass some of the current literature on bisexuality and (non)religion. We will then look specifically at how those in our study who identify as bisexual also talk about their (non)religious identities. Our findings are presented first quantitatively, reflecting comparatively on our respondents as a whole and those who identified as bisexual in terms of identifiers and practices. We then consider the ways our bisexual respondents elaborate and complicate their identities, in their own words. Finally, we offer some concluding remarks on the intersections of bisexuality and (non)religion.

Research on (non)religion, spirituality, bisexuality

Critical research in the areas of gender and sexuality studies continues to challenge the rigidity of normative expectations regarding gender and sexuality (Butler, 1993; Foucault, 1978), resisting dominant assumptions that there are inherently 'natural' aspects to maleness or femaleness (Rubin, 1994) that determine how one then portrays womanhood or manhood (Irigaray, 1984), or to sexual preferences and practices. Feminist critiques of gender binaries interrogate performative expectations (Butler, 1993; Halberstam 1998; Irigaray, 1984) as well as the expectation of 'compulsory heterosexuality' (Rich, 1980) that follows from these expected social norms. The expectation of heterosexuality is dominant within many religious traditions. It also bleeds into so-called secular norms through policy, law, education and the representations of what 'acceptable' couples, families and relationships 'look like' (Cossman and Ryder, 2001; Valverde, 2006).

There is a growing body of research on diverse religious and sexual identities as lived and experienced, as our chapter has widely referenced. When religion is part of the discussion, much research to date has focused on the ways religion (typified often by majoritarian religiosity) restricts and constrains sexuality and sexual identities, prescribing monogamous, heterosexual pairings intended towards procreating (Duggan, 2002; Valverde, 2006). This rigid conceptualization of the relationship between religion and sexual diversity derives from professional, doctrinal approaches to religion – the notion that 'religion' is something that is controlled by a select few, frequently religious authority figures, and must be understood within textual limitations of the teachings of the tradition (Strahn, 2014). However, research has long shown that religion as it is lived is always fluid, contextualized, contested and nuanced (Davie 2014; Ehrman, 2003; McGuire, 2008). Rarely do religious individuals see themselves as obliged to adhere only to strict religious teachings.

Sociology of religion and critiques of the categorization of religion (and secularism) point to the misappropriation, oversimplification and subsequent limitations in our understanding of the diversity of (non)religious, spiritual, secular experiences (Arnal and McCutcheon, 2012; Arweck et al., 2013; Beckford, 2003; Cragun, 2016; Lee, 2015; Wallis, 2014; Woodhead, 2013). Unpacking the historical assumptions embedded in 'religion' as a category offers insight into ideas about what is seen to count as real religion and what is denigrated or denied status – and how these valuations impact on the treatment of diverse traditions, beliefs and practices in multiple spheres, such as law and policy (Beaman, 2012; Berger, 2015; Sullivan, 2018).

Though understanding about the diversity of (non)religion is increasing, the same cannot be said for bisexuality, which is still an understudied topic (Toft, 2012, 2014). General assumptions about bisexuality – i.e. that it is not a 'real' sexual identity, but rather a confused or interim identity – continue to misrepresent and deny the experiences of bisexuals within an already heterosexually privileged environment (Carillo and Hoffman, 2018; Diamond, 2003). Kenji Yoshino (2000: 353) argues that the sociological absence of bisexuality in the landscape of research on sexuality and sexual diversity is explained by the 'overlapping political interests' heterosexuals and homosexuals have in keeping bisexuality invisible. Bisexual erasure is therefore not about the actual population of bisexuals in a given social group but rather is the result of social erasure (Yoshino, 2000: 357). Misunderstanding about bisexuality, in addition to assumptions about the privilege of 'straight passing' for bisexual individuals, has led to several consequences in the lives of those who identify as bisexual – and further, it has impacted on the research available on bisexuality. Where bisexuals are seen to be able to transcend discrimination and disadvantage via their heterosexual relationships (see, for example, Rehaag, 2009), a consequence of this assumption is that bisexuality as an identity is not seen as invoking the same concern that other sexual minority identities – such as lesbian, gay and trans – do. This kind of erasure perpetuates the challenges experienced by bisexual individuals, whose lives are understudied and underrepresented in research on sexuality and sexual minority identities, and subsequently who continue to face personal, political and legal obstacles as a result of their sexual identity (Monro, 2015; Rehaag, 2009; Toft and Yip, 2018).

Further, bisexuality as a fluid sexual identity is frequently paired with a resistance to 'naming' oneself bisexual which can lead to self-identifications as straight, with bisexual (or same-sex) attractions and engagements (Carrillo and Hoffman, 2018). Casual homophobia, including persistent tropes about prison sex,[4] contributes to the misunderstood, resistant and negative perceptions about bisexuality as an identity and places self-identification as bisexual within a fairly hostile environment. Perceptions that bisexual individuals can also 'straight pass' to avoid discrimination and harassment exacerbates the feelings of identity negation and misconstrues bisexual attraction as strategically selected (Hemmings, 2002; Pfeffer, 2014).

In a shifting landscape, such as in much of the Global North, where public policy, law and general public opinions have moved towards more accepting and nuanced understanding of sexuality and sexual diversity, there is still considerable research that demonstrates attitudes among adolescent men continues to stigmatize homosexuality (Anderson, 2014; Weeks, 2007). Several studies have demonstrated that sexual flexibility among young adults (particularly males) relies on resistance to adopting categories such as homosexual or bisexual, preferring instead to identify as 'mostly heterosexual' (Savin-Williams and Vrangalova, 2013; Scoats et al., 2018) or, as will be discussed momentarily, as MSM (men who have sex with men). Within this diverse landscape, the ways young men, in particular, reflect on and construct their sexual identities (beyond heterosexuality) warrants increasing analysis.

Resistance to rigid categories is evidenced across our full cohort of respondents. Young people do not feel obliged to limit themselves to narrow or restrictive notions about identity categories in general, or religion, gender and sexuality specific to our project. Instead, they challenge the boundaries of the categories and the expectations embedded in those categories, be they social or religiously prescribed expectations. The young people in our study are comfortable discarding aspects of (non)religious or spiritual traditions that do not reflect their own commitments and values; they are willing to reject the stereotypes associated with gender and sexuality, insisting on more contemporary frameworks in our understanding of identity (Shipley and Young, 2017; Young and Shipley, 2014, 2020).

Our bisexual respondents, as part of this trend, however, adopt the 'bisexual' label, while at the same time resisting it. The resistance is grounded in wanting to avoid stereotypes and misunderstandings and also in response to negative or misrepresented perceptions about bisexuality. The resistance in this instance is somewhat different from our overall cohort's resistance to being confined to identity labels because it is not just a refusal to be confined, but the resistance of a perceived negative identity category.

Bisexuality, (non)religion and spirituality: identities and relationships

In this section we concentrate on responses from the surveys. In a later section we look at the more qualitative data from our interviews. We do this because the data from the interviews further develop many themes found in the surveys. In general, the quantitative data line up with the interview data in terms of opinions, but categories of 'Nonreligious', 'Spiritual but Not Religious' (SBNR) and 'Other' are even more dominant in the bisexual interview participants than in the bisexual survey participants, indicating that interview participants had largely removed themselves from organized religion. In any event, we do not read 'bisexuality' as a different reason than other non-heteronormative sexualities for making specific religious choices (see Young and Shipley, 2020). Instead, we read bisexuality as a category that gets problematized alongside many other categories in our research.

Survey

Of the 486 respondents to the RGSY survey,[5] 12.1% identified as bisexual (n = 40). Of those who claimed bisexual identities and who also answered the questions about sex/gender identification, 87.5% identified as female (n = 35), 15% as male (n = 6) and 5% as trans (n = 2).[6] Of the 34 answers to a question about relationship status, 58.8% identified as single, 29.4% as in a heterosexual common law relationship, 5.9% were in a heterosexual marriage, 2.9% indicated they were in a same-sex marriage and 2.9% indicated a same-sex common law relationship. 94.9% identified as not having children.

Bisexual respondents have a higher number of self-identified females and people who self-identify as trans. The full cohort (n = 486) is represented as 71.6% female, 27.9% male, 1.4% trans. Further, in the full cohort (n = 399 respondents to this question), most of our survey participants were single (78.4%); 7.2% were married (one in a married same-sex relationship). A further 14.6% were in common-law relationships (2.78% of those were same-sex common-law relationships). Only 1.5% of survey participants had children.

Thus, proportionally more of the bisexual participants identified as female and as trans than in the full cohort. Proportionally more bisexual participants were in some sort of committed relationship, a significant number in heterosexual relationships. As demonstrated elsewhere, engaging in heterosexual relationships as a bisexual individual can be construed as part of the 'strategic' or selective decisions taken by individuals in light of perceptions that are made about bisexuality as a confused or less legitimate sexual identity (Pfeffer, 2014; Rehaag, 2009; Swim et al., 2007). The complexity of these dynamics, being bisexual but being viewed by society as 'heterosexual' by virtue of current or marital relationships, is explored by bisexual RGSY participants as they reflect on their own perceptions of claiming or resisting bisexual identities.

(Non)religion and spirituality

Participants were able to identify with more than one religious tradition and were able further to explore the category of 'Other' – some of the responses were: self-defined view of God, morality and purpose; I'm an atheist; I identify with Aboriginal beliefs; Paganism. Choices of Non-religious, Spiritual-But-Not-Religious or Other, alone or in combination with one another, account for 42.5% of the 40 bisexual respondents. And a further 10% of total respondents chose one or more of these categories alongside Christianity. On the liberal to conservative scale, these self-described bisexual respondents overwhelmingly identified as liberal (83.8%).

Table 2.1 Bisexual respondents' religious identities (n = 40)

Religious identity	*Percentage*
Buddhism (n = 1)	2.5%
Christianity (n = 18)	45.0%
Non-religious (n = 8)	20.0%
Spiritual-But-Not-Religious (n = 2)	5.0%
Other (n = 5)	12.5%
Christian and Non-religious (n = 2)	5.0%
Christian and SBNR (n = 1)	2.5%
Non-religious and Other (n = 1)	2.5%
Non-religious, SBNR and Other (n = 1)	2.5%
Christian, SBNR, Non-religious and Other (n = 1)	2.5%

Bisexual participants vary in their religious practices not according to sexuality, but according to their own religious choices. In the few sentences that follow, we look at only those bisexual participants who did not name multiple religious identities. Of those who name themselves bisexual and Non-religious, without any other complicating religious affiliation (75% or 8 of 12 who named themselves bisexual and Non-religious), not one engaged in private religious practice and 33% (n = 4) never engaged in public religious practice, 16.7% (n = 2) engaged in public religious practices on special occasions and 16.7% (n = 2) rarely. Those who named themselves solely SBNR (n = 2) showed more diversity of religious practice. One of them rarely engaged in public religious practices and the other did so on special occasions. Those who named themselves solely Christian (n = 18, of a variety of sorts) account for the bulk of both private and public religious practices in the bisexual group. Nearly half (47%) indicated that they engaged in public religious practices once a week or more and 70.5% indicated that they engaged in private religious practices once a week or more. In contrast to the bisexual but Non-religious group, every Christian participant attended public religious gatherings and only 0.6% indicated they rarely attended public religious activities. 17.6% of the Christian group indicated that they attended public services on special occasions. Further, 17.6% of those who named themselves bisexual and solely Christian indicated that they rarely engaged in private religious practices. For those bisexual persons who indicated more than one religious identity (15%), the responses about public and private religious activities were quite varied. Here the divergences seem not to have much to do with sexual identities. Bisexual Christians in general continued to practise their Christianity and the bisexual nonreligious in general abandoned religious practices.

We witness similar explanations both within our full cohort and in our bisexual cohort represented by participation in certain public practices, particularly as connected to family traditions and family religious practices – many identified they attended religious services during the holidays (Christmas and Easter) and engaged with public practice when they were visiting family. As compared with the full cohort of respondents, bisexual respondents self-identify as more liberal though their religious self-identifications are similar to those in the overall group (Christianity as the largest religious category selected, followed by Non-religious and SBNR).

These variations, within the full cohort and in the group self-identified as bisexual, are representative of the larger analysis that has emanated from this research project. Young people's identities are very much under construction, fluid and negotiated sometimes on a daily basis, and, as such, their current experiences and relationships to categories of identity represent the wide spectrum of diverse options available as they consider, reject and reflect on their values, ethics and ideologies. The language that is made available to them to analyse and represent their 'religious' (nonreligious, spiritual, atheist) identities also comes under scrutiny through this project; the grammar of religion as currently available limits rather than expands when exploring the interconnections and disassociations that are felt when considering: familial practices, doctrine, (non)religious authority, social norms, gender and sexual equality, and so on (Young and Shipley, 2020; see also Lynch, 2010; Shipley, 2019; Ursic, 2014; Wallis 2014). The choices that are accessible to explore identity and ethics offer young people an array of building blocks; however, much of the language regarding (non)religious identity and spirituality is felt to constrain. When we ask, 'What does your religion mean to you?' a common response is, 'Do you mean *my* religion? Or do you mean what the texts say?' 'Religion' continues to relate to doctrine and traditional attitudes; personal values and ethics that do not align with doctrine and tradition have yet to find a new placeholder.

Sexuality

Bisexual respondents were nearly evenly divided between those whose sexual identification was solely bisexual (21/40) and those who also identified across other sexual identity categories, sometimes several sexual identity categories (19/40). Participants had space to further describe their sexual identities, if the categories they selected above were not sufficient. The predominant comment (as an identity that was not available in the list) was pansexual. In comparison with the full cohort, the greatest variation in the responses are in relation to the categories of: heterosexual and queer. In the full cohort, 69.1% self-identified as heterosexual and 10.2% identified as queer. In the bisexual cohort, over twice as many proportionally identify as queer (10 of 40 or 25% of those who identify as bisexual also identify as queer; 3 of those 10 identify in the two categories of bisexual and queer; and another 7 of those 10 identify as bisexual and queer along with other identifiers). There is a significant reduction in the percentage who identify as heterosexual (5 of 40 or 12.5% identify as bisexual and heterosexual, one of these includes other identifiers as well). While it might not be surprising that bisexual respondents identify less as heterosexual, perhaps it is of note that still 12.5% selected that category at all. We conjecture that the use of heterosexual as an identifier by our bisexual participants points to several important analytic reflections that deserve further examination. Why, for instance, is it assumed, by researchers among others, that the category of heterosexual is less complicated than the other sexual identity categories? Because individuals are identifying as heterosexual and also bisexual, queer, pansexual, etc. further thought needs to be given to problematizing heterosexual as a category. Commonly held notions about bisexuality are still significantly underdeveloped, so perhaps our categories restrict rather than expand when it comes to offering bisexual individuals options for identification.

The use of queer as a self-identifier is both rapidly increasing among younger demographics (Steinmetz, 2016; Ven, 2018) and is also referenced by our survey and interview respondents (across sexuality identities) as being the best option to encompass the spectrum and fluidity with which they see their sexuality. As Monica (23, female, atheist or nonreligious) stated in her interview, she identified as queer because the rest of the categories were more problematic.

In terms of sexual practices, in our full cohort 74.8% of participants indicate they do not engage in casual sex (though 65% said they were sexually active). Among the bisexual participants, 57.9% say they do not engage in casual sex while 42.1% say they do. In the full cohort and among our bisexual participants, the use of 'casual' in the question itself has been challenged. Participants sometimes objected to the implication that 'casual' sex was somehow negative or less valuable that sex within the context of a relationship. In our interviews, both self-identified bisexual respondents and those who express fluidity regarding their sexual identities challenge the typical framing of casual sex. For example, Colin (26, male, bisexual and polyamorous, nonreligious) began questioning the practice of monogamy at the same time he realized that it would not bother him if another man had sex with his girlfriend. In the same vein, Haley (22, female, 'mostly straight', agnostic Catholic) identifies as 'mostly straight', states that while she 'likes girls' she would not go so far as to call herself bisexual. Haley also states that non-committal sexual relationships are both intentional and thoughtful; she was interested in sexual relationships with people she could trust but was not seeking long-term commitment.

Further, our bisexual participants identify their sexualities as less fixed than many of the participants in the full cohort. They are more likely to be in married or common-law relationships; as demonstrated in the quotes below they express much more exploration in terms of their sexual relationships and attitudes; and for some, they might have a same-sex or opposite-sex partner, but their sexual expression can involve sexual engagements with other intimate partners outside that relationship.

Religion and bisexuality

In a series of Likert scale questions, participants responded regarding bisexuality and sexuality and religion as follows:

Table 2.2 Respondents' responses to selected questions on religion, sexuality and bisexuality, separated by bisexual respondents and full cohort.

	Respondents	*Strongly agree*	*Agree*	*Neither agree nor disagree*	*Disagree*	*Strongly disagree*	*N/A*
Bisexuality is a distinct sexual orientation, just like homosexuality and heterosexuality	Full cohort: N = 403	37.4%	28.9%	18.2%	8.5%	5%	2%
	Bisexual respondents:	62.5%	22.5%	10%	5%	0%	0%
Bisexuality is a confused sexuality. Bisexuals should choose to be either heterosexual or homosexual	Full cohort: N = 404	2.5%	6.5%	13.9%	18.7%	55.5%	3%
	Bisexual respondents:	2.5%	0%	0%	2.5%	90%	5%

(Continued)

Table 2.2 (Cont.)

	Respondents	*Strongly agree*	*Agree*	*Neither agree nor disagree*	*Disagree*	*Strongly disagree*	*N/A*
My religion understands the issues lesbian, gay, bisexual and trans people face	Full cohort: N = 330	16.5%	23.5%	14.%	13.4%	13.4%	19.2%
	Bisexual respondents:	29%	22.6%	6.5%	6.5%	19.4%	16.1%
Religious teachings on sexuality should adapt to contemporary social and cultural values	Full cohort: N = 329	30.89%	29.36%	13.8%	8.9%	11.%	6.1%
	Bisexual respondents:	51.6%	32.3%	3.2%	3.2%	0%	9.7%
My religious tradition is significant in shaping my attitudes towards sex and sexuality	Full cohort: N = 327	14.2%	23.7%	8.7%	19.8%	15.1%	18.8%
	Bisexual respondents:	6.5%	16.1%	6.5%	29%	22.6%	19.4%
My religious tradition is significant in shaping my sexual practices	Full cohort: N = 323	11.8%	19.6%	13.7%	18.4%	18.4%	18.1%
	Bisexual respondents:	9.7	12.9%	0%	29%	25.8%	22.6%

Compared with the full cohort of respondents, bisexual participants are significantly more likely to see bisexuality as distinct (62.5% as opposed to 37.4%) and to reject the notion that it is a confused sexuality (rejected by 90% of those who claim bisexual identity versus 55.5% of the full cohort). Bisexual respondents, however, also feel more strongly that their religious tradition understands the issues LGBTQI+ individuals face and to feel that religious traditions should reflect contemporary values (see Table 2.2). Given the diverse ways bisexual respondents understand their own (non)religious and spiritual identities, often as very personalized, this feeling of understanding might emanate from the (non)religious identity they experience rather than being a question tied to traditional or doctrinal religion. That is, although some do struggle with conflict between their religion and their sexuality, many choose (non)religious options that support their sexual identities (such as nonreligious, SBNR or liberal Christianity) or they adapt their understandings of religious traditions so that their sexual lives are accounted for. As noted above, a huge percentage of bisexual respondents (83.9%) think religious teachings on sexuality should adapt to the contemporary world and only 3.2% disagree with that idea. Among our full cohort, respondents identified more of a conflict between 'my' religion and their integration of the teachings of their self-identified religious tradition into their sexual lives (Young and Shipley, 2014). It is only speculation, but perhaps this conflict is not felt the same way for bisexual respondents. They are correspondingly less likely to see their religious traditions as having a significant influence in shaping their sexual attitudes or practices, in part because they are overwhelmingly Nonreligious, SBNR or Other; and in part because when they are religious they have mostly chosen liberal forms of religion where societal norms and religious norms are closely correlated.

With a high response rate among bisexual respondents in the Nonreligious, SBNR and Other categories, indicating less of an influence from religious traditions on their attitudes and practices is not entirely surprising. For those who also identify with Christianity (see quotes below), unpacking their relationship with Christianity as an inherited or familial identity versus their current personal beliefs and values offers insight into the way these bisexual young people experience the relationship of their sexual identities to their (non)religious and spiritual identities.

At the end of the survey we asked open questions, specifically 'What does your religion mean to you?' and 'What does your sexuality mean to you?' Responses to these questions have offered rich and nuanced reflections on the ways our survey participants expand and feel limited by both of these concepts and the language available to explore these aspects of their identities (Shipley and Young, 2014). For our bisexual respondents, the relationship between these two questions offers further reflection on the ways they connect or separate their (non)religious and spiritual identities with their bisexual identity.

> My sexuality is a fact of who I am, a kind of aside in the big list of 'I'm a young adult white kid, who happens to be pansexual, not interested in sex, and bigender. How was your day?' It doesn't really affect my daily life besides my clothing, which does get interesting since I am a modest girl and am struggling with not being Muslim but wanting to follow their modesty code for privacy and comfort.
>
> (#394, 22, female/male/bigender, Christian/Islam/non-religious/SBNR, bisexual/queer/asexual/I do not define[7])

> It [my sexuality] has created the most special relationship I could have ever imagined, and as a side benefit, acts as a filter to keep away the religious nutjobs and bigots who hate people in same-sex relationships.
>
> (#284, 24, female, atheist, hitchensian anti-theist, bisexual)

> Religion for me is a sense of tradition that I can rely on, but also something that I know I am unhappy with and would like to eventually allow myself the time and freedom to come to terms with .... My sexuality is a constant source of stress at the moment. Identifying as bisexual makes it difficult to maintain either a homosexual or heterosexual relationship because to others' eyes, it automatically negates the possibility of the other. I am confident in my sexual orientation but am unsure about how to best fulfill my needs while still being happy with the structure of my life.
>
> (#182, 19, male, United Church of Canada, bisexual)

These variations in response demonstrate the complex relationships felt and experienced between (non)religion, sexuality and the negotiation of these categories. The tensions that persist in respondents' lived experiences of being bisexual, (non)religious or spiritual are felt daily in their interactions with others – how they present themselves in the world and how they feel they are received. As we see in these quotes, and as is expanded in the section on the interviews below, being 'in between' homosexuality and heterosexuality is often perceived as a lack of commitment, negating sustained romantic or sexual relationships (Anderson, 2008; Carillo and Hoffman, 2018). Bisexuality can also be a shield, to deflect and deter negative experiences and engagement. Bisexuality may be a 'safer' designation in contexts where gay, lesbian or queer are negatively perceived. But it also might bring with it questions about lack of self-knowledge or fear of more negatively perceived identities.

Interviews

Five of our 32 interviewees (Monica, Chelsea, Colin, Michelle and Teresa) identified either explicitly as bisexual or identified as engaging in both same-sex and opposite-sex relationships, while pushing back on the limitations of defining oneself by category. Some did not identify as bisexual but complicated their sexual identity category in the following ways: Haley (22, female, agnostic Catholic) identified as 'mostly straight'; Lauren (23, female, United Church of Canada) identified as 'probably straight'; and Andrea (26, female, nonreligious) said her sexuality rests in the middle of the spectrum.

Chelsea's (23, female, bisexual, nonreligious) first exploration of same-sex attraction was in middle school, which she describes as her 'first understanding of what even being attracted to somebody was' – complicated by the fact that the person was another girl; 'at the same time I was like wow she's awesome and also wow … I will never tell anybody'. Chelsea resisted the term bisexual for years, feeling that it reinforced the idea of binary gender identity and was therefore leaning towards transphobia in its usage, but has since settled on it as a term she can use that others will understand when she talks about her sexuality:

> I wanted a word that I could say and people would be, like, I have a vague idea of what you mean. It doesn't need to be a word that they have a perfect understanding, but, so … yeah, so, bisexual is the word I go with and it's still the one I use. I think my current understanding is that for me in the grand scheme of things, like, gender is just not very high on the list of things that are important to me in a partner. So that's maybe why I'm okay with a word that's imperfect.

Colin's high school experiences regarding the treatment of, in particular, gay males continues to make him hesitant to apply the term bisexual to himself – instead he prefers to describe himself as MSM (man who has sex with men):

> I still kind of struggle with this whole bisexual thing, like I mean I don't, I don't identify as gay, I identify as MSM, if you'd like, man who has sex with men, or bisexual, and I think that, and I still have a lot of discomfort, it takes a long time for me to warm up to a sexual partner who is male and I do really strongly associate that with … the sort of homophobic environment that maybe still exists in high school but it certainly did when I was going through, especially for men.

During the interview, Colin said he had been working to embrace the term and identity as bisexual; he identified 'strongly as being straight' and polyamorous until 'well, the way I tell it is until I met a man that I wanted to have sex with'. His first experience sexually with another man was in a group dynamic though he has been exploring 'solo' sexual experiences with other men over time. Although he does not relate his religious choices to his sexual preferences, Colin identifies as nonreligious, though he sees a spiritual element in his polyamorous philosophy.

Michelle (22, trans/genderqueer, queer, Muslim) identifies as pan-sexual but finds 'queer' to be a better catch-all term to describe her sexual identity. Michelle says she did not identify as bisexual until grade 10 because she thought people could only be 'straight or gay'.

> I just kind of assumed that because I had a crush on a boy first I was straight and then one day I was reading online and somebody mentioned being bisexual and I was like, wait, you're allowed to like both? That was pretty revolutionary. I went to school the next day and … my best friend was talking to me and I was, like, do you know what I found out? I'm bisexual. And then I was kind of out by default because I was so excited about it I told … everyone I knew.

Michelle identifies as trans and genderqueer, stating that bisexuality as a category is restricted to binary gender categories. Her identification as bisexual during her teenage years inspired her to become more active in social justice activities, including becoming involved in LGBTQI+ clubs. Michelle also identifies as Muslim, though her current practice is mostly in private or through online engagement. She thinks that Islam itself is a very open religion but that mosques and mosque leadership continue to be patriarchal and homophobic; while she hopes that will change over time, she describes herself as an 'online' Muslim for now. Identifying as trans, queer and Muslim is not experienced as conflictual for Michelle.

Monica (23, female but gender fluid, queer, atheist/nonreligious) describes her sexuality as fluid. Although she had initially engaged only in heterosexual relationships, she began an open relationship with a woman and described that as the transition of her identity 'from being straight'. Monica resists labels on her sexual identity or exploration, stating she does not see sexuality as a fixed identity and that she does not see herself now saying that she only dates women. Rather her sexual relationships are based on the people she is attracted to and their connections to one another. Monica identifies as atheist or nonreligious; she was raised in a very liberal household, with Unitarian Universalist, spiritual and Eastern religious influences. Although she found her religious upbringing to be quite open and progressive, she identified as atheist at a young age, problematizing the use of the category of 'spiritual' as ultimately her reason not to identify herself as spiritual although she continues to engage in various religious or spiritual practices, in private and with family.

The relationship of (non)religion and spirituality for our bisexual respondents is complex, connected to social pressures and negative perceptions about the category of bisexuality and further by perceived or experienced rigidity regarding religion and sexual diversity. In some cases, the negative associations about bisexuality emanate from experiences among peers in high school (as in Colin's case); in others, the experiences occurred in personal engagements within religious institutions (such as Michelle). These negotiations complicate our respondents' own exploration of their bisexual identities, an identity they both adopt and resist for various reasons. Although some of our bisexual respondents have turned away from the religions of their upbringing, others seek to integrate being religious with their bisexual identities. This falls into line, we think, with the generally liberal identities of our bisexual respondents and with their higher tendencies to claim nonreligious or SBNR identities.

Concluding remarks

In line with the increasing research available on young people's identities – religious, gendered and sexual – participants in the RGSY project demonstrate the complexity of identity construction as negotiation. Their identities are truly living; they are shifting and fluid and comprised of multiple influences, sources and engagements. For our self-identified bisexual participants, this complexity is further evidenced reflected in negative perceptions and misunderstanding about bisexuality in general. Social norms and expectations for young people are pronounced across religious, gendered and sexuality categories; for our bisexual respondents, social norms and expectations sometimes negate the sense that their sexuality is valid – the prescriptive expectation of monogamous pairings (opposite-sex or same-sex) continues to place bisexuality outside the expected matrix. Even within an increasingly accepting demographic regarding sexual diversity, bisexuality is often underrepresented and misunderstood. In combination with dominant religious teachings regarding sexual expectations, bisexual youth find themselves continually placed on the borders. For some of our bisexual participants, the use of the term bisexual to describe their sexual identities is done just to be able to use a term people describe – it is not necessarily a term they feel adequately captures their sexual fluidity.

Although some bisexual respondents have struggled with or continue to struggle with traditional religions that privilege heterosexuality, many have chosen (non)religious options that do not require them to question the realities of their sexual identities. Bisexual respondents across religious choices take seriously the idea that religion is malleable and should change with the times. Such a finding is certainly in line with Toft's (2014) exploration of bisexual Christians who usually did not adjust their sexuality in response to Church teachings but, rather, adjusted their view of what the teachings said in view of their sexuality. But, in general, we did not find a huge divide between those who named themselves bisexual and those whose sexuality was named in other non-heteronormative ways, in large part we think because our respondents rejected strict identity categories more generally, not just in relation to sexuality. Although the bisexual respondents know about the constraints imposed by certain forms of religion, they have generally chosen themselves out of or adapted those forms to their current lives. The question remains how the term and concept of bisexuality will continue to be adapted to people's lives and experiences.

Notes

1 We use (non)religious to challenge the rigidity of the category of religion in response to the results of our project; participants in the Religion, Gender and Sexuality among Youth in Canada project complicate the limitations of 'religion' as an identifier and expand its meanings related to values, ideologies, ethics, nonreligion and spirituality. That is, (non)religious expands the meaning of traditional religious categories by encompassing a broader range of meanings and values.

2 One of the key findings from the project has been our argument about the need for a new grammar of identity; specifically a new grammar of religion. RGSY participants' challenge to the restrictive language of religion has demonstrated that the categories of religion and nonreligion are in need of an overhaul. In line with similar studies conducted by Elizabeth Ursic (2014) and Gordon Lynch (2010), our findings suggest that religious studies scholarship would benefit from the learnings of gender and sexuality studies in the development of a more fluid and nuanced conception of what is meant by (non)religion.

3 The RGSY project team consists of Pamela Dickey Young (Principal Investigator, Queen's University), Heather Shipley (Co-Investigator, University of Ottawa) and Ian Alexander Cuthbertson (Research Assistant). It was generously funded by the Religion and Diversity Project, a Social Sciences and Humanities Research Council of Canada Major Collaborative Research Initiative led by Lori G. Beaman (Director) and housed at the University of Ottawa.

4 Though most of these tropes concern men, it is interesting to note that the latest season of *Orange Is the New Black* (a series on Netflix) invokes the notion of 'gay for the stay'.

5 Respondents were able to identify with more than one sexual identity and more than one gender identity. Further, not all participants elected to identify their gender or sexual identity. Participants did not have to answer every question in the survey for their data to be included; as such, we indicate here both the full cohort numbers as well as the number of individuals who answered the specific question we are analysing in order to reflect accurately the responses to each question. The percentages offered connect to the number of individuals who answered any given

question. The RGSY questionnaire was open from July 2012 to July 2013; interviews and video diaries were conducted in 2014–2015. We collected data from 486 survey participants, 32 interviews and 10 video diaries. See Young and Shipley (2020) for detailed discussion about the project, methods and findings.

6 Participants were able to select more than one category for their responses.

7 Participants were able to select multiple options for their (non)religious, gender and sexual identities. Those indicated in this chapter are the selections that the participants made, including any elaborations they provided on those categories. Survey respondents are identified by numbers while interview and video diary respondents are identified by pseudonym.

References

Anderson, E. 2008. 'Being masculine is not about who you sleep with …': Heterosexual athletes contesting masculinity and the one-time rule of homosexuality. *Sex Roles* 58(1–2), 104–115.

Anderson, E. 2014. *21st Century Jocks.* London: Palgrave Macmillan.

Arnal, W. and McCutcheon, R. 2012. *The Sacred is the Profane: The Political Nature of 'Religion'*. Oxford: Oxford University Press.

Arweck, E., Bullivant, S. and Lee, L. 2013. *Secularity and Non-religion.* London: Routledge.

Beaman, L. G. 2012. Battles over symbols: the 'religion' of the minority versus the 'culture' of the majority. *Journal of Law & Religion*, 28(1), 67–104.

Beckford, J. A. 2012. Public religions and the post-secular: critical reflections. *Journal for the Scientific Study of Religion*, 51(1), 1–19.

Berger, B. 2015. *Law's Religion: Religious Difference and the Claims of Constitutionalism.* Toronto: University of Toronto Press.

Beyer, P.F. and Ramji, R. 2013. *Growing Up Canadian: Muslims, Hindus, Buddhists.* Montreal: McGill-Queen's University Press.

Butler, J. 1990. *Gender Trouble: Feminism and the Subversion of Identity.* New York: Routledge.

Carrillo, H. and Hoffman, A. 2018. 'Straight with a pinch of bi': The construction of heterosexuality as an elastic category among adult US men. *Sexualities*, 21(1–2), 90–108.

Collins-Mayo, S. and Dandelion, P. (eds). 2010. *Religion and Youth.* Farnham: Ashgate.

Cossman, B. and Ryder, B. 2001. What is marriage-like like? The irrelevance of conjugality. *Journal of Family Law*, 18(2), 269–326.

Cragun, R.T. 2016. Defining that which is 'other to' religion: Secularism, humanism, atheism, freethought, etc., in *Religion: Beyond Religion*, edited by P. Zuckerman. New York City: Macmillan, 1–16.

Davie, G. 2014. *Religion in Britain: A Persistent Paradox* (2nd edition). London: John Wiley & Sons.

Diamond, L.M. 2003. Was it a phase? Young women's relinquishment of lesbian/bisexual identities over a 5-year period. *Journal of Personality and Social Psychology*, 84(2), 352–364.

Duggan, L. 2002. The new homonormativity: The sexual politics of neoliberalism, in *Materializing Democracy: Toward a Revitalized Cultural Politics*, edited by R. Castronovo and D.D. Nelson. Durham: Duke University Press, 175–194.

Ehrman, B. 2003. *Lost Christianities: The Battles for Scripture and the Faiths We Never Knew.* London: Routledge.

Foucault, M. 1978. *The History of Sexuality: Volume I.* New York: Pantheon Books.

Freitas, D. 2008. *Sex and the Soul: Juggling Sexuality, Spirituality, Romance and Religion on America's College Campuses.* Oxford: Oxford University Press.

Gareau, P., Bullivant, S. and Beyer, P. (eds) 2018. *Youth, Religion and Identity in a Globalizing Context: International Perspectives.* Leiden: Brill Academic Press.

Halberstam, J. 1998. *Female Masculinity.* Durham: Duke University Press.

Hemmings, C. 2002. *Bisexual Spaces: A Geography of Sexuality and Gender.* London: Routledge.

Hunt, S.J. and Yip, A.K.T. 2012. *The Ashgate Research Companion to Contemporary Religion and Sexuality.* Farnham: Ashgate.

Irigaray, L. 1984. *An Ethics of Sexual Difference.* Ithaca, NY: Cornell University Press.

Lee, L. 2015. *Recognizing the Non-religious: Reimagining the Secular.* London: Oxford University Press.

Lynch, G. 2010. Generation X' Religion: A Critical Evaluation. In *Religion and Youth*, edited by S. Collins-Mayo and P. Dandelion, 33–40. London: Ashgate.

McGuire, M.B. 2008. *Lived Religion: Faith and Practice in Everyday Life.* Oxford: Oxford University Press.

Monro. S. 2015. *Bisexuality: Identities, Politics, and Theories.* London: Palgrave Macmillan.

Page, S.-J, Yip, A.K.T and Keenan, M. 2012. Risk and the imagined future: Young adults negotiating religious and sexual identities, in *The Ashgate Research Companion to Contemporary Religion and Sexuality*, edited by S.J. Hunt and A.K.T. Yip. London: Routledge, 255–274.

Pfeffer, C.A. 2014. 'I don't like passing as a straight woman': Queer negotiations of identity and social group membership. *American Journal of Sexuality*, 120(1), 1–44.

Rehaag, S. 2009. Bisexuals need not apply: A comparative appraisal of refugee law and policy in Canada, the United States, and Australia. *International Journal of Human Rights*, 13(1/2), 413–436.

Rich, A. 1980. Compulsory heterosexuality and lesbian existence. *Signs*, 5(4), 631–660.

Rubin, G. 1994. Thinking sex: Notes for a radical theory of the politics of sexuality. In *Pleasure and Danger: Exploring Female Sexuality*, edited by C.S. Vance. Boston: Routledge & Kegan Paul, 267–319.

Savin-Williams, R.C. and Vrangalova, Z. 2013. Mostly heterosexual as a distinct sexual orientation group: A systematic review of the empirical evidence. *Developmental Review*, 33(1), 58–88.

Scoats, R., Joseph, L.J. and Anderson, E. 2018. 'I don't mind watching him cum': Heterosexual men, threesomes, and the erosion of the one-time rule of homosexuality, *Sexualities*, 21(1–2), 30–48.

Shipley, H. 2019. Apathy or misunderstanding? Youth's reflections on their religious identity in Canada. In *Youth, Religion, and Identity in a Globalizing Context: International Perspectives*, edited by P. Gareau, S.C. Bullivant and P. Beyer. Leiden: Brill Academic Press, 191–210.

Shipley, H. and Young, P.D. 2014. Values and attitudes: How are youth integrating religion and sexuality in their daily lives? In *Globalized Religion and Sexual Identity: Contexts, Contestations, Voices*, edited by H. Shipley. Leiden: Brill Academic Press, 276–294.

Shipley, H. and Young, P.D. 2017. Religion, youth and queer identities in Canada, in *Sexual Diversity and Religions*, edited by M. Jaime. Lima: PEG/Diversities Publishing, 219–234.

Smith, C. and Smith, P. 2009. *Souls in Transition: The Religious and Spiritual Lives of Emerging Adults*. New York: Oxford University Press.

Steinmetz, K. 2016. Why "LGBTQ" will replace "LGBT". *Time*, October 26, [Online]. Available at: http://time.com/4544704/why-lgbtq-will-replace-lgbt/ [accessed 21 August 2018]

Strhan, A. 2014. English evangelicals, equality and the city. In *Globalized Religion and Sexual Identity: Contexts, Contestations, Voices*, edited by H. Shipley. Leiden: Brill Academic Press, 236–255.

Sullivan, W. 2018. *The Impossibility of Religious Freedom: New Edition*. Princeton: Princeton University Press.

Swim, J. K., Pearson, N.B. and Johnston, K.E. 2007. Daily encounters with heterosexism: A week in the life of lesbian, gay and bisexual individuals. *Journal of Homosexuality*, 53(4), 31–48.

Toft, A. 2012. Bisexuality and Christianity: negotiating disparate identities in church life. In *The Ashgate Research Companion to Contemporary Religion and Sexuality*, edited by S.J. Hunt and A.K.T. Yip. Farnham: Ashgate, 189–203.

Toft, A. 2014. Re-imagining bisexuality and Christianity: The negotiation of Christianity in the lives of bisexual women and men. *Sexualities*, 17(5–6), 546–564.

Toft, A. and Yip, A.K.T. 2018. *Intimacy Negotiated: The Management of Relationships and the Construction of Personal Communities in the Lives of Bisexual Women and Men. Sexualities*, 21(1–2), 233–250.

Ursic, E. 2014. Bi the way: Rethinking the categories of religious identity. *The International Journal of Religion and Spirituality in Society*, 3(4): 29–34.

Valverde, M. 2006. A new entity in the history of sexuality: the respectable same-sex couple. *Feminist Studies*, 32(1), 155–162.

Ven, J. 2018. Why I use queer as my identifier, April 12. [Online] Available at: https://www.jonah-ven.com/blog/why-i-use-queer [accessed 21 August 2018].

Wallis, S. 2014. Ticking 'no religion': A case study amongst 'young nones'. *DISKUS: The Journal of the British Association for the Study of Religions*, 16(2), 70–87.

Weeks, J. 2007. *The World We Have Won*. London: Routledge.

Woodhead, L. 2013. Liberal religion and illiberal secularism, in *Religion in a Liberal State*, edited by G. D'Costa, M. Evans, T. Modood and J. Rivers. Cambridge: Cambridge University Press, 93–116.

Yip, A.K.T. and Page, S.-J. 2013. *Religious and Sexual Identities: A Multi-Faith Exploration of Young Adults*. Farnham: Ashgate.

Yoshino, K. 2000. The epistemic contract of bisexual erasure. *Stanford Law Review*, 52 (2), 353–461.

Young, P. Dickey and Shipley, H. 2014. Belief, not religion: Youth negotiations of religious identity in Canada, in *Handbook on Child and Youth Studies*, edited by J. Wyn and H. Cahill. Singapore: Springer, 861–873.

Young, P. Dickey and Shipley, H. 2020. *Identities under Construction: Religion, Gender and Sexuality among Youth in Canada*, Montreal: McGill-Queen's University Press.

3 Identifying as young, disabled and bisexual within evangelical Christianity

Abigail's story

Alex Toft and Anita Franklin

Introduction

Sexuality in the lives of young disabled people is an under-researched topic. This is due, in the main, to the failure of researchers to engage with disabled young people themselves; often focusing solely upon adults. The voices of disabled young people are largely missing from the research and they are not being asked about issues which affect their lives, although there are of course some exceptions (Henry et al., 2010; Kimbal et al., 2018; Sinecka, 2008; Toft et al., 2019a, 2019b). Research has consistently used expert opinion to form a consensus about what is important, and makes decisions on the behalf of young disabled people (Abbott and Burns, 2007).

Adding LGBT+ sexuality to the mix further reduces the research field as disabled people are not seen as sexual beings. Disabled people are consistently de-sexualised and infantilised (Dinwoodie et al., 2016; Martino, 2017) and this is reflected in the sex and relationship education that young disabled people receive which is often not accessible or inclusive and is also heteronormative (Blyth and Carson, 2007). Little is known with regards to bisexuality and disability, as bisexuality has been subsumed within labels of gay or LGBT+. Although such a collective LGBT+ voice is important for the visibility of non-heterosexual sexualities, Abigail's story, the focus of this chapter, suggests that there are aspects of her experiences that are uniquely related to her bisexual identity, particularly in relation to how others perceived her sexuality.

Being both bisexual and Christian is assumed to be paradoxical within religious and popular discourses, and indeed the messages from organised religion have not always been positive towards people who identify as bisexual (Toft, 2012, 2014; Shepherd, 2018). However, through negotiation and re-evaluation of both sexuality and spirituality, bisexuality and Christianity are able to be reconciled. Previous research has suggested that this has been achieved either through re-imagining bisexuality (Toft, 2014) where bisexual Christians work to downplay the sexual side of bisexuality in favour of other personal characteristics; usually in a response to the Christian Church's focus upon sex. Alternatively, and a much more common strategy enacted by respondents in Toft's previous research (2009, 2012, 2014) has been a reframing or reconceptualisation of Christianity in relation to sexuality. This is done through adopting a more flexible approach to Christianity where Christianity works for the individual's life and problematic teaching and scripture is understood within the context of the age in which it was written. Research has suggested that not resolving such identities could lead to mental health problems, including depression (Levy and Reeves, 2011). However, negotiation (or resolution) is difficult due to the tensions between the multifaceted identities which could potentially be in conflict.

This chapter explores the experiences of Abigail, an 18-year-old transgender woman who identified as bisexual and disabled. The objective of the chapter is to examine the challenges that she faced and the strategies she used to address these in order to understand what bisexuality and spirituality (specifically Evangelical Christianity) mean in her life and how these identities were negotiated. Of course, as the focus is upon one individual the purpose is not to generalise and conclude that all disabled bisexual young people face the same challenges; but as this an area of new research it is important to highlight what may be some of the key issues and what they could mean for disabled bisexual young people. We are aware that this chapter does not focus upon Abigail as a transgender woman in great detail or provide an overview of the literature in this area. This is beyond the scope of this chapter, and we will work to explore this further in future dissemination. However, we are also aware of the importance of intersectionality and specifically the impact that being transgender may have upon other identities; as a result, this will be discussed in the findings section. It is clear that the resistance she faced and her responses were focused upon her identities rather than specific aspects (such as solely her sexuality).

It is important to stress that the chapter explores a number of identities that are contested. Abigail identifies as being: young, bisexual, trans, disabled and religious. In this instance we explored with Abigail what it meant to be disabled and bisexual, and also being religious and bisexual, as a disabled young person. In order to speak to these aspects, we will present a brief overview of the literature which touches upon these issues.

The chapter will then provide a short methodological account. It then presents findings which speak to the overall aim of the chapter. The first section explores (bi)sexuality in Abigail's life, looking at her understanding of how society views her as someone who is bisexual and disabled; and then moving to explore how she understands sexuality in her life. The aim is to construct a picture of what it means to be both bisexual and disabled and to explore both private and societal pressures and the negotiations which take place. Having presented a picture of being bisexual and disabled, the second section then applies this to look at religion in Abigail's life and the challenges she faced as a religious, young disabled bisexual person. As an Evangelical Christian, Abigail had the desire to attend church and be part of a religious community, yet the congregation and their attitude towards her sexuality made this difficult. The chapter explores her religious life and the negotiations she made in order to lead a religious life as a young disabled bisexual person.

Bisexuality and disability

Historically, research on bisexuality has focused on understanding bisexuality and its relation to sex, gender and other sexual identities (Storr, 1997). More recent research has tended to explain bisexuality as relating to sexual attraction, behaviour and identity (Robinson, 2015), building upon important work by pioneers such as Klein (1993) and Rust (1995, 2001). However, it is clear that there are motivations for adopting a bisexual identity that do not relate solely to intimacy and relationships. As Hartman-Linck (2014) has shown, bisexual visibility is important not only for attracting sexual partners but also in terms of being visible as bisexual women (in this case), which might not be obvious in some situations (e.g. in monogamous opposite sex relationships). In this regard it is an identity shaped by political beliefs and ideology. Previous research has also shown that bisexual women and men also focus upon non-physical markers for attraction, and are therefore attracted to the person rather than their sex (McCormack, Wignall and Anderson, 2015; Ripley et al., 2011; Rust, 2001; Toft, 2014, forthcoming; Toft and Yip, 2018). Such a history is potentially questioned by the rise of intersectionality (Windsong, 2018) which stresses the importance of understanding that identities intersect and influence each other. Earlier research on bisexuality tended to view bisexuality in isolation with little exploration of intersectionality beyond gender (see Pennington, 2009) and religion (Levy and Harr, 2018; Toft, 2014, 2019).

This history of bisexual research is largely missing any consideration of individuals who identify as disabled (one exception being Caldwell 2010), although there is research with LGBT+ and disabled people. Our view is that bisexuality needs separate consideration. Although there are some overlapping and potential relevant issues that arise from this literature which is relatable for bisexual disabled people, in essence grouping individuals into the umbrella of LGBT+ potentially obscures and dilutes bisexual identity. Research on LGBT+ sexual identities and disability has focused upon how society has viewed sexuality in the lives of disabled people and has shown that they are consistently desexualised by wider society (Richards, 2017) and perceived as being non-sexual (Dinwoodie et al., 2016; Shakespeare, 2000). The wider research, from which this chapter originates, has shown that young disabled people are excluded from debates concerning sexuality. As a result, they often receive little or no information/support, due to the belief that it is not needed (they will never be sexual), it would not be understood (they lack capacity), or that sexuality is a passing phase; at times linked with their disability (they don't understand what LGBT+ sexuality is) (Toft et al., 2019a, 2019b). This lack of information/support results in young disabled people being left to explore without knowledge or information and the risk of abuse is potentially heightened (Franklin et al., 2015).

Christianity and (bi)sexuality in the lives of young disabled people

There is no literature that we know of exploring Christianity in the lives of young people who are bisexual and disabled. However, historically Christianity has been viewed as exclusionary towards disabled people in terms of its imagery. According to Hull (2003), such prejudice against disabled people is ingrained in Christianity and perpetuated through the Bible and church worship. Research from Iceland (Björnsdóttir and Traustadóttir, 2010) has suggested that disabled people are devalued and not seen as having the capacity to engage with God. Participants in the research reported being denied access to religious spaces. One young man was denied confirmation by a minister who stated that people who are developmentally delayed cannot have 'a meaningful relationship with God' (55). However, the young man in the story resisted such views and requested confirmation from his minister. The initial reaction from the minister confirmed for the authors that 'people with learning difficulties were, as a group, viewed as incompetent, dependent and eternal children (57). This is a common theme throughout the literature and can be traced at far back as the work of Craft who coined the term 'forever child' (1987: 14) to describe how disabled people were perceived.

Individuals who identify as both Christian and bisexual have to work to negotiate their identities and attempt to reconcile with a religion that is generally unaccepting of their sexuality. Toft's previous research (2014) shows that this is achieved either through adaption of spiritual beliefs or clarification about what bisexuality means. Strategies that individualise or adapt Christianity reflect a definite shift in contemporary religious life. A number of individuals in Toft's research moved away from organised religion and/or practised a faith which is more personalised and reflective. This reflects what Woodhead (2001) has noted in relation to the contemporary religious landscape, a shift towards asking what religion can do for you rather than what you can do for religion (Woodhead, 2001). Much of the Christian Church's understanding of bisexuality appears to be deeply flawed, with previous research (Toft, 2014) suggesting that bisexuality has been largely conflated with promiscuity and that bisexual lives are always polyamorous (House of Bishops, 2003).

Methodological account

The data used to construct this chapter was gathered during a 12-month project funded by the British Academy (SG163117). The project aimed to explore the experiences of young people (16–25 years) who were disabled and LGBT+, particularly in relation to how they negotiate their identities, their experiences of support and education and other aspects of their lives that played an important role (such as religion). We spoke to 13 young people during the project. However, the lead author has since continued work in this area conducting a number of focus groups and workshops to continue the research.

The data was collected using semi-structured interviews, which generally lasted around one hour. Interviews were guided by the responses of the young people in line with the exploratory nature of the research, but broad topic guides were constructed focusing upon the intersection of their age, sexuality and disability. Topic guides were framed to then explore the young people's life experiences, societal perceptions, challenges/barriers and education. The broad aim of the interviews was to allow the young people space to explore how they understood and negotiated their identities.

In order to make the interviews more accessible we constructed a series of innovative methods that would be used during the interview. This enabled us to move away from a reliance upon potentially anxiety-inducing question and answering sessions. These included word cards, role-play activities and vignettes. Word cards worked well in helping to build rapport with the young people. During the activity both the researchers and participants looked through cards with key research words such as 'gay', 'bisexual' and 'disabled', and selected those which applied to their lives. This was also useful in starting to unpick how such identities were used and the pressures young people felt. Role-play activities and vignettes were often used simultaneously and revolved around using real-life (or imagined) stories involving disabled and/or LGBT+ issues. The researcher and participant then worked through the issues raised to discuss aspects that related to the participants lived experiences.

Although we tried to work in a more sensitive and inclusive manner, with regards to collection data we acknowledge that our methods excluded those with complex communication needs. Our sample was also convenience based and not representative; as we used gatekeepers with access to young people via their established support groups.

Bisexuality in Abigail's life

The literature clearly shows that being LGBT+ and disabled is challenging. Abigail's story suggests that these challenges are as a result of societal misconceptions and ignorance. This section will now explore Abigail's perception of how society understood her sexuality and the challenges this posed. The section then moves on to explore how she responded to such challenges by using creative agency.

Everyday challenges

Abigail suggested that the biggest difficulty she faced is not being able to validate her own sexuality. Throughout her story she gave examples of when she was being denied a sexual identity, due in main to her disability and being seen as incapable of making such a decision. She described herself as having a statement of special needs[1] due to being learning disabled and having mental health issues but was clear that she understood her own sexuality: 'I always knew it was how I wanted to live [as bisexual]. So being LGBT and that young they always thought it was a phase.'

She noted that both family and friends did not believe her when she discussed her sexuality, questioning her ability to understand what being bisexual meant. In the following quotation Abigail suggests that people simply do not accept that she is bisexual because she is disabled:

> Because of my learning difficulties people [say] that because I am disabled that I don't understand it [bisexuality], and it is just a phrase.[2] I got told that a lot, that it is just a phrase, because I don't understand it because of my learning difficulties. You know, I may struggle with things but I am not completely stupid.

Abigail is clearly upset that people assume she does not have the capacity to understand her own sexuality and that as a result she has no sexual identity. As research has suggested (Toft et al., 2019), young people often experience others making a link between their disability and understanding their own sexuality, and this is exacerbated with regards to LGBT+ which Abigail suggested was more difficult for others to accept. This is most clearly shown with regards to her sexuality being seen as a phase. Although this is an issue faced by young disabled LGBT+ persons as a whole (Toft et al., 2019a, 2019b) this is clearly exacerbated in those who are bisexual, due to misconceptions about bisexuality as being either a path towards being gay or a period of uncertainty and experimentation.

Abigail explained how people in general see her bisexuality as a phase through which she will eventually pass. This also reflects discrimination against Abigail in terms of her age and makes a judgement regarding her maturity, seeing her too immature to grasp concepts such as bisexuality. This was also reflected in family reactions as they were unable to acknowledge that Abigail was indeed bisexual. This resulted in her family stating that her sexuality was a phase which she would grow out of:

> When I was a younger person and I came out. Mum always used to tell me it was a phase and I would grow out of it … Seeing comments [on Facebook] saying that parents are forcing it on their children. I think that does play a key role in people being themselves at a young age, that it is being forced on them and it is not. It is just who we are.

Abigail's mother in this instance was referring to both her trans and bisexual identities, about which her mother was in denial. For her mother, it was hoped that Abigail would no longer pursue her transition and that she was in a bisexual phase but would be straight at some point.

It was a common occurrence for people not to understand her sexuality, and she was used to explaining her sexuality and gender to people. During the interview Abigail stated that this was a daily occurrence, but she was receptive to such requests:

> There have been a few times when I have had to explain my sexuality and that [referring to her gender identity] to people. It can be frustrating but it is something I am really open about. So in that sense I don't mind talking to people about my whole transition and coming out and what not. That for me is something I am used to on a daily basis.

Although noted as being 'frustrating', there was a clear sense that she was willing to talk to people about her sexuality and gender. Abigail made a conscious effort to distinguish between people's interest in her sexuality and those who were being abusive. Interest and the desire to better understand was a welcomed interaction, as opposed to those who remained ignorant and did not attempt to understand her experiences. Abigail noted how her friends and associates tried to be supportive but they could not quite grasp the situation:

> Yeah, I think a lot of people didn't get it. When I came out [as bisexual and trans], I first came out on Facebook so I had quite a lot of comments on it. They were supportive but they were confused as well, so I had to explain the difference between my sexuality and my gender. That is something I have to explain a lot as well.

Reaction from the general public was not always so positive, and as previously suggested there were people who did not want to learn more about sexuality and what it meant to Abigail. She explored how people's reaction to her sexuality has often resulted in violence and open discrimination: 'I have been told to kill myself, to overdose, to slit my throat, to slit my wrists, yeah. I get that on a daily basis.'

These experiences reveal the severity of the responses and the everyday challenges that Abigail faced. However, such a response did not come from a specific community or group of people. In her experience abuse occurred either online or in a public place ('on the streets') and perpetrators were members of the public. The following exchange highlights this:

> *Abigail:* When I've been walking down to the shops and that. I've had my nose broken and everything.
> *Interviewer:* And is that people you knew?
> *Abigail:* Yeah. Well I've seen them round the area, but not personally.

There were no instances of discrimination and abuse from LGBT+ or disabled spaces, and Abigail was clear that she garnered great support from her LGBT+ friends. During the interview, Abigail noted that she does have a few other disabled friends who have been accepting of her journey. She suggested that disabled people are used to being discriminated against and are therefore understanding and supportive:

> I'm going on personal experience I think they have been more supportive because disabled people get discriminated quite a lot so they would understand what it is like to be discriminated against. So they would be more supportive in a way.

This is an interesting perspective which sheds light on the power of shared experiences. Abigail is suggesting that because other disabled people are likely to have experienced and suffered abuse from non-disabled people they are less likely to abuse others. This is pushed further by Abigail as she explains how she has in fact been a figure of encouragement for other people:

> I've been told that I am an inspiration because … I'm a person for helping everybody else. I've been called an inspiration, people look up to me. I've been told that people do look up to me and how much I'm an amazing person, and I've been told that by people. And for me that has made me feel a lot better about myself and that kind of wants to make me carry on with things.

These experiences represent a consistent denial of the validity of bisexuality in Abigail's life. She was told that her sexuality is a phase and that she cannot be bisexual because she does not understand LGBT+ sexuality because she is disabled. The abuse that she suffers is very real, although she continued to work to educate and inform others about what her sexuality means.

Responding to challenges

Against the misunderstandings and discrimination outlined above, Abigail worked to form her sexual identity and to be her 'true authentic self' – a phrase that she repeated a number of times throughout the interview. Abigail responded to the misunderstanding and misconceptions by working to understand her sexuality on her own terms. Although she attends an excellent support group for young LGBT+ people in central England, which provides her with support, education, community and a place to explore herself in relation to her sexuality and gender identity; her family have not been supportive. As a result, she leads a double life where she cannot be herself at home; juxtaposed with her social life amongst friends where she feels free to be herself. Without guidance and the support of her family, she worked with a sense of creative agency. It is clear that she is aware that others perceive problems with her being bisexual as a disabled person, but this is not reflected in how she constructs her sexual identity. For Abigail, the central tenet of her bisexuality revolved around being open to other people and wanting to form a special connection that is not dependent upon their sex.

For Abigail, bisexuality was conceptualised as falling in love with someone, and she did not put any filters or qualifiers upon this: 'I just tell them that I fall in love with whoever I fall in love with. For me that is the easiest way to put it really without getting complicated.'

Abigail preferred to understand her sexuality in terms of an openness to falling for a person rather than focusing upon their sex or gender. This often resulted in her preferring not to label herself, but she felt that overall bisexuality was probably the best way to frame her sexuality.

> Sometimes, most of the time, I don't tend to label myself, because for me I tend to fall in love with whoever I fall in love with regardless of their gender or whatever. But if someone doesn't understand I use these terms (referring to bisexuality and pansexuality) to make it a little bit easier for them to understand.

There was a consistent downplaying of the importance of sex and gender in terms of her attraction. Abigail preferred to think about her sexuality in terms of a romantic spark where personality and individual traits were more important than sex or gender:

> I think it is just about that instant spark with them and being able to get along with them, and just to be able to have a laugh, and just be myself around them. To me their sex and gender doesn't define who they are as a person. It is more personality and how they treat me, and how they see me as a person rather than basing it on gender and sex.

Abigail described her sexuality as being either bisexual or pansexual and was not insistent on either being a preference. However, she was clear that she tended to use bisexuality for ease as most people had a better grasp of what bisexuality means. She defined her sexuality as being able to fall in love with someone no matter what their gender. In this regard Abigail perhaps conflated pansexuality and bisexuality. However, it is clear that she saw pansexuality as a type of bisexuality where the focus was upon both the gender identity of the person and their sex. She was attracted to people not based upon their sex or gender identity, making the distinction with bisexuality historical focus and conceptualisation as attraction to 'either' (as opposed to any) sex.

In this regard she understood her pansexuality as bisexuality-plus, an updated and improved version of bisexuality that is less constrained by homonormative tendencies (Klesse, 2018). It is important to note, however, that understandings of pansexuality are not well established due to a lack of research on pansexual lived experiences. As Klesse points out, little research has been done with the pansexual community. Although the emergence of such intimate and erotic cultures could be signalling a generational shift, as the focus shifts more clearly upon 'non-binary gender and sexual experiences' (2018: 1363). The subsuming of pansexuality into the wider umbrella of bisexuality is problematic for some who suggest that identifying as pansexual is a conscious move away from mainstream identity politics. As Gonel notes:

> Faced with the new-homonormativist identity politics of the mainstream LGBTQ movements, pansexual identification through respondents' answers align with queer activism. Indeed, as queer activism criticises gay-only identity politics for their assumptions on fixed cores of identities, pansexuality embodies this criticism in that respondents suggest that their sexual identity is multiple, ongoing and transgressive.
>
> (2013: 56)

In line with such an assertion, Abigail continued by discussing the use of terms such as non-binary or queer. She noted that it is often preferable not to label herself, which appears to fit with Gonel's (2013) discussion. Sex and gender is often not the central force in forming relationships or intimacies and the idea of loving the person – regardless of their gender and sexual identities at a particular point of life – is accentuated in the life of bisexuals (Toft, forthcoming).

Abigail's sexual and gender identities were important to her, and she argued that not living her life truthfully and openly was inauthentic and damaging. This is perhaps best demonstrated through her coming-out story which she described as a life-changing journey which had to be made:

> I came out to save my life really. Personally for me it was to save my life and just kind of it was like a weight lifting off my shoulders. I felt I had to come out just to be able to be myself. I felt like I owed an explanation to people. I had to come out to save my life.

It is important here to recognise that Abigail is not talking in metaphor or hyperbole, and that coming out to save her life means that she felt that in order to continue living she had to come out. The only alternative she saw to coming out was suicide:

> I think because I couldn't hide away who I was. It was pushing me away more from society. I felt if I didn't come out I probably, as horrible as it sounds, I probably would have committed suicide… So for me it is either I come out and be myself or I live my life as a lie, be unhappy and commit suicide.

This is difficult to read but further highlights the challenges she faced and the internal struggles that she had to contend with. For Abigail, not coming out represents a deception and an engagement in an act which does not represent her correctly or authentically. The process of enacting false or closeted identities was too much pressure for Abigail and had a constant negative effect on her mental health.

Although coming out is often strategic (Orne, 2011) or something that is an ongoing process akin to a career (Guittar and Rayburn, 2015), for Abigail the pressure of not telling people about her sexuality and gender identity was too difficult. As a result, she revealed her sexuality and desire to transition in order to spare herself from such turmoil. This shows how, although she knew that coming out would be a difficult journey, it was preferable to living as someone else.

Religion in Abigail's life

Abigail was a Christian and started attending an Evangelical church with her mother in her childhood. The Church, according to Abigail, was very rigid in terms of its reliance on the absolute truth of the Bible and its teachings. However, after leaving the Church, due to them not accepting her sexuality (as will be explored in greater detail) Abigail took to practising a more individualised form of Christianity involving personal reflection and private prayer. She missed the community aspect of worship and wanted to be a 'real' Christian again, as she felt less Christian due to her non-attendance.

Alongside the challenges of being bisexual and disabled, Abigail was working to negotiate her religious identity and exploring ways to continue to be a Christian. She had been raised in an Evangelical Christian Church near to her hometown and had attended regularly until she began the coming out process. This section explores how Abigail framed her religious beliefs as a young disabled bisexual person, the reactions from the Church which ultimately led to her leaving the Church and, finally, how she saw her religious life presently and in the future. Exploring these aspects will highlight how religion, sexuality and disability intersect in Abigail's life and the negotiations that occur.

Religious belief

Abigail described her religious beliefs as initially rooted in her attendance at her local church. She aligned her beliefs with those of the congregation from an early age. Abigail requested in the interview that the church be anonymised. However, it is clear from the official messages promoted by the church that a literal interpretation of the Bible, specifically in regard to the New Testament, is taught. The Bible is God's word as inspired by the Holy Spirit. Believers' baptisms are crucial and that it is through understanding that Jesus is the only Saviour, the truth, the life and the way, that believers can enter the kingdom of God.

Although Abigail had been a regular attendee, she had recently begun to disengage and her attendance had reduced:

> I was just little and mum would take me every Sunday and every big church event I would go to as well. But it got to the point where I don't go anymore. Mum goes less often now too. But, I just don't go there, I don't feel that I can.

Although, as this quotation alludes to, Abigail has moved away from the Church and organised worship in general, Christianity is still a central part of her life and Christianity morality and belief in God contribute to how she understands the world. During the interview she explored whether she thought God was real and whether concepts such as heaven were useful. It is clear that for Abigail there is indeed an entity who oversees the world which she understands as God. The following quotation explains her core religious beliefs:

> I do actually believe that there is a God. I do believe that everyone is their own [person], everyone should be treated as God's children. Personally, I believe it. I do believe that there is a heaven. But I don't believe there is a hell. No matter how bad people have been, no matter how people have sinned they are still going to heaven because they are still God's children in my eyes.

Here Abigail is exploring some of the central tenets of her belief system, which appear to align with the teaching of the church she attended. It is clear for her that there is a God and a heaven and that we are all God's children. As God's children we should be treated fairly and all of us are special and unique. The distinction between heaven and hell is also made as she states that there is no hell and/or no one goes to hell because we are protected by God as his children. There is also a suggestion here that people are equal and ultimately the same because of the fact that we are God's children. Due in part to the length of time attending the Church, it was clear that her beliefs and those of the Church are intertwined. Much of her religious belief was a result of the teaching of the Church. The impact upon her life as she began to distance herself from the Church must have been substantial; however, she eventually left as their teaching on sexuality (in particular) no longer fitted with what she understood Christianity to be about. As will be explored in the next section, she saw the Church's reaction to her sexuality as a complete contradiction for her as they no longer loved her; something she viewed as entirely un-Christian. Her Christianity focused strongly around love and equality with an emphasis upon treating each other with respect. This exchange clearly highlights this:

> *Abigail:* Just to love everyone as they would like to be loved, and not treat them any different to how they would like to be treated.
> *Interviewer:* So do you think that Church is misunderstanding what being Christian is?
> *Abigail:* Yeah, because I personally think being Christian is about loving everyone, loving God and not treating anyone different.

Abigail clearly expressed a disillusionment with her Church who have, in her eyes, moved away from a key aspect of Christianity. If we are not open and loving to all people then this does not represent Christianity for Abigail. This is also reflected in Abigail's understanding of the communal aspects of religion. It was argued that belief in God places individuals within a collective family in which believers become like brothers and sisters working together for the good of the wider community:

> From what I've seen before, before I came out, people come together. They treat each other as family. To an extent there is no judgement, but then when it comes to LGBT stuff, that is when the negative side comes out. But other than that I do see a lot of positives like family, they class each other as family like brothers and sisters.

This quotation does, however, begin to touch upon the fall-out with her religious community who placed great emphasis on sexuality after she came out. As will be explored in the next section, the congregation came together to work against her sexuality which they saw as being incompatible with their beliefs.

Responding to and negotiating challenges

Abigail stated that she came out to save her life, as the pressures of being what she described as inauthentic and closeted began to take their toll on her mental health. However, upon vocalising her sexuality Abigail was met with open abuse from her religious community: 'I am a sinner for it, that is a word that I get quite a lot, that I am a sinner for it. God doesn't accept it.' The religious congregation which she had been part of for the majority of her life turned against her and labelled her as a sinner once she revealed her sexuality. Of course, this was a point of great confusion for Abigail who had always understood Christianity to be about love and equality; and yet the congregation continued to abuse and berate her about her sexuality:

> They tried praying it out for me in the hope that God would heal me. So … Yeah, they laid their hands on me and tried praying for me. I was like, you know, God says to love everyone as their own but I wasn't getting any of that. So I just stopped going because I felt I wasn't good enough to go.

The quotation above is very telling as it clearly shows the contradiction between the Christian message as understood by Abigail, and what was being practised in her Church. Abigail internalised this abuse and stopped attending as she felt she was not good enough to continue going to the Church. The discrimination and abuse she received shamed her into no longer attending. The quotation also reveals the extent to which the Church went in order to 'fix' Abigail. The scenario that she outlines almost resembles an exorcism where an attempt is made to remove the possessed essence of bisexuality through Christianity. There is a similarity here with reparative (or conversion) therapy (Mikulak, 2018; Reay, 2018) which treats non-heterosexual sexualities as psychological disorders which can be changed through workshops and prayer. Although the structure of this therapy is clearly different in Abigail's case, as there were no workshops and the process does not appear to be consensual, the underlying feature is that Abigail's sexuality was seen as something that could be changed and it would be beneficial for her to do so.

Abigail said that before she told members of her congregation about her sexuality, sexuality was never mentioned at the church and she did not think it was part of their teachings. However, after learning of her sexuality it became the main focus of church services. She reflected on how the congregation took to having sessions where they prayed for her in order to get rid of her sexuality. This was surprising to Abigail as before she vocalised her sexuality there had been no teaching in this regard. She found the situation 'weird': 'Yeah, they would talk about it and try and pray it out of me. It was really weird. Like you just said, that is something that is never talked about that often in Church, yeah.'

On reflection, Abigail felt that their constant focus on her sexuality after coming out was in line with a literal interpretation of the Bible. The Bible was projected as being the word of God which was incompatible with bisexual life and used as a weapon against her. The following quotation highlights Abigail's thoughts on this:

> I think because they followed the Bible quite a lot. Everyone has a Bible in the Church and the worship leader takes out the Bible, reads it out and then puts it into practice as well. But when I did talk about me being trans and bisexual it was like he focused just on that, and tried to pray it out of me.

The view that bisexuality is not accepted in a Christian life has been further confirmed by Abigail through conversations with preachers and representative of Churches with a similar denominational outlook to her old Church. She regularly engaged with street preachers to gauge their opinions on LGBT+ sexualities. For her this confirmed that it is not accepted:

> Yeah because it is not … in the Bible it is not accepted. I go to [UK city] and I don't know if you've seen preachers standing on the side and I have actually stopped to talk to someone about being part of the LGBT, and it is not accepted. I think it is hard to be religious and LGBT, it is just not accepted as much.

Further contradictions and uncertainties for Abigail are reflected in the Church's attitudes to her as a disabled person. Being disabled, unlike being bisexual, has not been an issue for her Church and she received support and compassion with regards to this aspect of her life. For her, being disabled had less of an impact on her everyday life as it was framed as being easier to accept and compatible with her faith: 'They are actually really supportive in terms of my disability, they love me for that still. So in that sense being disabled, that doesn't affect me on a day-to-day basis.' The acceptance of her disability but rejection of her sexuality further highlights her religious community's view that her sexuality was a choice and something that could be changed. The reparative work that the Church attempted with Abigail is a demonstration of this belief. Her disability was not seen as a choice, however, and was accepted as part of who she was.

The reaction from Abigail's religious community was extreme. She was driven away with feelings of inadequacy and made to feel like a sinner as the Church tried to pray her sexuality away. The Church focused intently upon this aspect of her life, whereas previously it had not been part of their teaching. This brings into question where she sees her religious life presently and in the future.

Religious life

> I want to be myself, to be my authentic self and to be able to go to Church as myself, and live my life as a normal person. I am a normal person but for society to see me as a normal person.

This powerful quotation highlights Abigail's desires. She desperately wanted to be able to worship and to be Christian but this had to be done on her own terms. Although this situation initially appeared to be hopeless, Abigail constructed a number of strategies or practices which allowed her to keep in touch with her Christianity. As Cusack (2011) has noted, young people exercise agency in the creation of their identities where religion is deregulated and recast in a market of choice. Abigail's story does reflect religion as adaptable and malleable in line with Rüpke's (2015) assertion that 'religion is a cultural resource articulated through the agency of individuals' (344). In this regard Abigail took guidance from Christian teachings and resources, but did this away from a communal church setting: 'But I do listen to a lot of gospel music still. I have a Bible at home that I read through. But in terms of going to church, for now that is something that I have stopped.'

This represents a desire to continue with traditional modes of worship but with an emphasis on distancing from her Church, a common strategy which is employed (Schuck and Liddle, 2001; Yip, 2000) Abigail explained that she still prayed and often combined this with her love of Christian gospel music. She explored how the music allowed her to be at peace and focus upon what she felt was important:

> I pray in my room. Like I mentioned earlier I listen to a lot of Church music. I put my earphones on, put it on and zone out really. Because that is what I am doing when I pray really, I zone out from everything. Kind of forget about everything.

Reading the Bible and her attitude towards the Bible were recurrent talking points throughout the interview. Although she clearly acknowledged that the Bible was the root of the problem with regards to her church's rejection of her sexuality; she felt that the Bible was central to Christian belief and it should not be used as a tool to put restrictions upon people's lives. Abigail explored why the Bible was important, specifically referring to Christian duty and the way that the Bible can reinforce essential Christian values:

> I think it is just part of my religion really. It is like respect to God that I will read it, and try and put it into practice. Treat Christian values really. I see it as a religious thing. Each Christian reads the Bible.

However, Abigail did not engage with aspects of the Bible that might be interpreted as being in contradiction with her understanding of Christianity. She worked to push such aspects or passages aside, selecting aspects that worked for her:

> I kind of push that to one side personally. But in the Bible it says to love each other as their own. So for me I love everyone as my own, as I would like to be loved. So in that sense I don't really tend to read that side of it. I kind of push it to one side.

It has been suggested that this level of individualisation is particularly prominent in the lives of young people. Religion in young people's lives is equated to individualisation due to the young adult period of life being the point at which people begin forming beliefs (Arnett and Jensen, 2002). Using the theory of emerging adulthood (Arnett, 1998), the key message is that late teens and twenties (Abigail was 18) in industrialised Western societies are characterised by an exploration of possibilities in life. In this regard, if the theory is accepted, young people are perhaps more likely to individualise faith (Collins-Mayo and Dandelion, 2010; Yip and Page, 2013).

In terms of her hopes for a religious life in the future, Abigail wanted to engage with religion as a force for good and not one which promotes exclusion. Although she has worked to construct a form of Christianity that fits with her life, it is clear that there remains a longing to engage with Christian communities. Abigail explained that she felt 'less religious' because she no longer attended Church. For her the ideal scenario would be to attend less regularly as she would have to travel to a different Church, but to be able spend time with other Christians and 'be a normal Christian in a way, to practice my faith'. Abigail is currently investigating more liberal Churches and hoped to start attending again soon.

Concluding remarks

Before vocalising her sexuality and her transition journey Abigail painted a picture of pressure, anxiety and poor mental health; where she lived, in her own words, 'an inauthentic life' which was unfulfilling and unsatisfying. For Abigail, telling others about her sexuality and gender identity allowed her to express herself and to resolve some of the internal struggles she faced. However, there were a number of new challenges that she had to negotiate. Her family viewed her as incapable of understanding bisexuality (due to her disability), and as a result, are unsupportive; seeing her sexuality as nothing more than a phase (Toft et al., 2019b). Their lack of support resulted in her living separate private and public lives. The pressures of misunderstanding and constant affirmation of disabled sexuality as childlike, therefore underdeveloped and negligible, has done much to weaken the possibility of LGBT + identities in the lives of disabled young people.

Adding a strong Evangelical Christian identity into this picture adds a further layer of complexity as she faced rejection from her congregation. Her experience with her Church is a harrowing story which resulted in her having to move away from organised religion. In its place, she worked to construct an individualised form of Christianity rooted in aspects of the faith which she could accommodate and integrate into her life. However, this has not been a satisfactory experience as she continued to explore alternative denominations to be, as she described it, Christian again.

Notes

1 From 2014 with the Children and Families Act Statement of Special Educational Needs have been replaced by Education, Health and Care (EHC) plans which are legal documents describing support needs. Abigail still preferred to refer to it as her statement.

2 Analysis of the surrounding data indicates that Abigail accidentally used 'phrase' when meaning 'phase'. This nuance in language is important to note as our research has also highlighted that disabled young people can be frequently accused of not understanding a word/phrase and lack capacity to understand, for example, bisexuality when they use this word to describe themselves.

References

Abbott, D. and Burns, J. 2007. What's love got to do with it? Experiences of lesbian, gay, and bisexual people with intellectual disabilities in the United Kingdom and views of the staff who support them. *Sexuality Research & Social Policy*, 4(1): 27–29.

Arnett, J.J. 1998. Learning to stand alone: The contemporary American transition to adulthood in cultural and historical context. *Human development*, 41(5–6): 295–315.

Arnett, J.J. and Jensen, L.A. 2002. A congregation of one: Individualized religious beliefs among emerging adults. *Journal of Adolescent Research*, 17(5): 451–467.

Björnsdóttir, K. and Traustadóttir, R. 2010. Stuck in the land of disability? The intersection of learning difficulties, class, gender and religion. *Disability & Society*, 25(1): 49–62.

Blyth, C. and Carson, I. 2007. Sexual uncertainties and disabled young men: silencing difference within the classroom. *Pastoral Care in Education*, 25(3): 34–38.

Caldwell, K. 2010. We Exist: Intersectional In/Visibility in Bisexuality and Disability. *Disability Studies Quarterly*. 30(3/4). http://dsq-sds.org/article/view/1273/1303 [accessed 1 August 2019].

Collins-Mayo, S. and Dandelion, P. 2010. *Religion and Youth*. London: Ashgate.

Craft, A. 1987. Mental handicap and sexuality: Issues for individuals with a mental handicap, their parents and professionals, in *Mental Handicap and Sexuality: Issues and Perspectives*, edited by A. Croft. Tunbridge Wells: Costello, 13–33.

Cusack, C.M. 2011. Some recent trends in the study of religion and youth. *Journal of Religious History*, 35(3): 409–418.

Dinwoodie, R., Greenhill, B. and Cookson, A. (2016). 'Them two things are what collide together': Understanding the sexual identity experiences of lesbian, gay, bisexual and trans people labelled with intellectual disability. *Journal of Applied Research in Intellectual Disabilities*. https://doi.org/10.1111/jar.12252 [accessed 3 August 2018].

Franklin, A., Raws, P. and Smeaton, E. 2015. *Under Protected, Over Protected: Meeting the Needs of Young People with Learning Disabilities Who Experience, or Are at Risk of, Sexual Exploitation*. London: Barnado's.

Gonel, A.H. 2013. Pansexual identification in online communities: Employing a collaborative queer method to study pansexuality. *Graduate Journal of Social Science*, 10 (1): 36–59. http://gjss.org/sites/default/files/issues/chapters/papers/Journal-10-01–02-HaleGonel.pdf [accessed 15 March 2019].

Guittar, N.A. and Rayburn, R.L. 2015. Coming out: The career management of one's sexuality. *Sexuality & Culture*, 20(2): 336–357.

Hartman-Linck, J.E. 2014. Keeping bisexuality alive: Maintaining bisexual visibility in monogamous relationships. *Journal of Bisexuality*, 14(2): 177–193.

Henry, W.J., Fuerth, K. and Figliozzi, J. 2010. Gay with a disability: A college student's multiple cultural journey. *College Student Journal* 44(2): 377–388.

House of Bishops. 2003. *Some Issues in Human Sexuality: A Guide to the Debate*. London: Church House Publishing.

Hull, J.M. 2003. A spirituality of disability: The Christian heritage as both problem and potential. *Studies in Christian Ethics*, 16(2): 21–35.

Kimbal, E., Vaccaro, A., Tissi-Gassoway, N., Bobot, S.D., Newman, B., Moore, A. and Trooiano, P. 2018. Gender, sexuality, & (dis)ability: queer perspectives on the experiences of students with disabilities. *Disability Studies Quarterly*, 38(2). http://dsq-sds.org/article/view/5937/4907 [accessed 15 March 2019].

Kinsey, A.C., Pomeroy, W.B., Martin, C.E. and Sloan, S. 1948. *Sexual Behavior in the Human Male*. Philadelphia: Saunders.

Klein, F. 1993. *The Bisexual Option* (2nd edn). New York: Haworth Press.

Klesse, C. 2018. Dancing on the waves or being washed away? Representations of bisexualities in Liquid Modernity. *Sexualities*, 21(8): 1360–1367.

Levy, D.L. and Harr, J. 2018. "I never felt like there was a place for me": Experiences of bisexual and pansexual individuals with a Christian upbringing. *Journal of Bisexuality*, 18(2): 186–205.

Levy, D.L. and Reeves, P. 2011. Resolving identity conflict: Gay, lesbian, and queer individuals with a Christian upbringing. *Journal of Gay & Lesbian Social Services*, 23(1): 53–68.

Martino, A.S. 2017. Crippling sexualities: An analytic review of theoretical and empirical writing on the intersection of disabilities and sexualities. *Sociology Compass*, 11(5): e12471.

McCormack, M., Wignall, L. and Anderson, E. 2015. Identities and identifications: Changes in metropolitan bisexual men's attitudes and experiences. *Journal of Bisexuality*, 15(1): 3–20.

Mikulak, M. 2018. Telling a poor man he can become rich: Reparative therapy in contemporary Poland. *Sexualities*. https://doi.org/10.1177/1363460718797543

Orne, J. 2011. 'You will always have to "out" yourself': Reconsidering coming out through strategic outness. *Sexualities*, 14(6): 681–703.

Pennington, S. 2009. Bisexuals 'doing gender' in romantic relationships. *Journal of Bisexuality*, 9(1): 33–69.

Reay, B. 2018. Straight but not straight: The strange history of sexual reorientation therapy. *GLQ: A Journal of Lesbian and Gay Studies*, 24(1): 159–161.

Richards, M. 2017. 'Angry, when things don't go my own way': What it means to be gay with learning disabilities. *Disability & Society*, 32, 1165–1179.

Ripley, M., Anderson, E., McCormack, M., Adams, A. and Pitts, R. 2011. The decreasing significance of stigma in the lives of bisexual men: Keynote address, bisexual research convention, London. *Journal of Bisexuality*, 11(2–3): 195–206.

Robinson, M. 2015. Bisexual people, in *The Oxford Handbook of Theology, Sexuality, and Gender*, edited by A. Thatcher. Oxford: Oxford University Press, 640–656.

Rüpke, J. 2015. Religious agency, identity, and communication: reflections on history and theory of religion. *Religion*, 45(3): 344–366.

Rust, P.C. 1995. *Bisexuality and the Challenge to Lesbian Politics: Sex, Loyalty and Revolution*. New York: New York University Press.

Rust, P.C. 2001. Too many and not enough: The meanings of bisexual identities. *Journal of Bisexuality*, 1: 33–68.

Schuck, K.D. and Liddle, B.J. 2001. Religious conflicts experienced by lesbian, gay, and bisexual individuals. *Journal of Gay & Lesbian Psychotherapy*, 5(2): 63–82.

Shakespeare, T. 2000. Disabled sexuality: toward rights and recognition. *Sexuality and Disability*, 18(3): 159–166.

Shepherd, C.A. 2018. *Bisexuality and the Western Christian Church: The Damage of Silence*. New York: Springer.

Sinecka, J. 2008. 'I am bodied'. 'I am sexual'. 'I am human'. Experiencing deafness and gayness: a story of a young man. *Disability & Society* 23(5): 475–484.

Storr, M. 1997. Introduction, in *The Bisexual Imaginary*, edited by Bi Academic Intervention. London: Cassell, 1–13.

Toft, A. 2009. Bisexual Christians: The life-stories of a marginalised community, in *Contemporary Christianity and LGBT Sexualities*, edited by S. Hunt. London: Ashgate, 67–85.

Toft, A. 2012. Bisexuality and Christianity: Negotiating disparate identities in church life, in *The Ashgate Research Companion to Contemporary Religion and Sexuality*, edited by S. Hunt and A.K.T. Yip. Farnham: Ashgate, 189–203.

Toft, A. 2014. Re-imagining bisexuality and Christianity: The negotiation of Christianity in the lives of bisexual women and men. *Sexualities*, 17(5–6): 546–564.

Toft, A. Forthcoming. Exploring the intersection of bisexuality and Christian identities: The negotiation of gendered attraction in intimate lives, in *Intersecting Religion and Sexuality*, edited by S. Page and A.K.T. Yip. Leiden: Brill.

Toft, A., Franklin, A., and Langley, E. 2019a. Young, disabled and LGBT+. *Journal of LGBT Youth*, 16(2): 157–172.

Toft, A., Franklin, A., and Langley, E. 2019b. 'You're not sure that you are gay yet': The perpetuation of the 'phase' in the lives of young disabled LGBT+ people. *Sexualities*. https://doi.org/10.1177/1363460719842135

Toft, A. and Yip, A.K.T. 2018. Intimacy negotiated: The management of relationships and the construction of personal communities in the lives of bisexual women and men. *Sexualities*, 21(1–2): 233–250.

Windsong, E.A. 2018. Incorporating intersectionality into research design: An example using qualitative interviews. *International Journal of Social Research Methodology*, 21 (2): 135–147.

Woodhead, L. 2001. The turn to life in contemporary theology and spirituality, in *Spirituality and Society in the New Millennium*, edited by U. King. Brighton: Sussex Academic Press, 110–123.

Yip, A.K.T. 2000. Leaving the church to keep my faith: The lived experiences of non-heterosexual Christians, in *Joining and Leaving Religion: Research Perspectives*, edited by L.J. Francis and F.Y. Katz. Leominster: Gracewing, 129–145.

Yip, A.K.T. and Page, S.J. 2013. *Religious and Sexual Identities: A Multi-faith Exploration of Young Adults*. Farnham: Ashgate.

4 Bisexual erasure and religious spaces

Experiences of young adults in the United Kingdom

Andrew Kam-Tuck Yip and Sarah-Jane Page

Introduction

Bisexuality is scary to many people. This is because it de-stabilises and disrupts entrenched and deep-seated cultural norms on not only sexuality, but also intimacy and relationships – in other words, the social order. Even for heterosexual, lesbian and gay people who are committed to the legal recognition and social acceptance of sexual diversity and difference, bisexuality challenges their often uncritically subscribed and unreflexively practised ideology of monosexism. As Toft and Yip have argued:

> Monosexism is a cultural ideology, a set of institutional practices and individual attitudes that demand a person's self-identification firmly and exclusively with one sexual identity. Monosexism operates on, and perpetuates, the hegemony of the hetero/homo dichotomy. Consequently, 'heterosexual' is a normative thus often unproblematized identity – and 'lesbian' and 'gay' are increasingly accepted identities – but this system of identification and stratification insists on an individual's attraction to either members of the same sex or opposite sex. This concretizes the exclusive occupation of one side of the hetero/homo and opposite-sex/ same-sex taxonomy.
>
> (2018: 234; see also Anderson and McCormack, 2016)

Rust rightly asserts that bisexuals are 'people whose common characteristic is their refusal to practice gendered exclusivity' (1995: 241; see also Rust, 2000, 2002). This positions them in a collision course with a society that obstinately hegemonises gender exclusivity and specificity in emotional and sexual relating. This gender exclusivity is reflected in the way we make assumptions about an individual's sexual identity from their current partnered arrangements. For instance, we uncritically assume that individuals in a cross-sex relationship are heterosexual, and those in a same-sex relationship are gay or lesbian. In other words, we label the relationship based on the gender of the individuals involved, and the individual's sexual identity based on the gender of their partner (i.e. a woman is firmly labelled as 'lesbian' because her partner is a woman, and the relationship is same-sex). In all these cases, the possibility that any of the individuals may self-identify as 'bisexual' is negated and eradicated. Bisexuality is simply squeezed out of the language, awareness and imagination. Such powerful assumptions underpin the pervasive and systematic invisibilisation and invalidation of bisexuality and bisexual people. This is the foundation of 'bisexual erasure' in language (i.e. social labelling), social norm and practice (Yoshino, 2000), undermining positive and sustained 'bisexual display' in everyday life (Hartman, 2013; Hartman-Linck, 2014).

In terms of relationship formation, even societies that legally and socially affirm sexual diversity (i.e. by legalising same-sex relationships as civil partnership and/or marriage) continue to homogenise dyadic or coupled relationships and the associated value of monogamy. Wilkinson (2013) calls this hegemonisation of dyadic relationships 'compulsory coupledom'. Consequently, polyamorous relationships are stigmatised and vilified. While there is a burgeoning corpus of research evidence that demonstrates incontrovertibly that bisexuality does not equate to polyamory (i.e. some bisexuals are committed to coupled relationship, whether it is monogamous or non-monogamous), the dominant discourse that bisexuals are 'promiscuous' and incapable of being committed to just one partner is constantly reinscribed in popular culture. In our view, 'compulsory monogamy' – closely associated with 'compulsory coupledom' (Wilkinson, 2013) as an aspirational narrative and a cultural norm – plays a significant role in the foundational characteristic of a 'committed' and 'faithful' (therefore presumably 'fulfilling') coupled relationship. It is precisely within this discursive frame that bisexuals – pervasively but erroneously constructed as having to be with members of the same and opposite sex simultaneously and in equal measure – encounter great difficulty in convincing people that monogamy is not antithetical to their sexuality and relationship aspiration, if so desired (Fielder and Ezzy, 2018; Shepherd, 2018).

This discourse permeates many heteronormative religious communities, especially those of Abrahamic traditions, typified by the infamous phrase from the Church of England's *Issues in Human Sexuality* (2003) that bisexuals are 'incapable of faithfulness', implying also that bisexuals should embrace heterosexuality exclusively, since they have a 'choice', compared to their lesbian and gay counterparts who do not. That dyadic monogamy and faithfulness are synonymised – and a 'choice' has to be exercised to embrace 'normality' – warrant many words of de-construction and problematisation. But this is not the aim of this chapter (see Shepherd, 2018 for further discussion of bisexuality in *Issues in Human Sexuality*). Nonetheless, it is crucial to stress that, such limited and limiting social constructions of sexuality, intimacy, relationship – and indeed religious and spiritual commitment – are challenges that bisexual people, religious or not, have to grapple with in everyday life.

In a nutshell, bisexuality, as a concept and an identity, is shrouded with ambivalence, confusion and indeed, fear (i.e. biphobia), leading to ongoing forces of bisexual erasure to eliminate the threat that bisexuality poses to the gender and sexual order (e.g. Flanders, 2016; Maliepaard, 2015; Monro, 2015, 2018; Monro, Hines and Osborne, 2017; Sears, 2014; Yost and Thomas, 2012). This is what Anderson and McCormack (2016) call 'the bisexual burden'.

The proliferation of social scientific research on minority sexualities in relation to religion in the past 25 years is undeniable. Hunt's (2010) five-volume collection of previously published works on this theme attests to this (see also Hunt, 2015). This has led to some scholars to assert that research in this area has reached a saturation point. We do not subscribe to this view. While we celebrate the research achievement in this area – to which we have also contributed – we firmly believe that there is more work to be done. There is an urgent need to dwell deeper into the lived experiences of people whose voices are often lost in research and discourse about minority sexualities, which in reality focus primarily on gay and lesbian people. Bisexuals and trans people are two cases in point (Page and Shipley, forthcoming; Yip, 2018; Young and Shipley, 2020). The specific focus we place on bisexual people with religious faith is an important endeavour. It generates insights that enrich our understanding of how they, as sexual and religious actors, engage with specific dominant discourses (e.g. monosexism, coupledom, monogamy) that often construct them in a negative light in secular and religious spaces and different sexual communities. On a general level, their experiences have much to teach us about how social actors live out their sexuality and religion by strenuously negotiating personal aspirations, religious norms and social ideologies. The specificities of their lived experiences should also caution us against homogenising minority sexualities, and their intersecting and interlocking relationship with religion.

The remainder of this chapter is divided into four parts. We begin with a methodological account of the mixed-method research on which this chapter is based. This is followed by two empirical themes. The first theme outlines the participants' self-identifications and the primary challenges they encountered in their everyday life, reflecting the circulation and reinscription of powerful discourses about sexuality, intimacy and relationships. In the second theme, which is the main crux of the chapter, we explicate the different outcomes of the participants' management of their sexual and religious identities, demonstrating that the intersection between them is not monolithic. We end the chapter with some concluding remarks.

Methodological account

This chapter presents qualitative and quantitative data from 55 self-identified bisexual participants in the United Kingdom, aged between 18 and 25, drawing on a larger study entitled *Religion, Youth and Sexuality: A Multi-*

faith Exploration. [1] All 55 participants completed an online questionnaire. In addition, a sub-sample of eight were interviewed individually. Four participants from the interviewed sub-sample also completed a video diary, over a period of approximately one week.

The online questionnaire was designed to collect primarily quantitative, but also qualitative data. It contained 38 open and closed-ended questions, organised into seven sections, aiming to document participants' views and experiences on a range of issues pertaining to their religion, sexuality, gender and being young adults in society. While the questionnaire aimed to provide an overview of each participant's perspectives and lived experiences, the interview served as a tool to generate 'thick description', using each participant's completed questionnaire as the primary but not exclusive basis. Each participant was interviewed for about two hours. As the video diary was designed to be largely participant-led, each participant was provided with a simple one-page guide. In essence, we wanted them to record their 'mundane' and significant reflections over approximately a week, with no interference from the research team during the process.

Thirty-five (63.6%) of the 55 participants self-identified as women, and the rest (20, 36.4%) self-identified as men. The vast majority of the sample (48, 87.3%) were 'white'. In terms of relationship status, the two primary categories are: 'single' (34, 61.8%) and 'unmarried partnered heterosexual relationship' (13, 23.6%). One fifth of participants (11, 20.4%) had a degree, with a further four (7.4%) having a postgraduate qualification. Most participants were students (39, 70.9%), with just over a fifth (12, 21.8%) of remaining participants in employment. The sample was geographically dispersed across the UK, with the highest proportion of individuals coming from Greater London, the East Midlands and North West (8, 15.1% in each respective location). In terms of religious identification, the biggest category is 'Christian' (34, 61.8%), followed by 'Buddhist' (7, 12.7%), 'Jewish' (6, 10.9%), 'Muslim' (4, 7.3%), 'Mixed faith' (e.g. 'Buddhist-Christian'; 3, 5.4%) and 'Sikh' (1, 1.8%).

Self-definitions and bisexual erasure in multiple spaces

In this section, we highlight the participants' self-definitions of bisexuality and their narratives of pervasive 'bisexual erasure' in different spaces.

Table 4.1 Participants who 'strongly agreed' or 'agreed' with statements about bisexuality

Statement	*Frequency*	*Percentage*	*Number of valid cases*
1 Bisexuality is a confused sexuality. Bisexuals should choose to be either heterosexual or homosexual.	2	3.6	55
2 Bisexuality is a distinct sexual orientation, just like homosexuality and heterosexuality.	48	87.3	55

The responses to Statement 1 are unsurprising: only two (3.6%) of the participants think that bisexuality is a confused sexuality, and that bisexuals should choose between the hetero-homo binary of sexual anatomy. The rest of the sample (53, 96.4%) 'strongly disagreed' or 'disagreed' with this dominant discourse of monosexism which, as we have discussed above, is the foundation of the invisibilising, silencing and marginalising force of 'bisexual erasure'. These responses highlight that, even in progressive spaces (religious or secular, heterosexual or lesbian and gay), the de-centring of 'compulsory heterosexuality' has not led to the deconstruction of 'compulsory monosexuality', which upholds that eroticism is fixed, and most of all, gender-specific and dichotomous.

One significant concomitant of 'compulsory monosexuality' is 'compulsory coupledom and monogamy'; i.e. that the most ethical and productive (i.e. 'faithful', 'committed') way to organise human intimacy is in the form of a monogamous coupled relationship, be it cross-sex or same-sex. The increasing social acceptance (e.g. the dominant 'love' discourse) and legalisation of same-sex relationships are predicated on this entrenched cultural norm. This reinscription of the seemingly unbreakable nexus between monosexuality, monogamy and coupled relationship constantly casts bisexuality in a negative light, as Klesse has argued:

> [D]ominant discourse constructs bisexuals as non-monogamous *by necessity* … the dominant definition of bisexuality demands people to be, at any particular time, behaviourally or actively bisexual … [that] people can only call themselves to be truly bisexual if they maintain relationships with people of both male and female genders at the same time.
>
> (2007: 78; emphasis in original)

The responses to Statement 2 clearly demonstrate the salient sentiment that the vast majority of participants (87.3%) attached to bisexuality, that it is a distinct sexuality, and not a derivative form, or combination, of heterosexuality and homosexuality. To them, bisexuality should be understood, not as an intermediary status between heterosexuality and homosexuality, but as a distinct affective and sexual expression in which heterosexuality and homosexuality co-mingle.

Indeed, there is a strong emphasis on transcending gender in terms of emotional and sexual attraction, as Petra, a single white Buddhist-Christian, explained in the interview:

> Generally, I am more into women but I have also been with men, and I would prefer women … It depends entirely on the person. I've been emotionally and sexually attached to both genders equally … I think that many people believe … you have to decide for one side [gender] … They prefer to categorise people because it makes life much easier and I think it also makes it much easier for them to deal with me.

As Petra's narrative clearly illustrates, the pressure to be categorised on either side of the heterosexual–homosexuality binary (i.e. monosexism) is immense, because it conforms to, thus reinscribes, the dominant sexual order. Conversely, defining oneself as bisexual – therefore putting emotional and sexual attraction on a spectrum rather than fixing it – disrupts and de-stabilises this dominant discourse of sexuality.

Against this backdrop, identifying oneself as 'bisexual' certainly generates the need to manage one's presumed lack of commitment to, and ability in, subscribing to monogamy, as James, a single Christian, expressed in the interview:

> The fact that I'm bisexual doesn't mean that because I'm dating a woman, I suddenly want to have sex with men … monogamy's fine. I don't mind monogamy at all. But yeah. No definitely if I was dating a woman, if I was married, I would be completely open to my wife, that I am bisexual. This is my sexual history. This is what I've been doing, end up doing in the past and things like that. But … I wouldn't be looking to have sex with men. No, definitely not. That wouldn't be an issue.

James's narrative shows that although he self-identified as bisexual on the basis of his sexual history, his religiously-informed commitment to monogamy was paramount in his practice of intimacy. In the next section, we shall explore more fully religious-informed commitments such as this and its differing impacts on participants' lives, including James's.

Given the prevalent misunderstanding of bisexuality, it is perhaps not surprising that, for some participants, this marked identity label ought to be avoided. Annie, a Buddhist woman in an unmarried cross-sex relationship, expressed this strongly in the interview:

> I came out as bisexual … If I had to choose [a label], you know, if I had to tick a box, I would say bisexual … [but] I didn't want to use the word 'bisexual'. I didn't like it because of this connotations of sitting on the fence, being promiscuous … You're actually one thing [gay or straight] but you can't admit it and all this kind of crap … If I had to choose, you know, if I had to tick a box, I would say bisexual, but almost in a way I don't want to negate, I don't want people to ever think that [ex-girlfriend] was a phase because I don't want to erase two and a half years of my life just because I'm somewhere different now.

Annie's reflection on her sexual identification is interesting. Although she opted for the label 'bisexual' for the purpose of our study, the interview has offered her the space to reflect more deeply on this issue. Further on in the interview, she asserted that she preferred the term 'pansexual' because it aligned more closely with her understanding of her own sexuality. Her understanding reflects scholarly literature which argues that, while 'bisexual' disrupts the hetero-homo binary, it nonetheless assumes a fixed position itself. 'Pansexual', in contrast, refuses to settle on any position, any exclusive identitarian belonging. Therefore, it is open to various permutations of sexual and emotional attachments. In short, it is even more transgressive of the normative sexual taxonomy.[2]

Like Annie, Emily also has serious reservations with the term 'bisexual' not because she is ashamed of it – in fact, she considered herself 'fortunate' in this respect – but because of the stigmatisation that is engendered in heterosexual, as well as lesbian and gay, communities. Emily is a white Christian woman in a monogamous unmarried cross-gender relationship, and she said in the interview:

> Some days I am happy both ways. But some days I wake up really 'anti-gay' and I can't be bothered with it. Some days I'll be completely gay and have the horn for girls. I can't explain that … It changes from day to day sometimes … I have kind of given up trying to define who I am because I just think if I like someone then I like someone. I really hate the term bisexual because straight people don't like you, gay people don't like you and lesbians don't like you. So I don't like this … If someone was to say to me, 'What are you?', I would say, 'I was just me'. If anything I would say I am gay. If someone catches me talking about an ex-girlfriend or going to a strip club they'll go, 'Are you bi?' I'll say, 'No, I am gay'. I would rather be associated with being gay than bi … I guess I am quite fortunate where I can have a relationship with either and I am open to that idea. I don't really think about it that much. Other people think about it more for me … If I fancy a girl, I don't think, I wonder what that means; it means I just fancy her. People worry about it more than I worry about it.

Taking the quantitative and qualitative data as a whole, we can learn three key lessons from the participants' views and experiences. First, far from being 'confused' about their sexuality, they embraced the authenticity of their bisexual identity. They acknowledged the presence of emotional attachment and sexual attraction to both genders, but often the expression of such an attachment and attraction was sequential rather than simultaneous. Many participants, like James, self-defined as bisexual because of their sexual history (i.e. having been involved with members of both genders), rather than the need to express the dual-gendered attraction simultaneously and equally at a particular point of time in their life. For those who were in a relationship, such as Annie, and those who aspired to be in one, such as James, being in a coupled relationship with a member of either gender, rather than both, was not perceived as a 'lack' or 'incompleteness' in their intimate lives. Indeed, being bisexual and being monogamous are not mutually exclusive. Therefore, consistent with other research findings (e.g. Anderson and McCormack, 2016; Barker et al., 2012; Monro, 2015), the participants' living out of bisexuality often defies the erroneous but recalcitrant discourse of bisexuality that its expression has to involve both genders simultaneously.

Second, in spite of the participants' positive self-identity, they were highly cognisant of – and indeed had to constantly manage – the social and psychological costs incurred in everyday social interactions. These costs took the form of stigmatising norms of biphobia, underpinned by monosexism and 'compulsory coupledom/monogamy', with their entrenched insistence on duality and binary in the social constructions of emotional and sexual relating, as we have discussed above. Therefore, some participants, such as Annie and Emily, had resorted to not socially identifying themselves as bisexual, precisely because they wanted to avoid the inconvenience and pain of having to deal with biphobic norms and practices. Of course, this resignation does not offer any resistance to the forces of bisexual erasure.

Third, the stigmatising norms of biphobia are produced, circulated and reinscribed in diverse spaces. Lesbian and gay and secular spaces, which are usually considered more respectful of sexual diversity – as opposed to heterosexual and religious spaces – are also implicated in this scenario. For example, bisexuals often encountered misperceptions that they were still 'undecided' about their sexuality in their sexual identity journey (due to, e.g., internalised homophobia) that should ultimately lead to coming out as gay or lesbian in order to achieve optimum sexual and emotional maturity and health. In other words, 'bisexual' is an under-developed or developing identity, en route to full flourishing as 'gay' or 'lesbian', as our participant Annie has frustratingly stated above. The other criticism that bisexuals often experience in lesbian and gay communities is that they, rather than being 'out and proud' gay or lesbian, are, at best, 'strategic', wanting to continue to partake in 'heterosexual privileges' in a still predominantly heteronormative society. Such narratives are well documented in a host of research literature (e.g. Anderlini-D'Onofrio, 2005; Barker et al., 2012; Enstedt, 2015; Friedman et al., 2014; Monro, 2015; Monro, Hines and Osborne 2017; Ross, Dobinson and Eady, 2010). As Barker (2014) has rightly argued, lesbian and gay politics itself emanates from a gender binary, affirming gender specificity. Consequently, it also reinforces monosexism.

This should caution us against adopting a monolithic view of such spaces and a simplistic understanding of their propensity for embracing the value of sexual diversity. Within this context, we shall, in the next section, focus on religious spaces and demonstrate the different ways the participants manage their bisexuality in relation to their religious faiths.

Negotiating the intersections: multiple outcomes

The intersection of sexuality and spirituality in participants' lives generate multiple outcomes, characterised by creative tension and adaptation, with differences emerging in how positively or negatively their identities are perceived in various sacred and secular spaces.

Table 4.2 Participants who 'strongly agreed' or 'agreed' with statements about their religious faith and bisexuality

Statement	*Frequency*	*Percentage*	*Number of valid cases*
1 My religion is positive towards sexuality	20	40.8	49
2 My religion restricts my sexual expression	22	44.0	50
3 My religious faith is significant in shaping my attitudes towards sex and sexuality	30	61.2	49

Table 4.2 demonstrates that, overall, the relationship between the participants' religious faith and sexuality is characterised by ambivalence. On the one hand, 40.8% of them reported that their religion was positive towards sexuality (Statement 1). On the other hand, 44.0% of them felt that their religion restricted their sexual expression (Statement 2). Nonetheless, a majority of 61.2% considered their religious faith significant in shaping their attitudes towards sex and sexuality (Statement 3). Based on this quantitative data, we can deduce that religion is by and large significant to most participants and it informs their understandings of sexuality.

However, how the two intersect, and the outcome of this intersection, manifest in diverse ways. In this regard, the qualitative data offers a more nuanced and layered picture. In the remainder of this section, we draw on data from interviews and video diaries to illustrate two primary stories. The first outcome, focusing on Saleem, Rachel and James, tell a story of conflict and tension. The second outcome, predicted on the experiences of Petra, Chloe and Lily, tell a story of accommodation and adaptation. Strikingly, the first group of participants came from Abrahamic religious backgrounds, while the second group consisted of those who self-identified as Buddhist or mixed-faith, featuring Buddhism prominently. We shall comment on this interesting observation later.

Conflict and tension

Saleem was a Muslim man in a same-sex relationship. In the interview, he told us at length how the dominant discourse of sexuality in Muslim spaces had generated much tension and conflict in his personal and social life:

> I found myself to be bisexual, I did find some guys attractive and some women. But I did try and pray to Allah, that these thoughts will get out of my head. I went onto online Islamic help chat rooms. I spoke with a few imams online. They would all tell me the same thing, they'd tell me it was *shaytan* [the devil], giving me bad, whispering into my ear, these sexual thoughts about men. They would tell me pray to Allah, or get married straightaway, and it will go.

It is rather significant to note the bisexual erasure embedded in the religiously informed advice that Saleem received from the imams. On the one hand, they disapproved of his sexual desire towards men, identifying it as homosexuality. On the other hand, they offered a solution: getting married; in other words, performing heterosexuality. Here, we see the reinscription of the heterosexual–homosexual binary. Bisexuality is not acknowledged, and is thus erased. This created tensions for Saleem, as he navigated his current secret partnership with another man, to whom he was deeply committed. To some extent, Saleem had absorbed some of the conservative teachings of the imam; although he did fervently reject the construction of his current partnership in such negative terms as an evil, he did view it as limiting, as he could not counter the idea that Islam would support same-sex marriage: 'I know that we can never get married; there's no imam [who] would marry us, and I would never get married by registry office because that's not seen as a marriage in the eyes of Allah.' Whilst the formalising of same-sex partnerships was a legal possibility, for Saleem, this was not good enough, as it did not receive sacred approval. At the same time he said, 'I really would like to get married in the future', with his meaning that this would be to a woman. He therefore pondered the idea whether, should he and his partner break up, it would be easier to forge a partnership with a woman, and be read through the lens of heterosexuality in his very conservative religious community.

Indeed, bisexual erasure is a pervasive phenomenon that heightens the complexity and intricacy in the participants' management of their bisexual and religious identities in relation to themselves and others. To illustrate this more fully, we want to focus on two participants – Rachel, an Orthodox Jewish woman, and James, an Evangelical Christian (whom we have introduced in the preceding section). We have deliberately drawn from the multiple entries of their respective video diaries to offer a nuanced and complex account of their experiences. As we explained in the methodological account, this method is primarily participant-led, in the absence of the researchers. Thus, their reflections are of particular value.

Rachel and James shared a key feature – they were in full cognizance of the unacceptability of same-sex relationship in their religious communities, and they were willing to conform to that. This approach has a significant impact on the ways they managed their sexuality and religiosity. Rachel went to extraordinary lengths to reduce such tension in both same-sex and cross-sex relationships that she had been in. The lengthy account below is based on her multiple video diary entries, which we have re-organised to enhance discursive continuity and clarity:

> I am bisexual, and my decision [is] that I want to actively try to limit myself to dating only men because I can't see myself living [in] a long-term relationship with a woman because of my community and my religion … I started having a relationship with a girl, and then at some point during the relationship I admitted to myself that I was gay. [But] I didn't

> feel comfortable being Orthodox Jewish and gay, in that I don't want to live in a fringe community. So my choices were: leave Orthodoxy and embrace myself as gay, and in that relationship in which I was very happy; or break off the relationship and embrace my Orthodoxy … I couldn't leave Orthodox Judaism. That was my home, my people, where I feel comfortable … My ex-girlfriend told me today that she was coming out to people, and this includes people who know both of us. Which means that even though it isn't explicitly said, presumably they could at least, you know, have a reasonable suspicion that I am interested in girls as well as boys. Or whatever they choose to think, whether I am lesbian or bi or whatever. So [that] threw me off a bit.

As we can see from the above account, Rachel's cognisance of the unacceptability of same-sex relationship within the Orthodox Jewish community significantly informed her decision to dissolve her relationship with a woman, despite her strong recognition of her emotional and sexual attachment. In her attempt to conform to religious and cultural norms, hoping for acceptance and belonging in return, she entered into a relationship with a man. However, this religiously and culturally accepted relationship type itself did not preclude other kinds of challenges to be managed, as she further narrated in her video diaries:

> [Referring to her current cross-sex relationship where the partner self-identified as Jewish and gay] I am more attracted to girls and he is more attracted to boys, so how do we really know that we are interested in each other? It is a difficult call so we decided to be physical in our relationship and it sort of opened the floodgates … [Initially] I had clear limits. I would go so far as kissing and perhaps some feeling, exploration, but I draw the line at mutual masturbation and any sort of penetrative, oral or anal sex because I have a religious objection to unnecessary ejaculation; ejaculation that won't lead to pregnancy … [But] in the past week there has definitely been some oral sex and ejaculation and that is a bit confusing to me … If you were to ask me straight out if it is allowed or forbidden, I would say forbidden.

Similar to Saleem, Rachel inhabited a religious culture that forbade same-sex relationships, so this affected her management of her bisexuality. She was working out her bisexual identity in relation to intimate sexual navigation, with the aim of conforming to the demands of belonging within her religious community. But in this endeavour, she further contravened the strict codes of conduct as dictated by Orthodox Judaism, where even touching a partner before marriage was forbidden.

Like Rachel, James was deeply committed to his religion's official teachings on sexuality. He spent a lot of time studying the Bible individually and with fellow Evangelical Christians in this regard. He shared his reflections on this in the lengthy account below, taken from multiple entries of his video diaries, which we have re-organised to enhance discursive continuity and clarity:

> I have a foot in two camps. I have a foot in the Evangelical camp and a lot of them don't know that I am bisexual, which I have chosen because I am completely celibate … I have made the decision to be celibate. I agree with the biblical rules on when and where sex is allowed: within the context of male and female marriage. I would say sex outside marriage is a sin the same for gay people and straight people. And I am fine with that … [My LGBT+ friends] assume I am single because I haven't found the right guy yet, or girl yet because I am bisexual … My gay and lesbian friends, a lot of them give the impression that they would be happier if I was just going out with a guy and could treat me as gay, rather than embarrassingly turning up to a gay club with a girl; too much straightness there … On the other hand though, the Evangelicals that I am with, a lot of them don't know that I am bisexual. I was thinking of telling them [but] … I found out [that at] a Christian camp a lot of teenagers go [to], they have a rule that if any are gay or bisexual, they can't stay overnight. That made me a little bit nervous about coming out, and telling people that I am bisexual but celibate because… I assume they don't think of me as bisexual. I want them to treat me as a fellow Christian, not because of my sexuality. I wouldn't even want my sexuality to be an issue. This is where it gets tricky. If I have made up my mind to be completely celibate anyway or to say that I am only going to marry a woman, do I count as bisexual? Just because I get sexual feelings towards men? I have already said I would never act on them and would never want to act on them. Do I even get the right to call myself bisexual anymore when there isn't even the chance of sexual activity? Again the answer would be yes technically because I still have sexual feelings but gay and lesbian people would prefer me to have a boyfriend. Bisexual people who … would say that no, if you are not open to a relationship with both then you are not really bisexual. That is probably the whole politics of the bi community.

James's reflections above raise several significant points. First and foremost, he self-defined as bisexual because of his sexual desires for women and men. Nonetheless, his commitment to the official teaching of Evangelical Christianity – that sex is only religiously acceptable within the context of heterosexual marriage – led him to make two decisions. First, he would only have sex within the specific context of marriage. Second, until that happened, he would remain celibate. Thus his commitment to celibacy was not only because he conformed to the official Evangelical line that any expression of homosexuality is wrong in all contexts, but also because of his belief that heterosexual sex should only take place within marriage. Being single and being celibate therefore go hand in hand.[3] His lament about the competing demands from friends of different sexual identities in terms of his public sexual identification also directly speaks to the monosexism – and its political implications – that we have already discussed. We can see that he sidelined his sexual desires to enable full participation in his various social networks. Therefore, friendship and social connections are prioritised over his personal sexual happiness.

Taking the experiences of Saleem, Rachel and James together, we can see that the conflict and tension they have to manage relates primarily to the ordering of social life around a heterosexual–homosexual binary. We would argue that this is precisely a reflection of the primary status and prominence of heterosexuality and homosexuality in the discourse and personal reflections on sexuality. Bisexuality is often negated in this scenario. Regardless of their self-definitions, these participants have to engage with a broader discourse of sexuality that is still obstinately binary and gender-specific. This binary logic was encountered in both religious and secular spaces, but because of the conservative nature of their religious traditions, they experienced significant censure here, where same-sex relationships had to be either concealed or abandoned. In order to be accepted in their religious communities, these participants saw engagement with a cross-sex relationship as the only option, thereby putting at risk the existing relationships that had been forged. We can also observe an ambivalence about the bisexuality label itself, especially as they navigated belonging and participation in different spaces.

Accommodation and adaptation

We now turn to Petra, Chloe and Lily, who have a strong affinity with Buddhism. Their experiences of the relationship between bisexuality and religion are in stark contrast to those of James, Rachel and Saleem. We have already introduced in the section above Petra, who is a white single woman, self-identifying as Christian-Buddhist. Her mixed-faith identity gives her an appreciation of Christian and Buddhist sexual ethics, and she certainly found the latter more inspiring and helpful, as she explained in the interview:

> In Buddhism it was basically like make up your own mind and my conscience told me no sexual misconduct as one of the precepts and misconduct would, for me, only comprise of being dishonest, betraying somebody I love … So [sexual misconduct] wouldn't [include] bisexuality or homosexuality … I think Buddhism is generally very positive towards experiencing life … Buddhism is also about experiencing joy … In Buddhism you are free to do with your sexuality whatever you want to do. So I always felt quite unrestricted then. So I felt quite happy with it … So I think Buddhism has a positive attitude to sexuality because the framework of Buddhism allows for that all. It's just your own responsibility … I prefer to carry my own responsibility.

Petra's account clearly illustrates the central and foundational tenet of Buddhist sexual ethics: avoiding sexual misconduct. Buddhists therefore strive to do no harm, including sexual harm. The sexual type (same-sex or cross-sex) and the legal status (married or unmarried) are of less significance. What constitutes a meaningful and acceptable sexual behaviour is the absence of sexual misconduct, a responsibility that each individual should carry. The freedom to exercise personal responsibility in living out one's sexuality, rather than having an institutionally-imposed injunction, is a value and an experience that many of our Buddhists found nurturing. Lily, a white Buddhist in an unmarried cross-sex relationship, argued in the interview:

> I'm bisexual, and I always have been. Yeah, it's not something I really think about to be honest … Yeah, I mean obviously I couldn't be part of a religion that didn't accept me, me being I suppose in a sexual sense bisexual. So I suppose yeah the two are kind of interlinked in a way. Yeah, you see I kind of think about it because it's so safe that I haven't even thought about it; it hasn't even crossed my mind that that's not acceptable in Buddhism, until you kind of asked that question. So I suppose they're very interlinked, otherwise I just wouldn't be a Buddhist.

Lily, like Petra, emphasised personal freedom, including sexual freedom, as an indispensable element to her practice of Buddhism. Chloe was also a white woman in an unmarried cross-sex relationship. She self-identified as Buddhist-Quaker-Pagan. She told us in the interview:

> If you compare [Quakerism], with other churches it's really very tolerant … I've never felt a need to hide my sexuality at Meeting … it's not an issue. And the Buddhist bit, I'm aware that some Buddhist groups have expressed opinions one way or another on sexuality but what I'd be interested in, in Buddhist teaching, is the material about, you know, the idea of not harming people and so that covers all sorts of issues around fully informed, open, willing consent and being honest with people. Honesty obviously, truth testimony is very important to Quakers as well. So the bits of Buddhism I'm interested in don't really have, they don't affect my position … my sort of religious commitments that move towards Goddess worship and being interested in feminine images of deity, affect my approaches to sexuality. And vice versa, that my sexuality in terms of being bisexual and non-monogamous perhaps makes me more open to there being deities who are of both genders and you know, I can cope with using metaphors that are about more than one deity. Although I can see theological problems for people committed to monotheism, I'm not committed to monotheism particularly.

Chloe also invoked the Buddhist value of the avoidance of sexual misconduct as the ethical principle of her own sexual behaviour. In fact, the emphasis on this principle is commonplace amongst our Buddhist participants. In addition, her comment about Quakerism shows that the denomination is more open to sexual diversity compared to, say, Evangelical Christianity that James embraced (Levy and Harr, 2018; Shepherd, 2018). Furthermore, her exploration of paganism through Goddess worship has also enhanced her appreciation of the fluidity, thus plurality and complexity, of spirituality, and life itself.

Taking the narratives of the Buddhist participants as a whole, we can see that they definitely perceived and experienced Buddhism as an agency-enhancing and democratic practice, privileging the centrality of the individual. In this respect, bisexuality, alongside other sexualities, are subsumed within the principle of the avoidance of sexual misconduct. It is an ethical principle that promotes individual agency, reflexivity and responsibility. Furthermore, in human (sexual) relating, it places the emphasis not on gender and sexual labels or gendered and sexed bodies, but on the value and effect of that relationality (for a fuller discussion of this and these Buddhist participants' management of religion and sexuality, see Page and Yip, 2017a).

We would like to conclude our discussion of the second empirical theme with a caution against the homogenisation of religion and the propensity to essentialise the intersecting relationship between (bi)sexuality and religion. As the narratives in this section have shown, participants within Abrahamic religious traditions demonstrated a strikingly different experience compared to their Buddhist counterparts. Participants in our study identifying as bisexual and aligned with Abrahamic traditions tended to be connected to the more conservative elements of their religious tradition. This is not to suggest that there are no bisexual-positive spaces within Abrahamic religion. Indeed, Chloe found Quakerism a positive space, and other research (e.g. Shepherd, 2018; Toft, 2014) has located a small number of bi-affirming religious spaces. But those traditions which were already negative or even hostile towards same-sex relationships were equally negative about bisexuality; indeed they created new layers of expectation, with the idea that bisexual people could 'simply' become heterosexual, without recognising the costs incurred to the bisexual person. By and large, Buddhist spaces were comparatively far more affirming. Overall, a more nuanced analysis of this intersection must take into serious consideration theological and cultural specificities within and across religions (Machacek and Wilcox, 2003; Page and Shipley, forthcoming).

Concluding remarks

It is indisputable that, just after half a century after the Stonewall Riots, the lives of many LGBT people have fundamentally changed for the better. Nevertheless, a closer inspection will reveal that the political, social and cultural benefits that come from this are unevenly distributed across the various sub-groups within the LGBT community. In this respect, bisexual people are often the forgotten ones; the losers. This is also reflected in the scant research attention given to bisexuality, compared to other sexualities (e.g. Shepherd, 2018; Toft, 2014).

In many ways, the findings of our study are unsurprising. However, we would contend that their unsurprising nature reflects precisely the silent and pervasive power of biphobia in our society and the systematic bisexual erasure that this precipitates. The first empirical theme – and part of the second theme – have demonstrated incontrovertibly the multiple challenges our participants had to navigate in their daily life. The study demonstrates the continued hegemony of monosexism and the ideology of compulsory coupledom which structures the participants' everyday lived realities in secular and religious spaces, and their tireless contestation of these ideologies.

These challenges often escalate when bisexuality intersects with religion. This is particularly true for participants of Abrahamic religious background (see also Bernhardt-House, 2012; Daniels, 2012; Levy and Harr, 2018; Shepherd, 2018). The narratives of Saleem, Rachel and James demonstrate the uncompromising nature of their religious communities' disapproval of homosexuality, and their strenuous effort to navigate that. The religious discourse they had had to navigate was narrowly framed within the heterosexuality–homosexuality binary, with a monolithic construction of heterosexuality as the aspired ideal, and homosexuality, the to-be-avoided 'Other'. In this discourse, bisexuality is conspicuously absent, erased.

Nonetheless, we must be cautious against generalising the relationship between bisexuality and religion. As our Buddhist participants have demonstrated, their understanding and practice of the Buddhist ethical principle of avoidance of sexual misconduct has led to the decentring and de-hegemonisation of gender/sexual specificity and labelling. Instead, the ethical core orients around the quality and effect of the encounter and relationship. This formulation facilitates the transcending of labels and the construction of an agentic and self-responsible sexual ethics (e.g. Gross, 2015; Keele, 2012; Page and Yip, 2017a; Smith, Munt and Yip, 2016). Compared to participants of Abrahamic faiths, they certainly embraced their religious and sexual identities with a much greater degree of ease and accommodation, even locating religious spaces that were potentially more inclusive of their bisexual identity than secular LGBT+-affirming spaces. This should also remind us that the ubiquitous but monolithic secularist discourse which constructs religions as inherently gender- and sexuality-restrictive should be resisted and contested.

We believe that everyday life is messy and complex, and an individual's identity is multiple, plural and contextual. While the advancement in social scientific research on LGBT+ sexualities and religion thus far is a cause for celebration, we would argue that it is of paramount importance to pay attention to the specific segments of the LGBT+ community who are often overlooked. In this respect, bisexuals, who currently constitute 'a minority within a minority', ought to be given far more attention than they currently receive (Page and Shipley, forthcoming; Yip, 2018).

Notes

1 The main study, conducted between 2009 and 2011, was jointly funded by the UK's Economic and Social Research Council and the Arts and Humanities Research Council under the Religion and Society Programme (Award no. AH/G014051/1). The research team consisted of Andrew Kam-Tuck Yip (Principal Investigator), Michael Keenan (Co-investigator) and Sarah-Jane Page (Research Fellow). The project, involving 693 participants of diverse religious backgrounds and various sexualities, aimed to examine the participants' management of their religious, sexual, youth and gender identities in different everyday contexts. The participants were recruited through a host of sampling strategies, including: publicity postcards/posters/emails to relevant groups, social media, snowball sampling, personal networks and the project website. A full methodological account of this project – as well as the contents of the three research tools: online questionnaire, interview guide, and video diary guide – can be found in Yip and Page (2013). Other key publications from this project includes Page and Yip (2012, 2017a, 2017b, 2019), Yip and Page (2014). This chapter is the first publication from this project that gives bisexuality an exclusive examination.

2 There is no space in this chapter to elaborate further on 'pansexuality'. For a good discussion, see e.g. Belous and Bauman (2017), Callis (2016), Klesse (2018) and Morgaine (2019).

3 For a more detailed discussion on singleness and celibacy, see Yip and Page (2013).

References

Anderlini-D'Onofrio, S. 2005. *Plural Loves*, New York: Harrington Park Press.

Anderson, E. and McCormack, M. 2016. *The Changing Dynamics of Bisexual Men's Lives: Social Research Perspectives.* Basel: Springer.

Barker, M. 2014. Bisexuality, in *Encyclopedia of Critical Psychology*, edited by T. Thomas. Basel: Springer, 170–175.

Barker, M., Richards, C., Jones, R., Bowes-Cotton, H., Plowman, T., Yockney, J. and Morgan, M. 2012. *The Bisexual Report: Bisexual Inclusion in LGBT Equality and Diversity*, Milton Keynes: The Open University. [Online] Available at: http://oro.open.ac.uk/52881/1/The%20BisexualityReport%20Feb.2012_0.pdf [accessed 1 February 2019]

Belous, C.K. and Bauman, M.L. 2017. What's in a name? Exploring pansexuality online. *Journal of Bisexuality*, 17(1): 58–72.

Bernhardt-House, P.A. 2012. Reinforcing binaries, downgrading passions: Bisexual invisibility in mainstream queer Christian theology, in *Sexuality, Religion and the Sacred: Bisexual, Pansexual and Polysexual Perspectives*, edited by L. Hutchins and H. Sharif Williams. London: Routledge, 22–31.

Callis, A.S. 2016. Beyond bi: Sexual fluidity, identity and the post-bisexual revolution, in *Introducing the New Sexuality Studies*, edited by N.L. Fischer and S. Seidman. London: Routledge, 213–224.

Daniels, M. 2012. Not Even on the Page: Freeing God from Heterocentrism, in *Sexuality, Religion and the Sacred: Bisexual, Pansexual and Polysexual Perspectives*, edited by L. Hutchins and H. Sharif Williams. London: Routledge, 12–21.

Enstedt, D. 2015. Blessing same-sex unions and the invention of a 'genuine homosexuality' in the Church of Sweden. *Sexualities* 18(5/6): 564–592.

Fielder, B. and Ezzy, D. 2018. *Lesbian, Gay, Bisexual and Transgender Christians: Queer Christians, Authentic Selves.* London: Bloomsbury.

Flanders, C.E. 2016. Bisexuality, social identity, and well-being: An exploratory study. *Sexualities* 19(5/6): 497–516.

Friedman, M.R., Dodge, B., Schick, V., Herbenick, D., Hubach Randolph, D., Bowling, J., Goncalves, G., Krier, S., and Reece, M. 2014. From bias to bisexual health disparities: Attitudes toward bisexual men and women in the United States. *LGBT Health*, 1(4): 309–318.

Gross, R.M. 2015. Buddhism, in *The Oxford Handbook of Theology, Sexuality, and Gender*, edited by A. Thatcher. Oxford: Oxford University Press, 467–483.

Hartman, J.E. 2013. Creating a bisexual display: Making bisexuality visible. *Journal of Bisexuality*, 13(1), 39–62.

Hartman-Linck, J.E. 2014. Keeping bisexuality alive: Maintaining bisexual visibility in monogamous relationships. *Journal of Bisexuality*, 14(2), 177–193.

Hunt, S. 2010. *The Library of Essays on Sexuality and Religion* (5 volumes). Farnham: Ashgate.

Hunt, S. 2015. *Religion and LGBTQ Sexualities: Critical Essays*. Farnham: Ashgate.

Keele, L. 2012. The third precept: Towards a Buddhist ethics of bisexuality, in *Sexuality, Religion and the Sacred: Bisexual, Pansexual and Polysexual Perspectives*, edited by L. Hutchins and H. Sharif Williams. London: Routledge, 159–170.

Klesse, C. 2007. *The Spectre of Promiscuity: Gay Male and Bisexual Non-monogamies and Polyamories*. Aldershot: Ashgate.

Klesse, C. 2018. Dancing on the waves or being washed away? Representations of bisexualities in liquid modernity. *Sexualities*, 21(8): 1360–1367.

Levy, D.L. and Harr, J. 2018. 'I never felt like there was a place for me': Experiences of bisexual and pansexual individuals with a Christian upbringing. *Journal of Bisexuality*, 18(2): 186–205.

Machacek, D.W. and Wilcox, M.M. 2003. *Sexuality and the World's Religions*. Santa Barbara: ABC-CLIO.

Maliepaard, E. 2015. Bisexual citizenship in the Netherlands: On homo-emancipation and bisexual representations in national emancipation policies. *Sexualities* 18(4): 377–393.

Monro, S. 2015. *Bisexuality: Identities, Politics, and Theories*. Basingstoke: Palgrave Macmillan.

Monro, S. 2018. Sexualities studies: The last 20 years. *Sexualities*, 21(8): 1229–1233.

Monro, S, Hines, S and Osborne, A. 2017. Is bisexuality invisible? A review of sexualities scholarship 1970–2015. *The Sociological Review*, Online First, 1–19. [Online] Available at: http://journals.sagepub.com/doi/abs/10.1177/0038026117695488 [accessed 9 March 2019]

Morgaine, K. 2019. *Pansexuality*. San Diego, CA: Cognella Academic Publishing.

Page, S. and Shipley, H. Forthcoming. *Religion and Sexualities: Theories, Themes and Methodologies*. London: Routledge.

Page, S. and Yip, A.K.T. 2019. The gendering of heterosexual religious young adults' imagined futures. *Journal of Contemporary Religion*, 34(2), 253–273.

Page, S. and Yip, A.K.T. 2017a. *Understanding Young Buddhists: Living out Ethical Journeys*. Leiden: Brill.

Page, S. and Yip, A.K.T. 2017b. Gender equality and religion: A multi-faith exploration of young adults' narratives. *European Journal of Women's Studies*, 24(3), 249–265.

Page, S. and Yip, A.K.T. 2012. Religious young adults recounting the past: Narrating sexual and religious cultures in school. *Journal of Beliefs and Values*, 33(3), 405–415.

Ross, L.E., Dobinson, C. and Eady, A. 2010. Perceived determinants of mental health for bisexual people: A qualitative examination. *American Journal of Public Health* 100(3): 496–502.

Rust, P.C. 1995. *Bisexuality and the Challenge to Lesbian Politics: Sex, Loyalty and Revolution.* New York: New York University Press.

Rust, P.C. 2000. *Bisexuality in the United States: A Social Science Reader.* New York: Columbia University Press.

Rust, P.C. 2002. Bisexuality: The state of the union. *Annual Review of Sex Research*, 13(1): 180–240.

Sears, J. T. 2014. Becoming and being: Bisexuality and the search for self. *Journal of Bisexuality*, 14(1): 3–6.

Shepherd, C.A. 2018. *Bisexuality and the Western Christian Church: The Damage of Silence.* Cham: Palgrave Macmillan.

Smith, S.E., Munt, S.R. and Yip, A.K.T. 2016. *Cosmopolitan Dharma: Race, Sexuality, and Gender in British Buddhism.* Leiden: Brill.

Toft, A. 2014. Re-imagining bisexuality and Christianity: The negotiation of Christianity in the lives of bisexual women and men. *Sexualities*, 17(5/6): 546–564.

Toft, A. and Yip, A.K.T. 2018. Intimacy negotiated: The management of relationships and the construction of personal communities in the lives of bisexual women and men. *Sexualities*, 21(1–2): 233–250.

Wilkinson, E. 2013. Learning to love again: 'Broken families', citizenship and the state promotion of coupledom. *Geoforum*, 49: 206–213.

Yip, A.K.T. 2018. Research on sexuality and religion: Some reflections on accomplishments and future directions. *Sexualities*, 21(8): 1291–1294.

Yip, A.K.T. and Page, S. 2014. Religious faith and heterosexuality: A multi-faith exploration of young adults, in *Research in the Social Scientific Study of Religion (Volume 25)*, edited by R. Piedmont and A. Village. Leiden: Brill, 78–108.

Yip, A.K.T. and Page, S. 2013. *Religious and Sexual Identities: A Multi-faith Exploration of Young Adults.* Farnham: Ashgate.

Yoshino, K. 2000. The epistemic contract of bisexual erasure. *Stanford Law Review*, 52(2): 353–461.

Yost, M.R. and Thomas, G.D. 2012. Gender and binegativity: Men's and women's attitudes toward male and female bisexuals. *Archives of Sexual Behavior*, 41(3): 691–702.

Young, P. Dickey and Shipley, H. 2020. *Identities under Construction: Religion, Gender and Sexuality among Youth in Canada.* Montreal: McGill-Queen's University Press.

5 Ritual and liminality

Bisexuality within Christianity and Paganism

Douglas Ezzy and Bronwyn Fielder

Introduction

Bisexuality embraces ambiguity and complexity. This chapter argues that this ambiguity is at the heart of what makes bisexuality uncomfortable for Christians, and why it is more easily embraced by Witches and Pagans. Seligman et al. (2008) develop a distinction between religions that focus on 'sincerity' and those that focus on ritual. They argue that religions that focus on 'sincerity' tend to see 'the "essential" or constitutive arena of action (often read as intention) as something *within* the social actor or actors, with the external, formal ritual seen as but the marker of these internal processes' (Seligman et al., 2008: 4, emphasis added). Seligman and associates argue that sincerity tends to be associated with traditionalist conservativism and fundamentalism, oriented towards overcoming or banishing dissonance. In contrast, religious movements oriented towards ritual tend to be more accommodating of dissonance and complexity: 'Ritual's repeated, performative, and anti-discursive nature, we have argued, provides a critical way of dealing with, rather than overcoming, the eternal contradiction and ambiguity of human existence' (Seligman et al., 2008: 129). Christianity tends to emphasise belief and sincerity, Paganism tends to emphasise ritual. This, in turn, shapes their responses to bisexuality.

Much research using the acronym LGBT subsumes the unique experience of bisexuals into that of lesbians and gay men, rather than giving it the distinct attention it deserves (Browne, 2010; Jeffries, Dodge and Sandfort, 2008; Richardson-Self 2012; Rodriguez, 2009; Rodriguez, Lytle and Vaughn, 2013; Toft, 2014; Yip, 2010). Despite a recent increase in studies into alternative sexualities and genders, bisexuality remains marginalised. According to Monro et al. (2017) research into bisexuality is often excluded and underrepresented within the social sciences, suggesting that in part, biphobia has contributed to its erasure in the social sciences. They also attribute this marginalisation to the development of dominant hegemonic discourses in identity politics. For example, Klesse (2018a: 1361) notes that within queer studies the reception of bisexuality is 'contested and uneven'. Many hoped queer studies would give rise to greater recognition of bisexuality, but were disappointed at its continuing erasure.

Toft (2010; 2014) suggests the dearth of research in this area is due to its complexity. Bisexuality is complex. It has proven difficult to categorise, define and threatens the Western binarised worldview. According to Toft and Yip (2018: 234) bisexuality problematises the broader sexual and gender order in two major ways: it challenges 'monosexism' and 'compulsory monogamy'. Monosexism is a complex cultural set of 'institutional practices and individual attitudes' (Toft and Yip, 2018: 234) which leads to a deeply ingrained insistence on limiting sexual partners to one gender, maintaining the binary of the normative heterosexuality and its dichotomy, homosexuality. There is thus resistance and even hostility towards bisexuality from both heterosexual and non-heterosexual communities (Eisner, 2013, with both, at times, viewing bisexuality to be transitory and their sexuality to be unformed (Gonzalez, Ramiro and Galupo, 2017).

A second problem bisexuality faces is the deeply embedded 'aspirational norm' (Toft and Yip, 2018: 234) of compulsory monogamy, that legitimises and idealises couple relationships. The popular imaginary is that bisexuals form simultaneous relationships with people of both genders, a misunderstanding that leads to its stigmatisation. Bisexuals are presumed to be promiscuous and as a consequence are mistrusted.

Mistrust and misunderstanding of bisexuality are even more pronounced within the Christian worldview. Official conservative church responses to bisexuality emphasise (mistakenly) that bisexuals are promiscuous (Toft, 2014). Toft and Yip's (2018) study indicated that this generalisation was not reflected in the real-life experience of their participants, many of whom were in long-term and committed monogamous relationships. According to Yip (2010) there is little theological argument within Western religious traditions that de-stigmatises bisexuality, suggesting it is even more subversive of heteronormativity than is homosexuality. Bernhardt-House (2010) points out that theologically, bisexuality undermines the dualistic argument of a 'natural God given' sexuality – an argument often used by lesbian and gay Christians to understand their sexuality within their Christian worldview. Yip names this 'theological capital' (2005: 50). The ambiguity of bisexuality remains in tension with this often binaried understanding of sexuality within Christianity.

There are two main responses to the problematic status of bisexuality for Christians. First, many bisexual Christians individualise their faith (Jeffries et al., 2008; Toft, 2014; Wilcox, 2002). According to Toft (2014: 548) belief is adapted as 'personal experience takes priority over traditional organised Christianity'. This enables many to live according to their Christian faith without compromising their sexual identity. Others find affirmation of their sexuality and spirituality in other religious traditions and spaces (Neitz, 2000). One such spiritual space is Paganism. The rich ritual element of Paganism can be a space where bisexuality is welcomed and celebrated, rather than merely tolerated, and possibly dismissed.

This chapter first examines the 'problem' that bisexuality presents for Christianity. Even progressive forms of Christianity and LGBT-accepting churches and groups tend to be uncomfortable with bisexuality. For example, the

Metropolitan Community Church, a Christian denomination catering specifically to the non-heterosexual community, struggles to encompass bisexuality as legitimate (Fielder and Ezzy, 2017). Christianity tends to seek to erase the ambiguity at the heart of bisexuality (Bernhardt-House, 2010). We next introduce Pagan responses to bisexuality through a discussion of teenage Witchcraft. Finally, we consider the experiences of ritualists at the Pagan festival of Faunalia, arguing that ritual is a mediating factor and that some people find liminal ritual spaces to be places of celebration of bisexuality. Ritual is queered, embracing ambiguity, and enabling a liberation from binaries and fixed identities. The chapter draws on three main empirical sources. First, it draws on a study of LGBT Christians conducted by Fielder and Ezzy (2017). Second, it draws on interview data with teenage Witches from a study conducted by Berger and Ezzy (2007). Finally, it draws on Ezzy's (2014) study of an Australian Pagan festival. We draw on both published and previously unpublished material from these studies to examine bisexuality.

Bisexuality

Alfred Kinsey (1948) was the first to recognise bisexuality as a separate sexual identity. Writing about men, Kinsey noted that:

> males do not represent two discreet populations, heterosexual and homosexual. ... not all things are black, nor all things white. It is a fundamental of taxonomy that nature rarely deals with discreet categories. Only the human mind invents categories and tries to force facts into separated pigeon holes.
>
> (1948: 633)

Prior to this, Freud (1905) had perpetuated the narrative that bisexuality was neither a sexual orientation nor a mature state of being – rather a passing phase leading towards a normal hetero or pathologised homosexual orientation (Eisner, 2013). In this respect, bisexuality was erased before it was recognised. The myth that bisexuality is a passing phase, unfinished and immature, lingers in the popular imagination (Eisner, 2013). However, as pointed out by Foucault, the pathologisation of sexualities, homosexual and bisexual, brought about their existence as separate identities. The 1970s saw the rise in identity politics with bisexuality beginning to 'reclaim its space' and celebrate its existence (Eisner, 2013; Klesse, 2018a).

There is no consensus on a definition of bisexuality (Toft, 2010; Klesse, 2005, 2007, 2018a; Flanders et al., 2017) and many resist the impulse to categorise (Eisner, 2013). Bisexuality came to be defined in general terms, as, 'of relating to, or characterised by sexual or romantic attraction to members of both sexes; also engaging in sexual activity with partners of more than one gender' (The Merriam Webster Dictionary, 2018). A more nuanced definition by the bisexual activist Robyn Ochs (2013, cited in Eisner, 2013:

loc 331), states that bisexuality is, 'the potential to be attracted—romantically and/or sexually—to people of more than one sex and/or gender, not necessarily at the same time, not necessarily in the same way, and not necessarily to the same degree'.

Ochs' (2013) definition seeks to dispel some of the myths of bisexuality. By using the phrase, 'potential to be attracted' she draws attention away from the requirement of sexual activity and immediate attraction. Being bisexual is an orientation – for many people, a way of being, a self-declared identity. With this definition she also addressed other popular myths, such as the idea that bisexuals always practise polyamory with partners of both sexes (see also Klesse, 2018a, 2018b). As Klesse (2018a), Toft and Yip (2018) and Robinson (2013) rightly point out, the lives of bisexuals are complex and varied. Further, in this definition Ochs draws attention away from binaries, emphasising that bisexuality recognises people of 'more than one sex/and or gender'.

As such, bisexuality challenges both heterosexuality and homosexuality – both of which are 'monosexual' – the cultural assumption that everyone is attracted to only one sex, be it different sex or same-sex (Falek, 2013: 36). Thus, bisexuality is often viewed with distrust and suspicion from both the heterosexual and homosexual community, within both the secular and religious world. The ambiguity is unsettling and for many, it transgresses cultural norms in unacceptable ways (Toft and Yip, 2018).

Bisexual Christians

Mainstream Christianity seeks to erase the ambiguity at the heart of bisexuality. For traditional Christians the ideal to be aspired to is the monogamous marriage between male and female (Shepherd, 2018). Within traditional Christianity, bisexuality is frowned upon not only because it encompasses homosexual relationships, but because it seemingly transgresses the cultural mores of monosexism and compulsory monogamy (Toft, 2014). The official teachings of the Church of England, for example, recognise bisexuality, but advise bisexuals to 'follow the way of holiness and chose heterosexual marriage rather than remain within an "ambiguous" sexuality' (Lingwood, 2010: 31; see also Toft, 2010: 13; Toft, 2014). The common assumption is that bisexuals can choose, in this case, heterosexuality. Certainly, this is the way for some bisexuals, given the virulence of the churches' stand against homosexuality. For example, in Jeffries' et al. (2008: 9) study of 31 black bisexual men who expressed interest in religion or religious affiliation in New York, three Christian participants stated that they intended to marry in a heterosexual relationship and remain monogamous as it was 'the Christian thing to do'.

Bisexuals also struggle to find a place within church groups specifically for gay and lesbian worshippers. Although bisexual individuals are welcomed within both gay and lesbian Christian groups such as Dignity (Catholic) and Affirmation (Mormon), and within the Metropolitan Community Church

(MCC), the spiritual needs of bisexuals are often not catered for within these organisations (Crapo, 2005). Margaret Robinson (2003: 30) describes her experience in a Catholic gay and lesbian group saying:

> [The group was] unsure of how to support a bisexual person. I was almost always a minority of one. Where I had intended to find a group of similar Catholics, I often encountered a group who were uncomfortable with, or dismissive of my bisexuality.

Even within the progressive MCC the standing of bisexuality is precarious. The MCC is a church created to enable spaces of worship for the LGBT community, but according to Reverend Martha Daniels, a practising bisexual Christian minister, bisexuals are 'not even on the page' (2010: 46; see also Shepherd, 2019; Wilcox, 2002). The bisexual experience is subsumed into that of the LGBT or queer banner. When Daniels became a minster at the MCC, she slowly began to understand that despite outward acceptance, her sexuality was not regarded as legitimate, that she really needed to 'find her true identity' (2010: 46). Toft (2014: 555) reports a similar finding from one of his participants in his study on bisexual Christians, who reported that the MCC is dismissive of those without same-sex partners.

Fielder and Ezzy (2017) find similar attitudes towards bisexuality within MCC church congregations in Australia. According to one MCC congregant, 'Even though it's LGBT it's never really.' In their study of four MCC congregations, Fielder and Ezzy found only one woman who identifies positively as bisexual. Two women say that they could identify as bisexual but do not, considering there to be a biased negative attitude toward it. One of these individuals says:

> I hate that term bisexual. I went to this talk and they said that bisexuals have the highest suicide rate, the highest depression rate, 'cause they don't really belong in either camp. Even though it's LGBT it's never really.
>
> (Fielder and Ezzy, 2017: 138)

Bisexuality and ambiguity

In the popular imaginary it is presumed that bisexuals practise polyamory, simultaneous multiple partners, as a matter of course. While this is sometimes the case, this is not necessarily so. Polyamory is practised more or less occasionally across all sexual identities: bisexual, homosexual and heterosexual (Anapol, 2012). Yip (2010) theorises that the misconception that bisexuals always practise simultaneous relationships with people of both sexes creates fear and mistrust of bisexuality within both the heterosexual and non-heterosexual religious community. Bisexuality thus appears to violate Christian values such as compulsory coupledom of the monogamous family and structured faithful relationships (Toft and Yip, 2018). The MCC (Metropolitan Community Churches, 2013), for example, overtly and covertly encourages a normative expectation of family, privileging monogamy over other organisations of sexual relationships and thus reproducing a new normative way of being, a homonormative ideal. Homonormativity, a term coined by Duggan (2002), is 'the assimilation of heteronormative ideals and constructs into homosexual culture and individual identity. It refers to politics that do not contest dominant heteronormative assumptions and institutions such as monogamy, procreation and binary gender roles' (University of Victoria, 2010: 26). Bisexuality is associated with non-monogamy, both in myth and sometimes in practice. It therefore challenges both the heteronormative and homonormative essential understanding of sexuality.

Bisexuality is seen to undermine the logic of essentialism that runs through the gay-affirming theology and discourse of LGBT Christian worship (Bernhardt-House, 2010; Toft, 2010; Yip, 2010). The knowledge that 'God made me this way' is central to the legitimation of self, within a traditionally hostile religious institution. As LGBT Christians strive for authenticity, identity essentialism is a critical management strategy (Fielder and Ezzy, 2017). The essentialist understanding of an authentic sexuality leads to bisexuality being viewed as an 'immature' state. Daniels (2011: 46) expresses the attitude she found among MCC members that her bisexuality was really homosexuality that is 'not quite formed'.

Further, the discomfort felt by others towards bisexuality is indicative of the emotional investment in normalcy and coherence. The response to the ambiguity associated with bisexuality in the MCC is indicative of the normative Christian thinking upon which individuals create meaning. Individuals feel safe in spaces that are unsurprising and, in some sense, 'normative'. Emotional bonding occurs in safe spaces, where beliefs and religious sensibilities are shared. Ambiguity disturbs individuals and threatens these safe spaces that are created in the MCC. Fielder (2015) concludes that the queering of religious space occurs only insofar as the individual and group needs are met in the desire to live an authentic life. The MCC, despite challenging heteronormative mainstream Christianity, creates its own 'homonormative' space.

Bisexual women

The experience of bisexual women in particular is compounded by the patriarchal nature of organised religion. The majority of institutionalised religions are patriarchal in nature, Christianity included (Bouma, 2006; Comstock, 1993; Raphael, 1999). According to Shepherd (2018: 5), binary thinking is 'the operating system of patriarchal hierarchies' and 'has had an enormous effect on the acknowledgment and visibility of bisexual people' (Shepherd, 2018: 5). Morrow (2003), for example, examined the impact of patriarchy on lesbians, and the difficulties they encountered. She firstly described how powerful the church remained as a social institution in legitimising broad moral constructs, particularly in regard to sexuality and gender. She reported that due to the conceptual construction of the deity as male, women were more likely to remain marginalised within religious institutions, a position that was magnified by being both a woman and a lesbian, which was regarded as 'particularly vile' (Morrow, 2003: 110).

This particularly colours the experience of bisexual women. Bisexual women are at greater risk than their male counterparts of stigmatisation as a result of their sexuality. In his qualitative study of in UK, Klesse (2005) determined that being 'out' as bisexual and non-monogamous is particularly stigmatising for women due to allegations of promiscuity that are embedded in popular discourse toward bisexuals (see also Klesse 2007, 2018b). Similarly, Ault (1996: 313) discusses the identity dilemmas bisexual women face as being 'doubly deviant'. Not only are they marginalised for being women and of non-normative sexuality, their bisexual status can lead to marginalisation by lesbian friends. Ault (1996: 454) quotes one of her interviewees as saying: 'all my lesbian friends dumped me when I came out as bi'. In other words, bisexual religious women have distinctive experiences of overlapping marginalisation and discrimination. As women, they experience discrimination in both religious and secular contexts due to their gender. As bisexuals, they experience marginalisation and discrimination in both secular and religious contexts due to their sexuality. Sexism and patriarchy intersect with essentialist and binary understandings of hetero/homosexuality for bisexual religious women.

This erasure of bisexuality moves beyond Christian churches and, at times can be observed in more liberal spiritual groups. A similar erasure of bisexuality is observed within liberal spiritual 'New Age' communities. Dinnie and Browne (2011: 1), in their research on bisexual women in Findhorn Community[1] in Scotland, discovered that even in this liberal spiritual New Age environment, the female participants' fluid sexuality was resisted by others, who continued to label and categorise them. Their fluid identity, the authors report, 'became re-subsumed into heteronormativity', leading the women to 'have to come out and identify all over again' (Dinnie and Browne, 2011: 1). They conclude that sexual fluidity is an unsustainable position in the heteronormative environment of this new-age religious group. This is particularly true for women.

Pagan spirituality and bisexuality

'Paganism' is an umbrella term that refers to a range of traditions including Heathenry, Druidry, Witchcraft and the various Pagan reconstructionist traditions that seek to reconstruct the pre-Christian religions of Egypt, Greece and Anglo-Saxon England, among others (Ezzy, 2014; Harvey, 1997; Hutton, 1999; Salomonsen, 2002). Witchcraft itself is split into various traditions, including the more traditionalist cultures of Alexandrian and Gardnerian Wicca (Hutton, 1999), the explicitly feminist, and sometimes separatist, traditions of Dianic Wicca (Griffin, 1995), the feminist, environmentalist and activist traditions of Reclaiming Witchcraft (Salomonsen, 2002) and a range of others. However, most Witchcraft practitioners are highly individualist and eclectic in their practice. Teenage Witchcraft is perhaps one of the largest subgroups of Paganism that came to prominence in the 1990s and 2000s (Berger and Ezzy, 2007).

For some bisexuals, Paganism can present a resolution and reinforcement of their spiritual life. Paganism both embraces gender equality and provides a community that embraces the ambiguity at the heart of bisexual identities (Ezzy, 2014; Pike, 2001). For example, Robinson (2003: 118) reflects that:

> The prospect of intimacy with a female deity offers intriguing possibilities for bisexual women's theology. Such a relationship, particularly if accompanied by ritual, could be a resource for those women in relationships with men, who find long-term bisexual visibility a challenge.

Some branches of Wicca, for example, offer a spiritual path for many bisexuals where bisexuality is celebrated and reinforced. Cheryl Dobinson, a bisexual Wiccan, summarised the positive aspects of her tradition:

> Some of the things that appeal to me are Wicca's focus on the goddess and the feminine, its queer and sex-positiveness, the lack of a hierarchy and 'one-right-way' of doing things, the creative and playful aspects, respect and care for the natural world, and the kind of loving, supportive and inclusive community I've found witches to be. For me, being feminist and queer-positive were two key things that I just didn't see in other religions or spiritual paths, and also that kind of room for questioning and independent thought are important to me. I need to be a free-thinker in whatever I do!
>
> (Cited in Robinson 2003: 30)

The experience of bisexuality for teenage Witches provides an excellent introduction to the typical experience of sexuality within Paganism. This is followed by a discussion of the role of bisexuality and liminal ritual at Faunalia, a more marginal Pagan festival.

Teenage Witchcraft and bisexuality

Teenage Witchcraft is characterised by young people searching for a form of religion that feels 'right' to them. Helen Berger and Douglas Ezzy (2007) interviewed 90 teenage Witches from Australia, the United States and the United Kingdom in the early 2000s. Individualism, feminism, environmentalism and magical realism all contribute to a sense that traditional religions are dissatisfying (Berger and Ezzy, 2007). Inspired by positive portrayals of Witchcraft in mainstream media, the availability of information about Witchcraft in mainstream bookstores and on the Internet, young people learn of the existence of the religion of Witchcraft and begin to practise and think of themselves as Witches, often without ever physically meeting another Witch. Many go on to join groups, both online and in their local area. Acceptance of sexual diversity, including bisexuality, is a key aspect of what makes Witchcraft attractive to young people:

> Repeatedly, the young people say that they felt different from others … About half the young men we spoke to are openly gay or bisexual, or had been thought to be gay in high school even if they are not … Witchcraft provides a group in which they do fit. This sense of finding a group of people similar to them, even if that group is only on the Internet or meets infrequently at Pagan gatherings, is one aspect of 'coming home' to Witchcraft. The religion, among other things, provides a venue in which being different is acceptable and even seen as positive.
>
> (Berger and Ezzy, 2007: 81)

The acceptance of sexual diversity is partly a product of the sacralisation of sexuality within the mythology of Witchcraft. For example, many Witchcraft rituals include a blessing of a cup of wine. This is traditionally done by inserting a ritual knife (*athame*) into the cup whilst blessing the wine – a symbolic sexual act (Hutton, 1999). The sacralisation of sexuality is bound up with the broader focus on 'nature' that is characteristic of Witchcraft. For example, the festival of Beltane is a fertility festival traditionally held on 1 May in the Northern hemisphere and 1 November in the Southern hemisphere. Beltane celebrates the fecundity of spring (this theme of fertility is also present in the chocolate eggs and rabbits that accompany the Christian festival of Easter). Similarly, because Witchcraft is polytheistic and deities are both male and female, sexual relationships between deities is common, and therefore sacralised. Some deities are bisexual and transsexual, such as Loki in the Norse pantheon (Lindow, 2002). A number of Witchcraft traditions and leading Witches have also been openly bisexual and polyamorous, including the Church of All Worlds and Starhawk,[2] one of the key founders of the Reclaiming Witchcraft tradition who also embrace same-sex relationships (Salomonsen 2002). As a consequence, young Witches are much more likely to encounter people who openly practise diverse forms of sexuality and gender. For example, Morgan is a 19-year-old American Witch. She reported:

> Just by being in the [Pagan] community, I have known more polyamorous people than anywhere else. I have known more adult gay men. I have known young gay men [laughs], the story of my life, and bisexual men, but older men living that life, I have met a lot more.
>
> (Berger and Ezzy, 2007: 222)

Similarly, Yvette[3] is a 17-year-old Australian Witch. Douglas Ezzy asked her about her attitudes to male and female roles:

> *Yvette:* I'm a lot more open to that now. I mean that I'm bisexual – proud to admit. Before I never really thought about it. I never really saw two guys holding hands or two girls the same, but now I like it. I like seeing two guys together. I think it's sweet, you know, and I get frustrated with other people saying 'Oh that's wrong, it's not meant to be. That's not how God made us' and all that kind of stuff. I think: 'They like it. They enjoy it. It feels right to them. Why not?'
>
> *Douglas:* Do you think that's a product of your Witchcraft?
>
> *Yvette:* Yeah, mostly. Yeah, it's made me more open minded about other people and how they view themselves as well.

The experiences of teenage Witches reflect the broader culture of contemporary Paganism and Witchcraft. For example, Neitz (2000: 372) reports that the goddess-centred theology and cosmology of Wicca is associated with norms of 'gender equality', and is a 'nonpatriarchal religion' often led by women. Heterosexuality is celebrated, but not in oppressive way. Rather, Neitz suggests it might be referred to as 'queer heterosexuality'. Neitz attended a large Pagan festival in 1996 in the Denver. She noted 'a significant gay presence' including rituals, paraphernalia and rainbow flags.

Not all Pagans are accepting of sexual diversity. As Neitz (2000: 374) observes, there are various Pagan traditions (such as some forms of Gardnerian Wicca) that have a heteronormatively oriented mythology based on the idea of sexual polarity. Similarly, some of the 'nativist' Paganisms have racist and homophobic aspects (Rountree, 2015). Nonetheless, Neitz argues, and others concur (Oboler, 2010), that Paganisms are typically more accepting of sexual diversity.

The embrace of sexual and gender diversity by Pagans is probably a mutually reinforcing product of individual seeking and cultural processes. Individuals do seek out subcultures where their desired gender and sexual expressions are accepted. Similarly, contemporary culture, including forms of Witchcraft in mainstream culture, encourage sexual and gender exploration and experimentation. The role of ritual in shaping self-understandings clearly has an impact

Sarah Pike for example, notes that a 1992 survey of one Pagan festival in the United States reported that of the 354 responses, 72% identified as heterosexual, 14% as bisexual, 5% as gay male, 3% as lesbian, 2% celibate and 4% 'other'. Compared to most Americans, 'heterosexuality is less emphasized as the norm in the Neopagan community' (2001: 84). Pike does not link this acceptance of sexual diversity to ritual, but her research does highlight the role of ritual in self-transformation. In particular, she highlights the ritualised dancing that occurred around fires late at night:

> Many women and men describe feeling 'freer' at festivals. At the fire they become less inhibited and more comfortable with their bodies. In this way the fire becomes a theatre for self-invention, and

> improvisational space to be 'outrageous' and 'attention-grabbing'. Men and women immerse themselves in the performance of dancing and drumming, releasing their bodies in ways unique to the festival setting. In so doing they make this space their own and redefine their bodies and movements to fit the space.
>
> (Pike, 2001: 191)

Pagan rituals tend to be experiences of the liminal (Turner, 1974). Rituals are often performed late at night, in special robes or unclothed, with incense, dancing, chanting, and other liminal characteristics (Ezzy, 2014). As such, they are potential venues for exploring alternative understandings of sexuality.

Liminal ritual

For Victor Turner, 'liminality' was the key component of ritual. It describes the stage where participants have been separated from an old status, but are not yet integrated into the new status. This includes the person who is no longer a child, but not yet an adult, in a life-cycle ritual, and the community that has been removed from ordinary everyday world and not yet returned to it, in rituals that mark seasonal festivals.

> Liminal entities are neither here nor there; they are betwixt and between the positions assigned and arrayed by law, custom, convention, and ceremonial .... liminality is frequently likened to death, to being in the womb, to invisibility, to darkness, to bisexuality, to the wilderness, and to an eclipse of the sun or moon.
>
> (1974: 81)

Turner's underlines the way in which ritual resists the heteronormativity, and perhaps also homonormativity, that is sanctioned in many societies. Liminal rituals have often been associated with promiscuity, hedonism, sexual pleasure and experimentation. More contemporaneously, raves and similar dance music events, for example, often have a liminal ritual character that enables experimentation with identities and performances, including sexualities, that would be considered 'other' in normative contexts (Brabazon, 2002; Tramacchi, 2000). D'Andrea (2004: 246) observes that the 'countercultural formations of Techno and New Age queer, transgress and reverse' culturally dominant sexual identities. Rave culture both facilitates 'experimentation', but also 'amoralize[s] desire by emphasizing degenitalized pleasures' (D'Andrea 2004: 246).

Pagan ritual and bisexuality

Some Pagan rituals can provide a context in which sexual experimentation is permitted, and as such contributes to the normalisation of bisexual identities.

In Ezzy's (2014) study of Faunalia this is clearly evident. Faunalia is a Pagan festival held in south-eastern Australia in which 80 people spend five days at a rural camp ground. It has some similarities to the festivals studied by Pike (2001). However, the depth and intensity of the rituals mark it as highly unusual. The two main rituals begin close to midnight and finish at dawn. The first ritual, on the second night, is a death rite, re-creating the myth of Persephone's descent into the underworld. The second ritual is a sex rite, based on a re-creation of the medieval Witches' Sabbath with the hermaphroditic deity Baphomet. The ritualist who embodies Baphomet has exposed breasts, a strap-on phallus, a goat-head mask and feathered wings. The first half of the ritual is scripted, with invocations, and ritual practices, such as the blessing and sharing of a sacred cup. The second half of the ritual becomes an extemporaneous improvisation involving dance and erotic encounters.

> Experimenting with erotic emotions and sensual interactions is the primary focus for most people in the second half of the Baphomet rite. Therion noted that the ritual provides a space where the social restrictions of everyday life do not apply. Participants are 'being more physically affectionate and emotionally open, playful and uninhibited about [their] bodies' … René noted that 'getting caught up in the energy' of the rite led her to: 'doing things like kissing women, which I had never done before'.
>
> (Ezzy, 2014: 120)

Similarly, Phoebe reported a same-sex encounter that led her to embrace a bisexual self-understanding:

> [At the Baphomet rite] I experienced a passionate kiss with another woman. That blew me away. The end result after many months of working with that was that I think that if had a different upbringing, I would have embraced bisexuality. I find women very, very appealing energetically.
>
> (Ezzy, 2015: 30)

Some men also reported same-sex encounters: 'Dale kissed Harrison, a moment of homoerotic relationship that "was just mind-blowing"' (Ezzy, 2014: 138).

René, Phoebe, Dale and Harrison all reported an expansion of their sexual self-understanding as a result of these encounters. These participants did not switch from heterosexual to homosexual self-understandings. Rather, the same-sex erotic encounter led them to embrace a bisexual identity, with same-sex attraction included alongside heterosexuality as part of their sexual identity. Among Ezzy's interviewees, there was one person who reported that a same-sex encounter during the festival led them to embrace an exclusively lesbian identity, but this experience was not that of the majority.

For Phoebe, René, Harrison and Dale, the ritual provides a context in which they can safely explore sexual desires that transgress their normative self-understandings. Marie, who identified as bisexual before the ritual, explains how this works:

> We start by dancing. We start by dancing with each other. As we dance, we explore. We explore by reaching out to others, and if other people are responsive to that, then going further in that exploration. It might be touching, it might be caressing, it might be kissing, it might be more sexual and more intimate. It might be with one person, it might be with a group of people. It might be whatever happens spontaneously within that experience. It is simply honouring and allowing that aspect of our primal sexuality to be free.
>
> (Ezzy, 2014: 119)

The festival organisers at Faunalia have made a deliberate effort to ensure that participants understand the importance of respecting each other's boundaries and the importance of consent. Before each ritual, there is a compulsory ritual briefing where many of these issues are discussed and explained. Participants are taught a number of techniques to ensure they listen attentively to the person they may be flirting with to ascertain whether the desire is mutual, or not. Marie goes on to explain how this works for her in the ritual:

> [Sexual exploration occurs] within the context of being conscious … If they are a little bit reserved about it, then move away. And then you pick someone else. And there's no problem with that, I think. If it's contained within that ritual space, it doesn't then impact on your relationship afterwards. Particularly if you have both been there, then there's nothing that's been done that's deceptive to your partner. [In the ritual] I've been more sexual [than in everyday life]. That's a challenge because it means that I'm more likely to be hit on by others. That does happen to me. But on the other hand, that challenges me to talk to my husband about it, and say, 'Well, how do we deal with this sort of stuff, you know? How do you feel about it? How's this going to impact on our relationship?' Maybe the rules of our relationship will change over the years, maybe they won't. If there's good communication, then hopefully that will be something that's about that whole growth of ourselves as a person.[4]

Marie says, 'If it's contained within that ritual space, it doesn't then impact on your relationship afterwards'. Well-structured rituals take people into a liminal space, where non-normative things happen, and then safely return them to 'normality'. This was Turner's (1974) point that ritual is not necessarily socially radical, even whilst it might be non-normative. Similarly, the ravers described by Tramacchi (2000) drive to a remote location, wear unusual clothing and dance all night to loud 'trance' music. They have emotionally powerful, even transformative experiences. Then, the next day, they drive home and return to their normal occupations. In a similar way, the rituals at Faunalia allow participants to experiment with same-sex erotic encounters, but then return to the pre-existing relationships afterwards. This is not always the case. Some relationships statuses do change as a result of participation in the festival. But most remain in their relationships.

For these Pagans, sexual exploration takes place within the liminal context of a ritual. As such, same-sex erotic desire can be safely explored whilst at the same time allowing them to continue to affirm pre-existing relationships, which are often heterosexual. Bisexuality is explicitly facilitated by this process. Embracing same-sex erotic desire does not require abandoning heterosexual desire, and the relationships that have developed out of practising heterosexual desire. As the quote from Marie above suggests, ritualists explicitly negotiate with existing partners about the parameters of what is permissible in the ritual. At the ritual pre-briefing organisers explicitly encourage this sort of discussion and open exploration. In contrast, lesbian and gay Christians legitimate their same-sex erotic desire through rationalising that they are 'born this way' (Fielder and Ezzy, 2017). This leaves little scope for bisexuality.

Marie also frames her sexual explorations as negotiated and consensual. Here she reflects the influence of polyamorous thinking such as that originally articulated by Easton and Liszt (1997) in *The Ethical Slut*. Bisexuality does not necessitate polyamory or promiscuity. However, the preparedness to allow people who are in committed relationships to express sexual desire for others in bounded and constrained ways does problematise monogamous understandings of sexuality. It also allows the expression of desire greater freedom because expressions of desire towards potential new partners are not understood to necessarily implying the termination of existing established relationships.

Identifying as bisexual is problematic because in most countries both heterosexuality and monogamy are normative. It is also normative to not express desire for other people when a person is in a committed relationship (see Toft and Yip, 2018). After experimenting with polyamory, Marie had decided that monogamy was preferable.

> One of the things that's very challenging for me is I'm bisexual. And what I've found over the years is that I find it very hard to be … having relationships with more than one person, and not end up with people getting hurt. So, what I've ended up doing is having one relationship with one person, and if that ends, then be open again to partners of both genders; but not having relationships with both genders at the same time, because I've tried that in the past and people just get hurt.

Others at Faunalia have embraced polyamory. Marie's rejection of polyamory needs to be placed alongside her comment that in the ritual she is 'more sexual' than in everyday life. The ritual provides a place for her to perform her polyamorous and bisexual desire, but where the consequences are explicitly not ongoing. This was the case for many participants. Their flirting and kissing during the ritual were transitory events, and understood as such from the very beginning by all who participated. Participants typically did not see the ritual as a place for finding new partners. Rather, they saw the ritual as a place to express and explore their desires, both bisexual and polyamorous. For some this did change the way they understood themselves, embracing bisexual identities. Others remained heterosexual or homosexual, and monogamous.

Perhaps the most significant outcome of the ritual for those involved, of whatever sexual or gender identity, was the experience of 'respect' (see Richardson-Self 2014 for a discussion of 'respect' and sexual diversity). The hermaphroditic deity Baphomet is confronting, and deliberately so. The ritual organisers, and the ritualists, deliberately seek out experiences that make them uncomfortable as an opportunity for self-discovery (Ezzy, 2014). Encounters with same-sex desire are part of this process of self-discovery. For some these experiences were confronting and revelatory. For Phoebe, for example, her encounter with same-sex desire required 'months' of work in order for her to understand the experience and its consequences. She, nonetheless, felt she had grown as a consequence, and valued the experience deeply.

Concluding remarks

Bisexuality embraces ambiguity and resists both hetero- and homo-normative assumptions. Some religious traditions are more comfortable with ambiguity than others. As Seligman et al. (2008) have argued, ritually oriented religions are much more comfortable embracing ambiguity than religions that focus on 'sincerity' of belief, such as Christianity. The pursuit of 'sincerity' of belief is linked to the pursuit of a true 'essential' core of a person that is also characteristic of Christianity (Seligman et al., 2008). In contrast, Paganisms are typically 'religions of practice' (Ezzy, 2016) that emphasise ritual experience rather than shared belief. We have argued that it is the centrality of ritual to Paganism that facilitates its embrace of ambiguity, and in turn its embrace of bisexuality. Paganism's embrace of bisexuality is manifest both in the experience of teenage Witches, which reflects the broad culture of Paganism, and in the ritual experience of Pagan festivals such as Faunalia, where intense forms of liminal ritual enable the exploration of bisexuality. For individuals already in committed heterosexual relationships, same-sex erotic desire can be performed in explicitly transitory encounters that are consensually negotiated without undermining a person's commitment to their existing relationship(s). These encounters sometimes lead to the adoption of gay, lesbian and bisexual identities, but this is not always the case.

Put another way, the focus on texts and beliefs characteristic of Christianity undermines engagement with the complexities of human experience that do not neatly fit into structured categories. This could be understood as an extension of McGuire's (2008) analysis of lived religion. She observes how the Protestant Reformation's focus on belief undermined the sacred understanding of women's engagement with the church. Activities such as childbirth, food preparation and family were desacralised when religion became primarily about belief and theology. In a similar way, we argue that the ambiguity of bisexual desire is erased as a possible identity when religion is understood to focus on 'sincere' belief rather than ritual practice and relational engagement.

Notes

1 Findhorn Community was founded as a liberal spiritual community in Scotland in 1962. It became famous for its horticultural 'wonders'. https://www.findhorn.org

2 The Church of All Worlds was a medium-sized Pagan tradition that began in the USA and had groups around the world that was inspired by Robert Heinlein's (2014 [1961]) book *Stranger in a Strange Land.* Starhawk was one of the founders of the Reclaiming tradition of Witchcraft that is one of the larger Witchcraft traditions worldwide and that brought together political feminism and Witchcraft (Salomonsen, 2002). Starhawk has published numerous books, with *The Spiral Dance* (1979) remaining one of the foundational texts for feminist and environmentally oriented Witchcraft.

3 Yvette's experience is discussed in the Berger and Ezzy (2007) book. This quote is from her interview for that project, but has not been previously published. Ezzy is grateful to Helen Berger for her collaboration on that project.

4 This quote, and those following, are from the transcripts for the study reported in Ezzy, 2014, but have not previously been published.

References

Anapol, D. 2012. *Polyamory in the 21st Century.* London: Rowman & Littlefield.

Ault, A. 1996. Ambiguous identity in an unambiguous sex/gender structure: The case of bisexual women. *The Sociological Quarterly,* 37(3), 449–463.

Berger, H. and Ezzy, D. 2007. *Teenage Witches.* New Brunswick: Rutgers University Press.

Bernhardt-House, P. 2010. Re-enforcing binaries, downgrading passions: Bisexual invisibility in mainstream queer Christian theology. *Journal of Bisexuality,* 10(2), 54–63.

Bouma, G. 2006. *Australian Soul.* Melbourne: Cambridge University Press.

Brabazon, T. 2002. Dancing through the revolution: The political and social meaning of the rave. *Youth Studies Australia,* 21(1), 19–24.

Browne, K. 2010. Queer spiritual spaces, in *Queer Spiritual Spaces,* edited by K. Browne, S.R Munt and A.K.T. Yip. Farnham: Ashgate, 231–245.

Comstock, G. 1993. *Gay Theology without Apology.* Cleveland: The Pilgrim Press.

Crapo, R. 2005. Latter-Day Saint lesbian, gay, bisexual and transgendered spirituality, in *Gay Religion,* edited by S. Thumma and E. Gray. New York: Altamira Press, 99–114.

Daniels, M. 2010. Not even on the page: Freeing god from heterosexism. *Journal of Bisexuality,* 10(1–2), 44–53.

D'Andrea, A. 2004. Global Nomads in Ibiza and Goa, in *Rave Culture and Religion,* edited by G. St John. London: Routledge, 236–255.

Dinnie, E. and Browne, K. 2011. Creating a sexual self in heteronormative space: Integrations and imperatives amongst spiritual seekers at the Findhorn Community. *Sociological Research Online*, 16(1). [Online] Available at: http://www.socresonline.org.uk/16/1/7.html [accessed 25 April 2012].

Duggan, L. 2002. The new homonormativity: The sexual politics of neoliberalism, in *Materializing Democracy: Toward a Revitalized Cultural Politics*, edited by R. Castronovo, and Dana D. Nelson. London: Duke University Press, 175–194.

Easton, D., and Liszt, C.A. 1997. *The Ethical Slut: A Guide to Infinite Sexual Possibilities*. San Francisco: Greenery Press.

Eisner, S. 2013. *Notes for a Bisexual Revolution*. New York: Seal Press.

Ezzy, D. 2014. *Sex, Death and Witchcraft*. London: Bloomsbury.

Ezzy, D. 2015. Reassembling religious symbols: The pagan god Baphomet. *Religion*, 45(1), 24–41.

Ezzy, D. 2016. 'Religions of practice': The case of Japanese religions. *Journal for the Academic Study of Religion*, 29(1), 13–29.

Falek, J. 2013. Compulsory monosexuality and the problematic nature of identity. *Sprinkle: An Undergraduate Journal of Feminist and Queer Studies*, 6, 34–42.

Fielder, B. 2015. *Queer Christians, Authentic Selves: The Negotiation of Religious, Sexual and Gendered Identities among Lesbian, Gay, Bisexual and Transgender Attendees of Four Church Congregations in Australia*. Unpublished doctoral dissertation, University of Tasmania, Australia.

Fielder, B., and Ezzy, D. 2017. *Lesbian, Gay, Bisexual and Transgender Christians: Queer Christians, Authentic Selves*. London: Bloomsbury.

Findhorn Foundation History. n.d. [Online] Available at: www.findhorn.org [accessed 5 September 2015].

Flanders, C.E., LeBreton, M.E., Robinson, M., Bian, J. and Caravaca-Morera, J.A. 2017. Defining bisexuality: Young bisexual and pansexual people's voices. *Journal of Bisexuality*, 17(1), 39–57.

Freud, S. 1905. Three Essays on the Theory of Sexuality. *The Standard Edition of the Complete Psychological Works of Sigmund Freud*, trans. J. Strachey (Vol. VII). London: Hogarth Press, 136–243.

Gonzalez, K., Ramirez, J. and Galupo, P. 2017. 'I was and still am': Narratives of bisexual marking in the #StillBisexual Campaign. *Sexuality & Culture*, 21, 493–515.

Griffin, W. 1995. The embodied goddess: Feminist witchcraft and female divinity. *Sociology of Religion*, 56(1), 35–48.

Harrod, H. 2000. *The Animals Came Dancing: Native American Sacred Ecology and Animal Kinship*. Tuscon: University of Arizona Press.

Harvey, G. 1997. *Listening People, Speaking Earth: Contemporary Paganism*. London: Hurst.

Heinlein, R. 2014. [1961] *Stranger in a Strange Land*. London: Hachette.

Hutchins, L. and Williams, S. 2010. Our hearts still hold these intimate connections: An introduction to the Spiritualities Special Issue of the *Journal of Bisexuality*. *Journal of Bisexuality*, 10(1–2), 4–17.

Hutton, R. 1999. *The Triumph of the Moon: A History of Modern Pagan Witchcraft*. Oxford: Oxford University Press.

Jeffries, W., Dodge, B. and Sandfort, T. 2008. Religion and spirituality among bisexual black men in the USA. *Cult Health Sex*, 10(5), 463–477.

Kinsey, A., Pomeroy, W., and Martin, C. 1948. *Sexual Behaviour in the Human Male*. Bloomington: Indiana University Press.

Klesse, C. 2005. Bisexual women, non-monogamy and differentialist anti-promiscuity discourses. *Sexualities*, 8(4), 445–464.

Klesse, C. 2007. *The Spectre of Promiscuity: Gay Male and Bisexual Non-monogamies and Polyamories.* Aldershot: Ashgate.

Klesse, C. 2018a. Dancing on the waves or being washed away? Representations of bisexualities in Liquid Modernity. *Sexualities*, 21(8), 1360–1367.

Klesse, C. 2018b. Bisexuality, slippery slopes, and multipartner Marriage. *Journal of Bisexuality*, 18(1), 35–53.

Lindow, J. 2002. *Norse Mythology: A Guide to Gods, Heroes, Rituals, and Beliefs.* Oxford: Oxford University Press.

Lingwood, S. 2010. Bi Christian Unitarian: A theology of transgression. *Journal of Bisexuality*, 10(1–2), 31–43.

McGuire, M. 2008. *Lived Religion: Faith and Practice in Everyday Life.* Oxford: Oxford University Press.

Merriam Webster Dictionary. 2018. Bisexual. [Online] Available at: https://www.merriam-webster.com/dictionary/bisexual [accessed 24 August 2018]

Metropolitan Community Churches. 2013. Governance. [Online] Available at: http://mccchurch.org/how-we-work/governance [accessed 20 February 2015]

Monro, S., Hines, S. and Osborne, A. 2017. Is bisexuality invisible? A review of sexualities scholarship 1970–2015. *The Sociological Review*, 65(4): 663–681.

Morrow, D. 2003. Cast into the wilderness: The impact of institutionalised religion on lesbians. *Journal of Lesbian Studies*, 7(4), 109–123.

Neitz, M.J. 2000. Queering the dragonfest: Changing sexualities in a post-patriarchal religion. *Sociology of Religion*, 61(4), 369–391.

Oboler, R.S. 2010. Negotiating gender essentialism in contemporary Paganism. *The Pomegranate*, 12(2), 159–184.

Pettaway, L., Bryant, L., Keane, F. and Shelley, C. 2014. Becoming down low: A review of the literature on black men who have sex with men and women. *Journal of Bisexuality*, 14(2), 209–221.

Pike, S. 2001. *Earthly Bodies, Magical Selves: Contemporary Pagans and the Search for Community.* Oakland: University of California Press.

Raphael, M. 1999. Monotheism in contemporary feminist goddess religion: A betrayal of early theological non-realism? In *Is There a Future for Feminist Theology?*, edited by D.F. Sawyer and D.M. Collier. Sheffield: Sheffield Academic Press, 139–149.

Richardson-Self, L. 2012. Questioning the goal of same-sex marriage. *Australian Feminist Studies*, 27(72), 205–219.

Richardson-Self, L. 2014. Same-sex marriage: Zero tolerance. *Parrhesia: A Journal of Critical Philosophy*, 21, 113–124.

Robinson, M. 2003. Bisexual women and lesbians: What will keep us in our churches? *Making Waves: An Ecumenical Feminist Journal*, 3(2), 30–32.

Robinson, M. 2010. Reading Althaus-Reid: As a bi feminist theo/methodological resource. *Journal of Bisexuality*, 10(1–2), 108–120.

Robinson, M. 2013. Polyamory and monogamy as strategic identities. *Journal of Bisexuality*, 13(1), 21–38.

Rodriguez, E. 2009. At the intersection of church and gay: A review of the psychological research on gay and lesbian Christians. *Journal of Homosexuality*, 57(1), 5–38.

Rodriguez, E., Lytle, M. and Vaughn, M. 2013. Exploring the intersectionality of bisexual, religious/spiritual, and political identities from a feminist perspective. *Journal of Bisexuality*, 13(3), 285–309.

Rountree, K. (ed.) 2015. *Contemporary Pagan and Native Faith Movements in Europe: Colonialist and Nationalist Impulses (Vol. 26)*. New York: Berghahn Books.

Rountree, K. 2017. Magic spaces: The symbolic construction of sacred space in contemporary goddess rituals. *Sydney Studies in Religion*. [Online] Available at: https://openjournals.library.sydney.edu.au/index.php/SSR/article/view/12111 [accessed 15 August 2018]

Salomonsen, J. 2002. *Enchanted Feminism: The Reclaiming Witches of San Francisco*. London: Routledge.

Seligman, A., Weller, R., Puett, M. and Bennet, S. 2008. *Ritual and its Consequences: An Essay on the Limits of Sincerity*. Oxford: Oxford University Press.

Sell, I. 2005. Intermediaries: Spirit and transcendence in a sample of 'third-gendered' North Americans, in *Gay Religion*, edited by S. Thumma and E. Gray. Walnut Creek: AltaMira Press, 303–312.

Shepherd, C. 2018. *Bisexuality and the Western Christian Church: The Damage of Silence*. New York: Springer.

Shepherd, C. 2019. *Bisexuality and the Western Christian Church: The Damage of Silence*. London: Palgrave.

Starhawk. 1979. *The Spiral Dance*. San Francisco: Harper & Row.

Toft, A. 2010. *Bisexual Christian Identity: A Sociological Exploration of the Life Stories of Female and Male Bisexual Christians*. Unpublished PhD thesis, University of Nottingham.

Toft, A. 2014. Re-imagining bisexuality and Christianity: The negotiation of Christianity in the lives of bisexual women and men. *Sexualities*, 17(5–6), 546–563.

Toft, A. and Yip, A. 2018. Intimacy negotiated: The management of relationships and the construction of personal communities in the lives of bisexual women and men. *Sexualitie*s, 21(1–2), 233–250.

Tramacchi, D. 2000. Field tripping: Psychedelic communitas and ritual in the Australian Bush. *Journal of Contemporary Religion*, 15(2), 201–213.

Turner, V. 1974. *The Ritual Process: Structure and Anti-structure*. Harmondsworth: Penguin Books.

University of Victoria, Canada. 2010. *Positive Space Network Resource Person Manual*. [Online] Available at: http://web.uvic.ca/psn/wp-content/uploads/PSN-Resource-Person-Manual.pdf [accessed 23 February 2015].

Wilcox, M. 2002. When Sheila's a lesbian: Religious individualism among lesbian, gay, bisexual, and transgender Christians. *Sociology of Religion*, 63(4), 497–513.

Wilcox, M. 2003. *Coming out in Christianity*. Bloomington: Indian University Press.

Wilcox, M. 2005. A religion of one's own: Gender and LGBT religiosities. In S. Thumma and E. Gray (eds) *Gay Religion*. Walnut Creek: AltaMira Press, 203–220.

Yip, A. 2005. Queering religious texts: An exploration of British non-heterosexual Christians' and Muslims' strategy of constructing sexuality affirming hermeneutics. *Sociology*, 39, 47–65.

Yip, A. 2010. Coming home from the wilderness: An overview of recent scholarly research on LGBTTQI religiosity/spirituality in the West, in *Queer Spiritual Spaces*, edited by K. Browne, S.R. Munt and A.K.T. Yip. Farnham: Ashgate, 35–50.

6 Negotiating sexuality and spirituality

The lived experiences of bisexual persons

Alex Toft

Introduction

As part of my doctoral research project I embarked on a large-scale mixed-methods study, looking to explore how bisexual Christians in the UK negotiated what, at first glance, appeared to be contradictory and conflicting identities. This was driven by an academic interest in identity and gender and a personal interest in Christianity and bisexuality. Due to the unique nature of the research and the specific focus upon bisexuality as opposed to lesbian and gay experiences, the data led to a number of publications and contributions to knowledge. The purpose of this chapter is to bring together the main findings from this research project that have been noted elsewhere but have not been articulated in relation to the project as a whole. It is hoped that this will highlight the contribution of the research to those with interests in religion, sexuality, gender and identity studies. I believe that the life stories of bisexual Christians highlight the uniqueness of bisexuality as a sexual identity, and shed light on how gender, sexuality and identity are enacted. Furthermore, the chapter shows the fluidity of Christianity, in contrast to the official teaching of organised denominations.

Uniquely, this chapter will explore how the participants' religious and sexual identities inform and interact, taking a more reflective approach. Although the two main sections – *Negotiating bisexual in Christian lives* (foregrounding bisexuality in the analysis) and *Bisexual Christianity* (foregrounding Christianity in the analysis) – centralise one identity over another, the aim is to present an analysis that is more intersectional and illuminate how bisexuality is informed by Christianity (during the first section) and how Christianity is informed by bisexuality (second section). Of course, such exploration should also explore other aspects of the participants' lives such as race/ethnicity and gender identity which will also impact upon such identities; however, due to the focus of the original research, such an analysis is not possible.

The chapter begins by outlining the theoretical underpinnings of the research to do two things: First, to give an overview of my position in relation to identity, bisexuality and Christianity, when the research took place, whilst exploring new advancements in these areas, particularly in relation to the move towards considering bisexual Christianity. Second, to briefly outline how the research was conducted. Following this the chapter moves to explore what was found during the research and a re-examination of these findings; and this has been divided into discrete but interconnecting sections for clarity. The focus beings with an exploration of how bisexual Christians do (or enact) their sexual identity in *Negotiating bisexuality in Christian lives.* Here the focus is upon how the participants negotiated and understood their bisexuality and what this tells us about their Christianity. The chapter then moves to explore *Bisexual Christianity.* Throughout this section I attempt to explore the participants' lived experiences in relation to the negotiation of their spirituality in light of their bisexuality.

Theoretical positioning

Identity

The overarching goal of the research was to understand how identity (specifically bisexual and Christian identities) are 'done'. I use the word 'done' as a shorthand to refer to the presentation of identity, the management and negotiation of our selves. Although Goffman's theory of the presentation of the self (Goffman, 1971) has been the focus of criticism, specifically the assertion that identity is a performance in which we can change characters at will (Layder, 2009), I feel that because of the pressures of institutions (the Church) and a lack of social blueprints for bisexuals, Goffman's work sheds light upon what is occurring. Goffman understands identity as a game in which individuals constantly work to display or conceal their selves dependent upon the situation. In the lives of bisexual Christians, where concealment and self-censuring play an important role, this is a useful perspective. There has also been some advancement in understanding bisexual identity specifically with the exploration of 'bisexual display' (Hartman, 2013; Hartman-Linck, 2014). Bisexuality, as Hartman-Linck (2014) notes, is particularly difficult to signal because heterosexuality is presumed unless people either verbalise or signify that they are otherwise. Even in same-sex relationships, bisexuality remains invisible. Although this work post-dates my research it is important to recognise this attempt to explain identity in bisexual lives, where due to bisexual erasure and invisibility in certain quarters, bisexuality has to be visualised and other aspects beyond sex and gender including political motivations play an important role (Toft, forthcoming).

Of course, my epistemological perspective was not to adopt Goffman's perspective uncritically. Importantly, I feel that there were two other aspects of identity that needed exploration, and these would have an impact upon those who identified as bisexual Christians: how identity can be constructed through reflexivity and the importance of the use of narrative in constructing identity. Both aspects are important for individuals who have to work with and against dominant structures such as the Church and bring their identities, which are seemingly at odds with hegemonic discourse, to life through narration. Using the work of Giddens (1991) as an entry point, due to de-traditionalisation, identity is more agency driven (Bauman 2001). As Elliott (2007) argued, identity draws upon memory, desire and society but also what other people do in their own cultural and societal practices.

To be bisexual is to identify as bisexual and this is enacted through telling stories. Using the work of Plummer (1995) and Lawler (2009), I argue that identity is produced by the stories we tell in everyday life – although, as Layder (2004) highlights, such an approach is problematic as it opens us up to creating fictitious versions of who we are. Understanding identity in this way is useful because it allows us to explore the negotiations that take place and the decisions and process behind such negotiations.

Bisexual identity

It is clear that the concept of bisexuality is somewhat imprecise and open to interpretation. Historically this has been due to the fact that bisexuality has traditionally been ignored in academia (Monro, Hines and Osborne, 2017). Definitions provided by Hemmings (2002) and Bi Academic Intervention (1997) indicate that bisexuality could be used to describe a combination of maleness and femaleness, a combination of masculinity and femininity or emotional and physical attracted to any gender. I understood that bisexuality related those who have the capacity for emotional, sensual, sexual relations with members of the any gender (Off Pink Collective, 1988; Robinson, 2015; Rust, 2004). The focus may be upon loving the person regardless of the gender (Clausen, 1990) and relationships may be monogamous or polyamorous (see Klesse, 2016). Bisexuality challenges the binary systems of gender and sex (Rust, 1996). It could be seen as radical and an attempt to move away from identification which relies on binary opposites (Highleyman, 1995); explored in Toft, forthcoming). Bisexuality remains ambiguous and recent work has shown that much research continues to debate its meaning and place within wider debates (see Klesse, 2018). Bisexuality continues in the main to refer to behaviour, attractions, identification and history (Rust, 1996; Robinson, 2015); although there is clear space to explore more nuanced examinations of bisexuality's unique positioning towards monogamy and compulsory monogamy (Toft and Yip, 2018; Toft, forthcoming).

Christian identity

Religious individualism was the dominant and most accurate way of understanding the Christian landscape at the time the research began, and this framed the focus of the work. Religion (Christianity specifically) is filtered through the self (Wilcox, 2003) and has switched to become an active attribute, with the emphasis on religion doing something for the individual rather than what the individual can contribute (Woodhead, 2001). This idea has been framed as the 'Turn to Life' (Woodhead and Heelas, 2000; Heelas et al., 2005).

I also tapped into work with LGB Christians, particularly the work of Wilcox (2003) and Yip (2000), as there were themes and ideas that could be consistent for other marginalised groups (such as bisexual Christians). Wilcox's notion of the 'Bible Buffet' resonated strongly as it was a technique which could be used to incorporate compatible aspects of religion into life. Yip's work is vital in understanding that official Church's understandings and/or teachings on sexuality are often viewed as being incompatible with modern society because Christianity has not evolved at a similar pace (Yip, 2003). As Davie (2000, 2002, 2012) has noted, and will be reflected throughout this chapter, this does not necessarily represent a reduction of belief but rather a shift in how belief is enacted. Faith in this regard becomes more personalised, with less reliance upon institutional guidance, in what is referred to as believing without belonging.

Furthermore, what Christianity means to individuals has shifted towards teaching about love and justice rather than control. Yip notes this in relation to Jesus.

> Jesus, for instance, is often constructed as being critical and subversive of unequal socio-political structures, and was unafraid to challenge them in the pursuit of justice. Thus, such reading of the texts instils pride and a sense of belonging to the family of believers. Far from being outcasts, LGBTQI people, as these texts evidence, have always been a part of religious communities.
>
> (Yip, 2010: 39)

Christianity is framed as an identity which is negotiable and adapts to change and progress, although this can conflict with traditional Christianity.

Methodological account

When the project began in 2007, the research with bisexual Christians was mainly autobiographical and theoretical in nature. It was therefore important to consider work in which bisexuals were included such as Yip (1997a, 1997b, 2002), Dillon (1999) and Wilcox (2002, 2003). Examination of such research showed a use of mixed methods often with a quantitative phase to act as scoping into areas which are under-researched. This approach would also allow a triangulation of methods where interview schedules are informed by the literature and the questionnaires. As a result, 80 questionnaires were collected which gave an overview of the participants' sexual and religious identities but also included large open-ended questions to explore what issues were important for them. This informed 20 individually constructed interview schedules which were based upon the questionnaires. Interviews were very loosely semi-structured which would produce rich and detailed life stories.

It is important to note here that the sample was constructed mainly through advertisement and personal networks, and was largely purposeful in nature. Although interviewees were selected to cover different locations and Christian denominations; genders and understandings of bisexuality were not purposefully targeted. Participants were split almost evenly between women (52.5%) and men (47.5%) – all were cisgendered; as noted, this was not by design but represents a limitation. The majority were in coupled relationships (66.7%), with 11.5% being in relationships with at least three people. A range of Christian denominations were represented including Anglican, Roman Catholic, Evangelical, Metropolitan Community Church and those who no longer attended.

Negotiating bisexuality in Christian lives

The research showed that most of the respondents felt their sexuality was central to who they were as people, at times referring to this as their core identity. In everyday life it was this identity which took precedent and which acted as a filter for all other important aspects of life. However, some negotiation of what bisexuality means, and how it was enacted, took place. The data suggests two main negotiations which they enacted and used in their everyday life: the flexibility of bisexuality; and/or a 're-imagining' of what bisexuality means in their lives.

Flexibility

Research has worked to show that bisexuality should not be encapsulated as 'fence-sitting' or enabling individuals to access heterosexual privileges (Kaplan, 1995; Hemmings, 2002). However, for bisexual Christians this flexibility, particularly with regards to issues of coming out, was often useful in spaces where they would face hostility and possible exclusion. Participants left their sexuality at the door to their church, downplaying bisexuality and allowing others to assume they were straight.

Half (40) of the participants said that it was not important to be out within their religious communities as they felt they it was most important to worship as human beings. Although this raises interesting points with regards to being defined as a person in relation to sexuality, in times of perceived difficulty a number of participants preferred to not highlight their sexuality. For some this was discussed in relation to vocalising their sexuality. One respondent, Jim, a 26-year-old Anglican from the Midlands, noted that bisexuality was flexible and allowed you to 'come out when you want to'. He continued: 'I am pretty much out to everyone but it was gradual and, like I said I had to be careful. Because my sexuality isn't always clear it was probably easier to do.' Jim went on to suggest that, although he would disclose his sexuality if asked, this wasn't often likely: 'It's not something that is mentioned at Church either, so I don't see the reason why I would talk about it. It's just easier and I don't really want to argue with people, it might not be safe.' Jim was tactical in presenting himself as a bisexual Christian and did not do so when it could be potentially difficult for him. Although it could be argued that Jim was being deceptive here and allowing others to see him as straight when it suited him, it was a strategy that was employed, due to issues of personal safety.

Several of the respondents found this flexibility a useful tool to explain how they enacted their sexuality. Richard, a 45-year-old man from Surrey, talked about bisexuality giving him access to feminine and masculine personas. Richard subsumed sexuality with gender, arguing that he was bisexual because of his more even blend of masculinity and femininity in his personality. For Richard, this bisexuality helped him in his religious work:

> But I'm not a church leader, and I wasn't that good a missionary when I did that. But I'm good as a carer because I am using my bisexuality, my female persona at times as a God-given gift and then at times I will use my male side.

This flexibility of gender was a part of what he felt made him bisexual. As Stoller (1972) notes, such conceptualisations of bisexuality appear to originate from the work of Freud, who understood bisexuality as an unformed sexuality. For Freud, the link between gender and sexuality was tangible, and in the case of bisexuality the failure to move towards either femininity or masculinity results in bisexuality. Viewing bisexuality as a failure to develop into a gender ideals (e.g. femininity in females) remains a point for discussion within psychoanalytic development theory (Elise, 1997). However, such theories and the work of social constructionists have shown such approaches to sexuality as not being aligned to real life experiences (Anderson, 2008).

Other respondents talked about having 'sides' to their personalities which reflected their sexuality. Adam, a 63-year-old Anglican man, explained that although historically he had been in relationships with women, he was currently only interested romantically in men, arguing that he was pursuing his 'gay side'.

> I wander around both [heterosexuality and homosexuality]. I'd say nowadays in practical terms I might as well be gay. But I also know from my side of it, my sex life when I was married was fine. I know guys who have been married and would say they are gay and I'd say you must have had a reasonable sex-life and they'd say 'No I used to hate it', and that just wasn't me, so that's why I think bi suits me.

The bisexuality that the participants presented is not often represented in modern exploration of bisexual identities. As previously noted, the conflation of gender with sexuality is no longer understood to be an accurate representation of lives (Weeks, 2002). However, the bisexuality that Adam and Richard refer to appeared to be informed by their understanding of

Christian values and morality in relation to gender, which the participants saw as reflecting their bisexuality. The focus upon the separation of masculinity and femininity or, in Richard's example, the combination of the two appears to be in part informed by their understanding of what it is to be a good Christian, in a rather traditional sense. As Richard notes, his bisexuality allowed him to move between the two, emphasising a binary view of gender. As an ex-missionary and carer, he argued that this helped him to engage with people on a personal level and spread the word of God. Of course, this is a clear example of his religious and sexual identities informing and influencing each other. A number of classic articles have highlighted the gender divide within conservative/traditional Christianity, particularly in terms of gender roles and responsibilities (e.g. Bartkowski, 1999; Sherkat, 2000; Wilcox and Jelen, 1991). This is very much still present in Richard's understanding of Christianity. However, Richard suggested that there is a unique bisexual take here, and explained that he was able to take this Christian view of gender and enact this through his sexuality.

Re-imagining

The stories above all explore bisexuality in terms of its flexibility and malleability, particularly in relation to the conflation of gender and sexuality. However, this does not effectively capture what all the respondents were doing. I suggest that in their everyday lives they were in fact re-imagining bisexuality. This is in many ways similar to the flexible approach outlined above but suggests more permanency and also a focus upon sexuality beyond sexual activity. Re-imagining refers to understanding bisexuality not solely upon sexual behaviour but as being able to relate to partners as close friends. It also should be reiterated that this re-examination of bisexuality was not common. As previously noted, participants usually adapted their faith to match their sexuality.

The focus upon non-sexual aspects of bisexuality meant that some participants were able to reconcile their sexuality and faith with little impact upon their religious lives. One respondent, Phillip, suggested that for him having some same-sex time through close friendships was enough for him to maintain his bisexual identity:

> I'd rather have friends than have sex … because friends are there for me and sex can actually sour it. So gradually I've become more coherent about who I am and where I am [prompt regarding the relationship between bisexuality and friendship], it's a blurred line but at this time in my life I want close friendships with people and I'm bisexual.

This focus upon emotional attachment over sexual attraction is present previous research. As Diamond and Savin-Williams (2000) have noted, attraction based upon emotion has been one key way that sexual-minority women have disrupted typical narratives of coming out. Furthermore, strong emotional attachments with one individual are common traits of non-heterosexual stories. As Phillip's story suggests, for him, this emotional aspect of attraction is very much part of his sexual life.

This did sometimes result in celibacy as a tool for reconciliation between faith and sexuality, but this approach was exceptional. During the interviews I met Jessica, a 38-year-old woman from London, who had been living with a female partner for over five years and had a civil partnership; however, they were both celibate. Jessica suggested that she was attracted to her partner on a spiritual level, and it was this deep connection that kept their relationship strong. The partnership was not based upon sexual activity: 'We relate because of our beliefs and the community that we are a part of … we don't have a sexual side to our relationship but we've been together for a while and all is good.'

Such stories have obvious and strong resonance to notions of sexual celibacy as an important factor in religiosity. Also, as I will suggest, bisexuality is uniquely placed with regard to this celibacy. The work of Isherwood (2006) here is of importance. Isherwood's focus of celibacy is in relation to sex's reinforcement of gender norms and the way that celibacy can disrupt heteropatriarchy: 'the world of sexuality is not an exchange of equality and mutuality in the pursuit of erotic pleasure but rather a highly stylized pornographic dance of domination' (Isherwood, 2006: 3–4). Isherwood then poses the question that in order to respond to this difficulty, should the 'twenty-first century, post-feminist movement women adopt celibacy as the counter to the worst excesses of heteropatriarchy?' (Isherwood, 2006: 4). Isherwood suggests a queering of Christ enables a bypassing of binary categorisation, and actually challenges the way we act and engage with others. The focus upon a queer understanding of Jesus and an erotic Christ has resonance with Jessica's story. In Jessica's relationship bisexuality is informed by the fact that the gender of a person is not the focus of attraction, she is bisexual because the gender of her partners is of no importance, challenging or queering this system. Therefore, celibacy for Jessica was also a necessary part of building a stronger bond with Christ, whereas sexual activity held no importance in her life. But, additionally celibacy here resonates strongly with the disruptive nature of bisexuality with regards to binary gender and sexuality categorisation.

Bisexual Christianity

The majority of the participants had to adjust their understanding of Christianity. This often led to practising a Christianity different from that which is often presented through official teaching or Church life. It could be argued that the respondents were less willing to dilute themselves as sexual beings and felt that Christianity, if properly understood and then negotiated, was entirely compatible with their sexuality. However, their Christianity was influenced by their sexuality and this was reflected in how they understood and enacted their faith. Here I will explore how the participants negotiated their faith and how this relates to their sexuality.

The research suggested that bisexual Christians used a number of strategies or negotiations in order to fit their sexual selves with their religious selves. There were two main findings which were revealed strongly in the data which will be the focus here:

1 To understand Christianity in terms of its moral values and teachings, moving away from more rigid and literal interpretations of Christianity: Refocussing Christianity;
2 To leave organised religion and construct a more individualised and personal form of Christianity: Individualised Christianity.

Refocussing Christianity

Refocussing Christianity refers to focussing upon aspects of Christianity which are compatible with everyday lives and working to silence aspects of Christian teaching which are no longer useful. Specifically, Christianity is forged in relation to sexuality and their intersection is viewed as inseparable. This refocussing, however, is different from selecting aspects scripture which fit, as with the Bible Buffet (Wilcox, 2003); which in essence is concerned with taking what works for you from the Bible whilst not using others. Here the focus is upon Christianity as a moral guide, moving away from teaching and worship. Refocussing then disrupts conventional understandings of doing Christianity (e.g. worship) in favour of being a Christian and living in a Christian fashion. Of course, cues are taken from established Christian norms and morality, but the focus shifts belief in God towards Christianity as a lifestyle and ideology.

For many this refocussing may be a step too far from traditional understandings of what Christianity is, and it could be argued that the participants were in fact no longer recognisable as Christians. Yet participants argued that Christianity's strength lies in its ability to speak to them personally and to help them gain understanding of their life. In everyday life, the participants in my research suggest that this has been presented in two ways: as an internalisation of God, where Christianity is about inner peace and finding meaning through personal reflection and meditation; or as focussing upon Christianity as a force for love and equality. Such refocussing has been noted in previous research in relation to religious texts. Yip (2010), in his research with LGB Christians, noted a shift from more traditional interpretation of texts that are not accepting towards LGB lives, towards a more flexible approach. Yip (2010: 37–41) highlights three strategies: 'defensive apologetics', a re-contextualisation of texts; 'cruising texts', uncovering same-sex lives within texts; and 'turning theology upside down', where religion is refocussed with the self at its centre.

For some of the participants Christianity had become a very personal and reflective process. Participants explored how their Christianity relation to a quest for inner peace most concerned with self-healing and learning to be comfortable in your own skin. The life stories of Kimberley and Florence are most relevant here as they both explored how Christianity is not related to belief in an external supernatural God but as a process of finding yourself as a whole being, including, of course, sexuality. Kimberley spoke about how God was metaphoric and referred to a journey or process of getting to know yourself and your purpose:

> The God I feel is more real and I must admit I'm going on feelings way more than the Bible, or everything I've ever been preached, or maybe it's the sum total of everything I've ever been preached. I just don't know. But I just know he feels real and loving and not condemning and I just can't imagine him making me choose.

The choice that Kimberley is referring to here is between her faith and her sexuality, in relation to her local Church's insistence that she must choose in order to be accepted within the congregation. However, Kimberley argued that this did not fit with her understanding of God or God's purpose for her. Believing in God was about believing in a 'force which gives me peace and lets me understand that we are all connected' (Kimberley's words). Florence explored this rather more explicitly during the interview and was able to articulate that her faith was consistent and compatible with her sexuality due to re-focussing Christianity towards an internal process of self-acceptance and peace.

'Finding God is finding myself. So, religion is like a quest to find who I am and where I am.' Here Florence is exploring how for her God represents a something to work towards and to aspire to and through self-reflection and Christian values she gets close to this. From the stories of the participants in does appear that this approach is perhaps the most radical proposed, in terms of re-focussing religion. However, a number of participants were a lot more prescriptive about using these Christian values to underline their belief; placing this at the centre of the belief system. This was reflected in understanding Christianity in terms of acceptance of others, being fair and working to equality. Here the focus is upon living a good Christian life guided by love above selfish drives. Michael, a 27-year-old man who had not attended church since he was 18, explained this in relation to his worship style. This does relate to the ideas put forward by Kimberley and Florence but with a greater emphasis on Christian values:

> I basically put aside an hour a day for meaningful time … it's like a relaxation time where I sit … perhaps with candles and so forth … sometimes I will have music … the candles aren't important either really none of it is really … I just need a space to be alone with me and God and to think about the correct thing to do … the Christian thing to do.

This refers to Michael's desire to be quiet and reflect inwards upon his life. However, Michael places his Christian values with an emphasis upon doing what he sees as the Christian thing. Through meditation and relaxation Michael felt able to reflect on the best way to be a Christian whilst being guided by his faith. Throughout the interview Michael referred to this refocussing as a centralising of his Christian values rather than being restricted by Christian teaching and doctrine. He stated that his beliefs were 'guided by being a good person, a Christian person who values all people … and does this through love'. Love was a recurrent word throughout the interview and represented a need for fairness and acceptance. For Michael enacting these values was what made him a Christian and as a result he felt free from any exclusionary practices that the Church may partake in.

Individualised Christianity

Whereas 'refocussing' refers to shifting the focus of Christianity towards other, more salient aspects of life, 'individualising' refers to revising or editing what aspects of traditional Christianity speak to bisexual Christians. In relation to religious texts, Wilcox's (2001) Bible Buffet is a good example of how this is enacted in religious life, as passages which affirm sexuality are embraced, whereas others that conflict are rejected. However, individualisation relates to all aspects of Christian life (e.g. attendance, community, support and scripture).

A good proportion (25%) of the participants in the research no longer attended church on a regular basis and this was often the first step in constructing a more individual form of Christianity. However, it is important to note that of those who still attended regularly (around 40%), they all practised some negotiation of their Christianity. Unlike their sexuality, religion was seen as being open to interpretation and malleable in terms of its meaning. A more individualised Christianity often is less reliant on official doctrine or teaching and is more selective of what aspects are adopted. For those who leave the Church, there appeared to be two main reasons for doing this. Firstly, the participants felt that there were too many conflicts between official teaching and their lives, perceiving the Church as unwelcoming towards bisexuals. Secondly, that Church practices were not compatible with bisexual life particularly in terms of the emphasis on coupled relationships.

The participants did not feel that adapting their faith or disengaging with the Church completely, made them any less of a Christian than those who attended regularly. The experiences of Elanor are most striking here, as she explored her Christianity in terms of a selection process: 'Christianity has so much to teach us and I take what I need, but I don't labour on what I don't need, and it's that choice for me to make.' Later in the interview, we explored this idea in relation to a conversation she had had with a friend:

> She was talking about the word of God and all that, saying I can't challenge those ideas, ways of being … but I'm here, living now. Things can only make sense if they are in relation to how I am living now.

It is clear that for Elanor this is no less Christian than adopting a literal interpretation of religion. Elanor's point is that the majority of the Church's teaching refers to societies that are entirely incompatible with our own. Although there are certain universal truths within Christianity, it is inevitable that such a religion will have aspects that do not fit with life today. For Elanor this referred to aspects of teaching on same-sex marriage, sexuality, gender and things that she perceived the Church to still hold archaic views on. A number of the participants justified this selective or individualised approach to their faith in relation to contradictions or problematic passages in the Bible. One participant, Joseph, explored how Leviticus was written to prevent incestuous sexual activities, which for him were irrelevant today. As sections like this exist, Joseph argued that it is only right to be selective in what parts of the Bible are accepted. Another participant, Cornelius, explained how the Old Testament prohibits the eating of meat on certain days, questioning why Christians would follow teaching on sexuality but not about eating meats.

The individualisation strategies practised by the participants were done out of perceived necessity, rather than being as a result of sexual identity. Such strategies would not be distinct from other Christians although of course, individual motivations and experiences would be unique. Individualised Christianity in this regard, then, is rooted in traditional understandings of Christian beliefs and worship, but the participants highlight how this was done in relation to contemporary life. Participants discussed ignoring aspects that they felt were incompatible with life today and focussing upon teaching they viewed as being useful.

Concluding remarks

This chapter has done two main things. Firstly, it has explored how the participants understood and then negotiated their sexuality in light of their Christianity. Importantly, and in contrast to some of my previous work (Toft 2009a, 2009b, 2014), it has attempted to do this in an intersectional manner in order to explore what it is about Christianity that has led to such negotiation. The stories of the participants suggest that sexuality was not usually the main focus in terms of negotiating or adapting identities to reconcile any potential conflicts. Bisexuality was often seen as something which was vital to understanding their 'selves' and an aspect of their character that was not up for negotiation. However, some participants explored how bisexuality could be seen as flexible and at times of potential risk to personal safety, sexuality could remain hidden. The participants recounted ideas around the connection between gender and sexuality, suggesting this helped them as Christians. Bisexuality was also 're-imagined' in reference to faith, where sexual activity and behaviour is downplayed, although such an approach was rare. Here the influence of Christian belief on gender had a direct impact upon how participants saw their sexuality. Traditional gender roles were adapted into some of the participants' lives and clearly influenced how they enacted their sexuality. Additionally, celibacy was explored as a lifestyle choice which reflected spiritual closeness in relationships but also in regard to its potential to disrupt binary categorisation, a key feature in bisexuality.

Second, the chapter has shown that in general the participants all engaged in some kind of adjustment of their religion, which was seen as the main reason for any conflicts they felt. Such negotiations were often seen as unavoidable due to what they perceived as rigidity in official Church teaching.

Through a re-focussing or individualising of what Christianity means, participants were able to conceptualise their faith as supporting their sexuality. A number of participants focussed on a Christianity which centralises messages of love and acceptance. Although many of the tenets of Christianity may not be present in the lives of the respondents who did this, they argued that the central messages of Christianity remained clear for them. Importantly, they identified as Christian and felt that their morals and approach to life represented what could be called a Christian ethic. Others, again through necessity, aligned themselves with strategies used by lesbian and gay Christians, individualising and restricting what aspects of Christianity to use in their lives.

The overall aim of the chapter has been to re-evaluate and add to my previous work, which has tended to explore Christianity or bisexuality in isolation. This chapter has attempted to present such identities intersectionally and to acknowledge that in everyday lives such identities will inform and impact upon each other. In simple terms, Christianity for a bisexual person will be understood and negotiated differently from a gay person. It is important to explore such strategies as this can teach us much about religion and sexuality.

References

Anderson, E., 2008. "Being masculine is not about who you sleep with…": heterosexual athletes contesting masculinity and the one-time rule of homosexuality. *Sex Roles*, 58 (1–2), 104–115.

Bartkowski, J.P. 1999. One step forward, one step back: 'Progressive traditionalism' and the negotiation of domestic labor within Evangelical families. *Gender Issues*, 17, 40–64.

Bauman, Z. 2001. *The Individualised Society*. Cambridge: Polity Press.

Bi Academic Intervention. 1997. Introduction, in *The Bisexual Imaginary*, edited by Bi Academic Intervention. London: Cassell, 1–13.

Clausen, J. 1990. My interesting condition. *Journal of Sex Research*, 27(3), 445–459.

Davie, G. 2000. *Religion in Modern Europe: A Memory Mutates*. Oxford: Oxford University Press.

Davie, G. 2002. *Europe: The Exceptional Case*. London: Darton.

Davie, G. 2012. From believing without belonging to Vicarious Religion: Understanding the patterns of religion in Modern Europe, in *The Role of Religion in Modern Societies*, edited by D. Pollack and D.V.A. Olson. London: Routledge, 171–182.

Diamond, L.M. and Savin-Williams, R.C. 2000. Explaining diversity in the development of same-sex sexuality among young women. *Journal of Social Issues*, 56(2), 297–313.
Dillon, M. 1999. *Catholic Identity: Balancing Reason, Faith and Power*. Cambridge: Cambridge University Press.
Elise, D. 1997. Primary femininity, bisexuality, and the female ego ideal: A re-examination of female developmental theory. *The Psychoanalytic Quarterly*, 66(3), 489–517.
Elliott, A. 2007. *Concepts of the Self*. Cambridge: Polity Press.
Garber, M.B. 2000. *Bisexuality and the Eroticism of Everyday Life*. New York: Routledge.
Giddens, A. 1991. *Modernity and Self Identity: Self and Society in the Late Modern Age*. Cambridge: Polity Press.
Goffman, E. 1971. *The Presentation of Self in Everyday Life*. Harmondsworth: Pelican.
Hartman, J.E. 2013. Creating a bisexual display: Making bisexuality visible. *Journal of Bisexuality*, 13(1), 39–62.
Hartman-Linck, J.E. 2014. Keeping bisexuality alive: Maintaining bisexual visibility in monogamous relationships. *Journal of Bisexuality*, 14(2), 177–193.
Heelas, P., Woodhead, L., Seel, B., Tusting, K. and Szerszynski, B. 2005. *The Spiritual Revolution: Why Religion Is Giving Way to Spirituality*. London: Blackwell.
Hemmings, C. 2002. *Bisexual Spaces: A Geography of Sexuality and Gender*. London: Routledge.
Highleyman, L. 1995. Identity and Ideas: Strategies for Bisexuals, in *Bisexual Politics: Theories, Queries and Visions*, edited by N. Tucker. New York: Harrington Park Press, 73–92.
Isherwood, L. 2006. *The Power of Erotic Celibacy: Queering Heterosexuality*. London: A&C Black.
Kaplan, R. 1995. Your fence is sitting on me: The Hazards of Binary Thinking, in *Bisexual Politics: Theories, Queries and Visions*, edited by N. Tucker. New York: Harrington Park Press, 267–279.
Klesse, C. 2016. *The Spectre of Promiscuity: Gay Male and Bisexual Non-Monogamies and Polyamories*. London: Routledge.
Klesse, C., 2018. Dancing on the waves or being washed away? Representations of bisexualities in liquid modernity. Sexualities, 21(8), 1360–1367.
Lawler, S. 2009. *Identity*. Cambridge: Polity Press.
Layder, D. 2004. *Social and Personal Identity: Understanding Yourself*. London: Sage.
Layder, D. 2009. *Intimacy and Power: The Dynamics of Personal Relationships in Modern Society*. London: Springer.
Monro, S., Hines, S. and Osborne, A. 2017. Is bisexuality invisible? A review of sexualities scholarship 1970–2015. *The Sociological Review*, 65(4), 663–681.
Off Pink Collective. 1988. *Bisexual Lives*. London: Off Pink Publishing.
Plummer, K. 1995. *Telling Sexual Stories*. London: Routledge.
Rust, P.C. 1996. Managing Multiple Identities: Diversity Among Bisexual Women and Men, in *Bisexuality: The Psychology and Politics of an Invisible Minority*, edited by B.A. Firestein. London: SAGE, 53–83.
Rust, P.C. 2004. Two Many and Not Enough: The Meanings of Bisexual Identities. *Journal of Bisexuality*, 1(1), 31–68.
Robinson, M. 2015. Bisexual People, in *The Oxford Handbook of Theology, Sexuality, and Gender*, edited by A. Thatcher. Oxford: Oxford University Press, 640–656.
Sherkat, D.E. 2000. 'That they be keepers of the home': The effect of conservative religion on early and late transitions into housewifery. *Review of Religious Research*, 41(3), 344–358.

Stoller, R.J., 1972. The bedrock of masculinity and femininity: bisexuality. *Archives of General Psychiatry*, 26(3), 207–212.

Toft, A. 2009a. Bisexual Christians: The life-stories of a marginalised community, in *Contemporary Christianity and LGBT sexualities*, edited by S. Hunt. London: Routledge, 67–85.

Toft, A. 2009b. Negotiating identity–Life narratives of bisexual Christians, in *Narrative, Memories and Identities*, edited by D. Robison, P. Fisher, T. Yeadon-Lee, S.J. Robinson and P. Woodcock. Huddersfield: University of Huddersfield Press, 127–135.

Toft, A. 2014. Re-imagining bisexuality and Christianity: The negotiation of Christianity in the lives of bisexual women and men. *Sexualities*, 17(5–6), 546–564.

Toft, A. Forthcoming. Exploring the intersection of bisexuality and Christian identities: The negotiation of gendered attraction in intimate lives, in *Intersecting Religion and Sexuality*, edited by S. Page and A.K.T. Yip. Leiden: Brill.

Toft, A. and Yip, A.K.T. 2018. Intimacy negotiated: The management of relationships and the construction of personal communities in the lives of bisexual women and men. *Sexualities*, 21(1–2), 233–250.

Weeks, J. 2002. *Sexuality and Its Discontents: Meanings, Myths, and Modern Sexualities.* London: Routledge.

Wilcox, C., and Jelen, T.G. 1991. The effects of employment and religion on women's feminist attitudes. *The International Journal for the Psychology of Religion*, 1(3), 161–171

Wilcox, M.M. 2002. When Sheila's a lesbian: Religious individualism among lesbian, gay, bisexual, and transgender Christians. *Sociology of Religion*, 63(4), 497–513.

Wilcox, M.M. 2003. *Coming Out in Christianity: Religion, Identity and Community.* Bloomington: Indiana University Press.

Woodhead, L. 2001. The turn to life in contemporary theology and spirituality, in *Spirituality and Society in the New Millennium*, edited by U. King. Brighton: Sussex Academic Press, 110–123.

Woodhead, L.J. and Heelas, P.L. 2000. *Religion in Modern Times: An Interpretive Anthology.* London: Blackwell.

Yip, A.K.T. 1997a. Attacking the Attacker: Gay Christians talk back. *British Journal of Sociology*, 48(1), 113–127.

Yip, A.K.T. 1997b. Dare to differ: Lesbian and gay Catholics' assessment of official Catholic positions on sexuality. *Sociology of Religion*, 58(2), 165–180.

Yip, A.K.T. 2000. Leaving the Church to keep my faith: The lived experiences of non-heterosexual Christians, in *Joining and Leaving Religion: Research Perspectives*, edited by L.J. Francis and Y.J. Katz. Leominister: Gracewing, 129–145.

Yip, A.K.T. 2002. The persistence of faith among non-heterosexual Christians: Evidence for the neosecularisation thesis of religious transformation. *Journal for the Scientific Study of Religion*, 41(2), 199–212.

Yip, A.K.T. 2003. The self as the basis of religious faith: Spirituality of gay, lesbian, and bisexual Christians, in *Predicting Religion: Mainstream and Margins in the West*, edited by G. Davie, L. Woodhead and P. Heelas. Aldershot: Ashgate, 134–146.

Yip, A.K.T. 2010. Coming home from the wilderness: An overview of recent scholarly research on LGBTQI religiosity/spirituality in the West, *Queer Spiritual Spaces*, edited by K. Browne, S.R. Munt and A.K.T. Yip. Aldershot: Ashgate, 51–66.

7 Ambiguities, authenticity and actualisation

Life story research with a bisexual Christian

Chris Greenough

Introduction

> At the age 34 I started to question what I believed and I asked myself questions such as, 'Could I live a life for God and be gender-fluid/bi?', 'What does God actually think about my gender and sexuality?', 'How would the church react to me if I did come out?'

Queer theology has emerged as a critical framework which embraces re-examinations of God, the Bible and religious beliefs and practices in light of non-normative gender and sexualities. Therefore, queer theology is a site acutely aware of how there can be an almost tangible tension between bisexuality and Christianity, as noted in Sam's citation above. Despite the burgeoning field of queer theology within the academy, the lives of non-normative identifying Christians are significantly under-researched, especially in relation to bisexual lives. Margaret Robinson observes that 'what is missing from even the bi-friendly queer theologies is the focus on experience' (2015: 648). The few existent explorations into the life stories and experiences of bisexual Christians have often detailed the various experiences of those identifying as bisexual within their various churches (Kolodny, 2000; Robertson, 2017; Toft, 2009, 2012, 2014; Wilcox, 2002, 2009; Yip, 2003a, 2003b).

Sam chose to use the pronouns 'they', 'their' and 'them'.[1] This chapter presents the story of Sam, who identifies as bisexual, gender-fluid and Christian. They describe their experiences in church as 'fragile' and they are conscious of the ambiguities of their gender, sexual and faith self-presentations. This chapter begins with an overview of how life stories are a source for Christian theology. As Sam's story is interwoven with the literature throughout, I explore Sam's 'coming out' and attention then turns to how bisexual ambiguity is a truly queer concept. It is unstable and unfixable and it is precisely what challenges normativity. Underpinning my examination of ambiguity, I explore how issues of authenticity and actualisation characterise contemporary understandings of religion, gender and sexuality. Authenticity is often thought of as experienced through the process of coming out while actualisation is explicitly linked to bisexual identifications through having bisexual feelings and/or acting upon them. One idea that germinates in this chapter is that authenticity and actualisation are important concepts for individuals who are negotiating being Christian with non-normative sexuality and gender identifications. The chapter then addresses the notion of a 'Bi/Christ' in the work of Marcella Althaus-Reid. This offers original critical insights on how an epistemology of bisexual ambiguity reveals the temporality of human understandings of identity. Althaus-Reid states, 'Bi/Christology walks like a nomad in lands of opposition and exclusive identities, and does not pitch its tent for ever in the same place' (2000: 119). Furthermore, it becomes apparent that the examination of the role of ambiguity in the lives of bisexual Christians illustrates how the concept of 'identification' offers more nuanced possibilities than the term 'identity', as it allows for fluidity. In the concluding section, the theme of fluidity is also extended to religious identifications, noting the subjective turn to personalised beliefs and the temporality of these beliefs.

Sexual storytelling

This chapter mobilises the sexual story from a bisexual, gender-fluid Christian to offer an example of the 'moving and powerful stories' which is advocated by Andrew Yip:

> [T]he emergence of anecdotal narratives and personal biographies… often offer moving and powerful stories of courage, resilience, and wisdom. In many ways, they could be more effective than scholarly writings precisely because they are not wrapped in academic language.
>
> (2010: 48)

Yet, despite embracing queer theology as a much-needed area of study, my disquiet around the area of queer theology is that it largely exists in theoretical form, rather than engaging with aspects of practical theology to explore the living experiences of those on the margins of social and religious normativity. I remain concerned about the accessibility of queer theological texts, which often employ dense, opaque language. Such theorisation fails to engage with individuals for whom 'queer' serves as a marker of identification. Deryn Guest shares this concern, noting how queer theory 'will prove to be an elitist discourse, hardly accessible to the lay person or in touch with the lived realities of the grassroots communities' (2005: 51). David Halperin would seem to agree too, as revealed in his comment about queer theory: 'Who ever could have guessed that we would come to saddle it with so much pretentious baggage?' (2003: 339). By engaging queer theology from a living experience perspective, the life story within this chapter provides a source for theology as it speaks back to the Christian tradition.

Althaus-Reid states that 'at the bottom line of Queer theologies, there are biographies of sexual migrants, testimonies of real lives in rebellions made of love, pleasure and suffering' (2003: 8). It is this bottom-up theology which reveals how life stories are potent forms of theology. James Nelson first used the term 'sexual theology' as different from 'theology of sexuality' in his significant volume on sexuality and theology *Embodiment* (1979). Rather than looking at what traditional source of theology (Bible, tradition, church) say about sexuality, Nelson revealed how examining sexual embodiment is a source for theology. Elsewhere, I argue that exploring and sharing one's life narrative in relation to sexuality is an act of practical theology (Greenough, 2018). Practical theology is about faith as a living practice. This is a call to do theology differently, a bottom-up approach from individual life stories, rather than a top-down approach from traditional Christian theology.

Sharing sexual stories are messy because human lives are messy, and therefore they challenge the stabilised and sanitised discourse of traditional theology. Life-story research is transformative as it is a relational process: narrating a story can help individuals make sense of their messy lives. In *Undoing Theology* I note, 'Sexual stories provide a catalyst for transformation from self-hate to self-love for individuals who have been shamed by their sexual selves, as they have been regulated by Christian discourse which is obsessed with policing sex' (Greenough, 2018: 30).

Stories also speak to others. Althaus-Reid observes how 'theology as a critical bisexual art can still be thematic and particular' (2003: 16), and this chapter looks at the themes relating to an individual life story of its protagonist. Although the story in this chapter is necessarily structured in a coherent, presentable form, Althaus-Reid is right to remind us that such a life story 'may resemble minor earthquakes or tremors occurring through a life story at the points of reflection where the bisexual theologian introduces a metaphorical third person into the discourse' (2003: 16). For Sam, the introduction of this third person is revealed as God.

Sam's 'coming out'[2]

Sam is 37 and they have two children. They came to faith at the age of 15 and were brought up as a Christian. Sam says:

> I came out as gender-fluid and bisexual to my ex-wife, friends and family over two years ago, which came as a big shock to the people around me as I had hidden this from everyone for all of my life. I found coming out to my sisters really easy. However, coming out to my mum and dad was something that struck fear into me, as we had always been a really close family and the thought of upsetting them or being rejected by them was something that I couldn't get my head around.

In terms of their marriage, Sam says, 'I was happily married to my ex-wife for 13 years but she is very old school in her thinking and she believes that I choose to be gender-fluid and bisexual, and that who I am is a sin against

God'. Sam's coming out therefore marked the end of their marriage, as their former wife's conservative Christian attitudes influenced her thoughts on their new self-identifications. In terms of their religious identifications, Sam's coming out also saw the church in which they had grown up become 'fragile':

> It feels good to no longer have to live a life with secrets and cover things up even if that does mean that church life has become harder. My prayer is that one day I'll be able to walk into church and feel free to worship God without feeling the pressure of what those around me are thinking.

Leanne McCall Tigert notes how 'coming out to oneself and others flies in the face of the conspiracy of silence perpetrated by homophobia and heterosexism' (1999: 75). Similarly, Althaus-Reid refers to the closet as a place of exile:

> A Queer theologian is a theologian in/of exile; she is hidden in the note-book, or the lover who does not phone at weekends, or cannot hold hands with her in church: she is the one who knows her closet, but also the complexities of it. Bisexuals may have more than one closet in their lives.
> (2003: 21)

Sam's story turns the spotlight on this closet, demonstrating the conflicting responses and feelings they had on coming out. For Sam, coming out signalled the end of a marriage and a new, renegotiated relationship with the church community; it also signalled the end of a long, lonely period of self-examination and self-denial. Brendan Robertson notes how 'when your theology and your reality come into contradiction, often it's time to rethink your theology' (2017: 4). Throughout their adolescence, Sam recalls how their expression of gender and sexuality was regulated by their understanding of Christian teaching relating to gender and sexuality. During their early adolescence, the traditional heteronormative teaching from the church actually served to regulate the confusion Sam felt. Sam says, 'coming to faith at 15 actually took away a lot of the confusion that I had, because my early encounters with church and God led me to believe that God made man and woman and that a man should be with a woman'. Heterosexuality was compulsory: a rule that had to be adhered to. For Sam, this was destined to unravel, as they add, 'it was only as the years went by that I began to question this theology and way of thinking because no matter how hard I suppressed my feelings or prayed about them, they would always come back stronger'. It was a period punctuated by inner conflict and emotional distress, as Sam reconciled multiple paradoxical identifications and multiple closets: Christian, bisexual, gender-fluid:

> I came to understand and know by the age of 16 that I was transgender and bisexual without knowing the terminology and labels at the time. But this was still something that I kept hidden away and never spoke about

> because I was under the impression that the church welcomed anyone that was LGBT but to love God and the church you had to be straight. So, for 19 years I fought my feelings of being transgender and bisexual and suppressed them the best I could. I would often beat myself up and pray about it in the hope that God would somehow cure me or take away my feelings and thoughts.

The emergence of Sam's sexuality and gender-questioning during their adolescence is pitted against the perceived hostility within their church. More significantly, however, is the idea that Sam perceived such hostility in relation to their obedience to God. The dawning of Sam's non-normativity was hidden and had to be effaced, using prayers as a process to beg God to 'cure' them.

The ambiguity of bisexuality

Within the UK-based context of Sam's self-narrative, we note how the Church of England describes bisexuality as 'ambiguous': 'there are those whose sexual orientation is ambiguous, and who can find themselves attracted to partners of either sex … it is clear that bisexual activity must always be wrong for this reason' (Church of England House of Bishops 1991: 42). This statement is repeated in *Some Issues in Human Sexuality*, yet it is expanded to state how 'bisexuality is always wrong, principally because it inevitably involves infidelity' (2003: 215). Both documents (1991 and 2003) go on to state that the choices for bisexual Christians are celibacy, abstinence or heterosexuality. Robinson claims that 'describing bisexuality as "ambiguous" effectively defines it as the failure to have a clear orientation at all' (2015: 645). In this context, bisexuality is a potent sexual disruptive marker, as it breaks binaries and dualisms. Rather than working within binaries of male/female, heterosexuality/homosexuality, bisexuality blurs this boundary and is a challenge to monosexuality (Gammon and Isgro, 2006; Gooß, 2008; Layton, 2008).

Bisexuality also moves us away from didactic thinking of heterosexuality/homosexuality as sexual categories. Rather than characterise the definition of 'ambiguity' by failure, as Robinson does, I would state that the inexactness of ambiguity means it offers rich potential for more fluid, open interpretations of sexuality. The absence of 'clear orientation' means both bisexuality and ambiguity cannot be fixed, stable, ontological concepts. Elsewhere, Robinson cites Althaus-Reid who states that bisexuality 'cannot be pinned down in a stable or fixed way' (Althaus-Reid, 2000: 16). Robinson adds that 'this is also true of other sexualities. Their fixity is an illusion' (2010: 110). Stable sexuality is revealed as being illusionary, while the sexual imagination allows ambiguity. In this sense, ambiguity is just as authentic as any perceived clarity of stability.

Adrian Thatcher and Elizabeth Stuart highlight how 'bisexuals undermine the whole sexual system, the neat classification of people into homo and hetero, the pathologising of homosexuality as a heterosexual disorder and so on' (2004: 34, cited in Toft, 2009: 77). Within the life story of the protagonist of this chapter, we note how Sam defines themselves as 'bi', and they are currently in a relationship with a woman. This reveals an encounter between complex gender and ambiguous sexuality.[3] Of course, bisexuality is truly queer in the disruption of the normative sexual imagination. Ambiguity evades normativity.

Within the very first issue of the *Journal of Bisexuality*, Paula Rust discusses the difference between 'technical bisexuals' (2000: 45) as those who self-identify as bisexual in relation to their sexual history or sexual activities at present, against those who have a capacity for bisexuality but may not actualise this capacity. Indeed, Klein (1978), Garber (1995) and Rust (2000) emphasise the non-behavioural, affective dimension of bisexuality, pointing to feelings or attitudes rather than actions. Rust does not offer a neologism for a non-'technical' bisexual, but it is helpful to highlight how bisexuality moves beyond the actualisation of sexual activity. Rust's participants demonstrate how the potentiality of bisexuality is important in an individual's self-identity as bisexual, rather than it being a physical expression through sexual activity. Within the survey of her participants, she concludes that 'bisexual identities are based solely on their feelings and potentials and not on their behavior' (2000: 46). Therefore, bisexuality is not only ambiguous because it challenges normativity, it remains ambiguous in terms of its own actualisation. In this regard, the capacity for bisexuality can be considered a critical epistemological tool within theology and religion. Bisexuality is about attraction, rather than actualisation. Sexuality can be cerebral and/or physical and similar examinations of gender have been undertaken, which have shaken the foundations of binary concepts of gender. Sexuality cannot be reduced to physical intimate activities, it is part of our self-expression and self-identification.

The performativity of Sam's gender contests the essentialist nature of 'identity', as they resist the constraints of heteronormative social representations. Bronwyn Fielder and Douglas Ezzy observe the cycle of re-creation that exists through queer gender and sexuality: 'Queer maintains that the self is in continual creation, a self that can be consciously created and recreated iteratively once heteronormative structural constraints are uncovered' (2018: 22). The notions of ambiguity and actualisation arise with regard to Sam's identifications, as bisexual and gender-fluid identifications are connected to visibility. Julie Hartman-Linck (2014) explores the notion of bisexual display, noting how bisexuality is rendered visible through the choice of a partner, yet for bisexuals in monogamous relationships, bisexuality is unsatisfactorily invisible as one is considered either heterosexual or homosexual. Therefore, sexual orientation is often perceived through the gender of someone's partner. For Sam, they note how their gender-fluid and bisexuality identifications are rendered invisible when they present as male because their current partner is female. This demonstrates a conflict between self-identification and social representation for Sam. Nonetheless, this assumption actually queers the cis/heteronormative imagination demonstrating how visibility and representation are inadequate markers of gender. For Sam, the issue of non-normative sexuality arises when they present as female:

> I'm quite fortunate in the fact that the person I fell in love with is female and that shields me from having to deal with the whole bisexual issue. However, I am quite open to talking about it and it's not something that I shy away from.

Sam describes their current relationship as 'fortunate' as it allows them to evade the issue of bisexuality, yet this does not deny the articulation of their capacity for bisexuality. Kathleen Jowitt describes such 'passing' as tiring: 'Perhaps it's easier knowing that one does, after all, have the option of passing as straight if it gets as bad as all that. I don't know. In my experience passing as straight is almost as tiring as repeatedly coming out' (2017: 116).

Sam came out to their pastor first, before the rest of the church community. They disclose how the level of acceptance in their church community has been limited:

> My pastor was one of first people that I came out to after my close friends and family as I have a lot of respect for him and I'd been an active member of that church since 1996 … I told him my story and how I had struggled with my gender identity and sexuality and that I've come to a point in life where I am not prepared to keep lying to myself and the people around me. He sat and listened to everything that I had to say and sympathised with the struggles that I had gone through. After a lot of questions he did say that he still wants me to be around in the church but he couldn't agree with my decision to accept that I was transgender and bisexual. Which to be fair was the response that I expected.

Rather than focussing on negative relationality, as illuminated in the comments Sam received from others in their church, Alex Toft notes how bisexuality offers a model of positive relationality in Christianity. Toft states: 'bisexuality represents the ideal way to live and relate to people. Taking the life of Jesus Christ as the ideal template for human existence, respondents argued that the relationships and the ethos expressed in Jesus' teaching was bisexual' (2009: 77).

Regrettably, the people in Sam's church clearly do not see how bisexuality is a Christ-like quality. For Althaus-Reid, a bisexual Christology offers an insight into the living experiences of bisexual identifying individuals, as well as being a theological trope to challenge traditional theology. She asserts: 'In a Christology of a Bi/Christ we are considering two things. First, the reality of people's identity outside heterosexualism, and second, a pattern of thought for a larger Christ outside binary boundaries' (2000: 117).

Althaus-Reid's Bi/Christ and authenticity

A Bi/Christ releases the divine from the shackles of compulsory, vanilla heterosexuality which has been repeated throughout Christian history and thought. It breaks the monotonous repetitions of the heteronormative tradition, allowing for a visibility of what has often been repressed in theology. It is a queer force, which serves to dismantle the representations of binary gender and heterosexuality as marginalising forces within the Christian traditions:

> The bisexual theologian (or the theologian who thinks critically bi- or polyamorously) is in the unique position of acting and reflecting in a theological praxis based on two basic elements: first, the relation of the closet, and second, the way of transcendence via the instability of God, sexual identity and humanity.
>
> (Althaus-Reid, 2003: 15)

A Bi/Christ therefore relies on the authenticity gained through the process of coming out.[4] The relationship to the closet renders visible what has previously been hidden. For some, the act of coming out actualises sexuality and activates authenticity of self. For Sam, the act of coming out has been life changing; as they note: 'I have no regrets in making the decision to come out publicly, my life is in such a better place now.'

Fielder and Ezzy's work details the pursuit of authenticity in the life of LGBT Christians (2018). They comment how 'the ethic of authenticity is lived through the relationships with God, with Jesus and with neighbours' (2018: 73). With regards to authenticity, Fielder and Ezzy's work describes the actualisation of coming out as a reconciliation of sexuality based on personal faith in Jesus. They state, 'the performative act of coming out, for example, is central to the attainment of authenticity, as is living a good life, following the example of Jesus' (2018: 12–13). This resonates profoundly in Sam's story, as they say:

> I began to accept that God loves me the way that I am and that I don't have to live according to what anyone else thinks. With that in mind I decided to stop fighting and suppressing who I really am and come out and be honest with myself and everyone else about my true gender and sexuality.

Of course, Althaus-Reid's theological troublemaking in conceptualising a Bi/Christ is not without its critics, even within the queer community. Robinson, as a bisexual-identified theologian, expresses her reluctance in accepting the potential disruptive marker a Bi/Christ would encompass. Robinson states that 'Althaus-Reid's critical bisexual theology is a method and not an identity', and that she has 'concerns about it being co-opted by non-bisexuals, to our detriment' (2010: 110). Robinson does not make reference to 'technical' bisexuals, but I would seek to revise her notion of bisexuality as an 'identity', and to this point I will return later in this chapter. She is, however, right in asserting that the bisexual theology advocated by Althaus-Reid is a method. Althaus-Reid herself does not claim it as an identity, but rather a critical epistemological endeavour. Althaus-Reid asserts:

> independently of the sexual identity of the theologian as an individual, theology is the art of a critical bisexual action and reflection on God and humanity. The interesting thing about this is the bisexual critical epistemology could be considered one of the main challenges for any theologian.
>
> (2003: 15)

Similar to Robinson's critiques about bisexuality as a method, Mary Hunt states how she is 'not persuaded that bisexuality challenges binary categories. To the contrary, it seems to reinforce the heterosexual–homosexual split precisely in claiming – thus re-inscribing – both' (2010: 23). Yet, it is Mary Hunt's positionality itself which seems ambiguous. In her Foreword to *Blessed Bi Spirit* (2000), published ten years earlier, Hunt states that bisexual theology actually moves us beyond dualisms. She argues that bisexuality means that 'binaries are no longer operative because something has come along to break their spell' (2000: xv). Hunt's position clearly changes, without her acknowledging this revision. This critical examination of Hunt is not offered as an exposé of inconsistency, or to highlight a flaw in her arguments. Rather, Hunt's reversal demonstrates perfectly how there is a fluidity of identification and positionality. The evolution and renegotiation of Hunt's position simply shows how identifications, positionalities, beliefs and allegiances change.

What can be inferred from Althaus-Reid's Bi/Christ as a critical epistemology is that there is a difference between authenticity and actualisation in terms of identifying as a bi-theologian. Hunt oscillates between one earlier view that bisexuality breaks the binary and a later view that states bisexuality reinforces the binary. Perhaps so. Perhaps bisexuality both breaks and reinforces the binary – now that would be queer! Aside from theoretical musings, in reality the point of bisexuality is that it encompasses the idea of 'both' and therefore embraces duality. The contradiction remains that despite the tsunamis of efforts of sexologists in establishing the accepted notion of a sexual continuum, and queer theorists who disrupt normalised ideas of gender and sexuality, bisexuality is often discussed as if it were a capturable, static, crystallised marker of identity.

The concern from Robinson (2010) about a bisexual positionality being adopted by non-bisexuals seems to imply there is something collective and shared about bisexual experience, which may be lost or diluted if used by non-bisexuals. What is at the essence of Robinson's critique, in my view, is that there is a dangerous notion of privilege when adopting a non-normative identification as a critical, heuristic tool yet with limited knowledge of how such an identification is lived and rooted in quotidian experiences. This chapter therefore massages some of the tensions between critical theory and living experiences. A limitation to those who engage critically by adopting a non-normative positionality or method is that they do not also share the living experiences and impact of such identities. Trauma is one such experience.

Trauma as non-normative experience

Ruard Ganzevoort, writing from a practical theology perspective, observes how 'identity is taken as the narrative construction of who the person is vis-à-vis her or his own life course and vis-à-vis other persons … Identity is the story one tells about oneself' (2008: 19–20). Ganzevoort reflects on trauma as part of the process that aids identity development. In theological terms, he notes how 'the Christian tradition has a traumatic experience as its nuclear story' (2008: 19). For now, attention returns briefly to Sam's story. Sam notes the traumatic experiences of hidden childhood experimentation.

> I knew from a very early age that I was different but I could never quite put my finger on why. Growing up I had a lot of female tendencies and I'd often enjoy spending time alone as a teen in my sister's clothes when my family were out.

Sam's story reveals how the dawning of their gender and sexual identifications was a process which can be aligned to Ganzevoort's theology of trauma, as trauma is not demarcated by referring to one specific past event, but by a process or series of repeated events that impact on an individual's life. For Sam, the impact was the realisation of their gender and sexual expressions as being non-normative:

> There was never a defining moment or an event that shaped me, I just always was this way and as much as I fought against my feelings and instincts I just naturally grew into the person that I am now.

Ganzevoort's position is helpful, as it firstly highlights trauma as 'an "alien" intrusion that calls for resistance' and it 'sees trauma as integral to identity development' (2008: 10). This trauma can be defined as the space between ambiguity and self-authenticity. Tigert observes how trauma is an experience common to non-normative identifications: 'Queer people understand the ordinariness of trauma all too well. It is a never-ceasing trauma, or traumatization to be rendered one-down, second-class, disempowered, and less safe just because of who we are and whom we love' (1999: 21). For non-normative Christians, the trauma is exacerbated by the heteronormative expectation and regulations which are articulated and repeated within the mainstream traditions. One example of this is found in the response of Sam's persistence to remain in the church, despite negative comments and feedback from others:

> I made the decision to stay strong in my faith and remain within my church despite some of the comments and feelings that have been made known to me. I love God and I love my church and I'm not prepared to let a few people steal that away from me just because I am different from them.

Identity and identification

Much ink has been spilled on the theme of 'identity' and sexual identities. Categories of identity are still conceived as stable entities, with identity being heralded 'the loudest talk in town' (Bauman, 2004: 16). Steve Epstein comments that 'queer' is 'the maintenance of identity and difference in tension' (1994: 197). Queer challenges the stability of the constructs of identity. In these terms, following Brubaker and Cooper, I agree that the term 'identification' is a more appropriate term than 'identity' when referring to bisexuality:

> As a processual, active term, derived from a verb, 'identification' lacks the reifying connotations of 'identity'. It invites us to specify the agents that do the identifying. And it does not presuppose that such identifying (even by powerful agents, such as the state) will necessarily result in the internal sameness, the distinctiveness, the bounded groupness that political entrepreneurs may seek to achieve. Identification – of oneself and of others – is intrinsic to social life; 'identity' in the strong sense is not.
>
> (2000: 14)

Sociologist Steph Lawler is correct to point out that 'processes of identification are increasingly important in how people produce their identities' (2014: 35). For Lawler, *identification* is a fluid process towards what is regarded as a collective entity: *identity*. It is the process of identification which has potency. Of course, post-structural and postmodern theories all serve to reveal the instability of identity. Aside from noting how she disagrees with Brubaker and Cooper, Lawler does not contest their preference for the term 'identification' rather than 'identity', but she uses the concepts of 'identifications' and 'disidentifications' to argue the ways in which identity is constructed (2014: 12). Indeed, Lawler does not engage with Brubaker and Cooper in any critical way throughout her text. Nonetheless, where they agree is that it is an individual's process of identification (including disidentifications) that reveals their continuing nature of self-understanding.

'Identification' is particularly important when considering bisexual lives and experiences as it allows for plurality and describes something which can be unfixable. It refuses allegiance to 'identity' and negotiates living bisexually as fluid, ongoing, continuous. 'Identification' reveals how the category of 'identity' can be conventional, stereotypical, overly generic, unimaginative and obfuscate. In contrast, 'identity' invokes assumptions. The semantic relative of 'identical' to 'identity' assumes that individuals are the same with a shared 'identity'. Indeed, Fielder and Ezzy agree that queer identity is 'anti-identitarian': 'The pursuit of "authenticity" assumes an essential unchanging self, while a queer self is continually created and a transformed self. In this sense, "queer" is anti-identitarian, in which the self is never crystallized' (2018: 15).

For bisexuality, the plurality of 'identifications' allows for an openness to temporality and to paradoxes which allow individuals to narrate their self-understanding without holding allegiances to past identifications or promises of future ones. 'Identification' allows a process of becoming; it does not offer the same trappings as 'identity'. Indeed, it allows an individual to change their mind. The move away from a crystallised concept of identity to a more fluid idea of identifications is useful, as Sam describes the visibility of their gender presentations:

> Overall my life is a bit of a mixed bag really when I comes to gender, I don't know from one day to the other what gender I'll be and what socially I can get away with. Some days I'm female, some days I'm male and others I'm just stuck somewhere in the middle.

Sam's definition of being 'stuck somewhere in the middle' provides a lens of ambiguity in terms of presenting binary gender, which is actualised based on their mood, feelings and the degree of social acceptability they envisage. The choice of the verb 'stuck' is striking, as there is a level of choice in the presentation of self, yet 'stuck' is entirely appropriate when self-disclosure and self-presentations are restricted based on acceptability.

This notion of being able to change one's mind offers a powerful example to the mainstream Christian churches, to encourage and allow them to change their minds in terms of the homonegative positional statements which have tarnished the traditions. Moreover, these statements have tarnished lives, as the negative and hostile attitudes from conservative Christians has led to episodes of upset for Sam. They reveal:

> I've had people tell me that I'm believing a lie from the devil and that Jesus doesn't approve of my choices in my life. I do find that hard to deal with and it does make me feel at times like I no longer belong there but I've never been tempted to turn my back on my faith over the opinions of a few.

Changing our mind not only leads to authenticity for individuals, but for the church. Just as coming out is an example of true authenticity of self, for the churches, full acceptance would demonstrate true authenticity of the mission of Christ.

For a moment, let us return to Hunt's critique of Althaus-Reid's Bi/Christ, and whether bisexual identity is important as a Christian theological tool which can transgress the binary. The focus on binary and identity means that we are arbitrarily moving about imaginary pieces of furniture which others claim to be a solid, fixed identity. We are making claim to imagined constructs which are revealed as being truly unstable in any case! In reality, what we need to be doing is creating space for liminal processes of identification which can lead to self-understanding in both spiritual and physical terms. These liminal processes offer a space where ambiguity, disorientations, disidentifications and negotiations occur. Elizabeth Whitney notes the importance of liminality to her own self-identification, as she states, 'perhaps this liminal desire to belong and yet retain fluidity of identity is the very thing which exemplifies my bisexuality' (2001: 112). 'Identity' smacks of fixability, using binary binds of categorisation which unavoidably point to 'other'. 'Identification' allows for the focus on a continuum, particularly in terms of sexuality. The continuum allows for process and multiplicity; it is a liminal space away from cis/heteronormative rules. So, moving away from a destructive metaphor of 'breaking the binary', I advocate a metaphor of 'cruising the continuum' in relation to engaging with authentic life stories.

Timothy Koch advocates a methodology of 'Cruising the Scriptures' (2001), defining cruising as 'using our own ways of knowing, our own desire for connection, our own savvy and instinct, our own response to what attracts and compels us' (2001: 175). In cruising the continuum, we are aware of many and multiple 'others' but rather than being plural opposites, in binary terms, the continuum allows identifications to sit among one another. For Sam, it allows for a release from being 'stuck'. Therefore, we are able to reconfigure the conceptualisation of Althaus-Reid's Bi/Christ in non-binary terminology, but using Christological understandings of Christ as dwelling among us: 'the Word was made flesh, and dwelt among us, (and we beheld his glory, the glory as of the only begotten of the Father,) full of grace and truth' (John 1:14).

Flexibility in individual religious beliefs

> Reconciling my faith to my gender and faith is somewhat of a rollercoaster for me, some weeks I don't have an issue with who I am and truly believe that I am who God created me to be and then other weeks I really question and doubt it.

Sam's current positionality in relation to their identifications and faith reflect the temporality of religious beliefs. Mobilising the ruptures of queer theory in relation to identity theory, Christian identities are also revealed as being unstable. Lawler says, 'identification can only be imaginary' (2014: 36) and I would add that the identification-imagination exists because it acknowledges its own temporality and spatiality, the multiplicity of its own term, the inconsistencies of the category it purports to represent. The perceived stability of organised religion is precisely because of how it has been repeated throughout history. The instability of identifications means that there is no crystallised concept of 'Christianity', and what emerges are Christianities which highlight the individualisation of faith, over institutional religion. Althaus-Reid points to this instability as we return to the notion of displacement of the theologian as an 'exile' (2003: 20). She states:

> She is the theologian who confesses to being away from home not even knowing where home is … A theologian who can participate in the contingent processes of representation of people in transit, nomadic subjects who follow their longing for different forms of purity and holiness and especially find their grace in the land of the sexually exiled.
>
> (2003: 21)

The lack of geographical 'home' is used as a metaphor for the struggle for representation of non-normativity within theology. Similarly, Sam explains above how their conception of who they are in God's image fluctuates, which results in an oscillation between acceptance and doubt. They state:

> I still get my good and bad weeks, some weeks I'm 99% comfortable in who I am with God and then other weeks I just don't want to be around church and I'm not sure what God makes of me but I guess it's a journey and I just doubt things like everybody else.

For Sam, the fluctuation is due to the hostility received from the other Christians in their church. They say:

> there are times when I leave church angry and confused and comments that have been made to me do play on my mind but I have to remind myself that it is only a handful of people at the end of the day and I can't let that come between my relationship with God.

In this context, it is almost ironic that Sam uses what is perceived as a stable building block of theology, the Bible, to be able to articulate their own self-understanding in relation to God. They cite the scriptures that have relevance to their life:

> In the end I came to the conclusion that I was created by God and he's the one that I need to look to for answers, so I turned to scriptures like:
>
> Psalm 139:14 – I praise you because I am fearfully and wonderfully made; your works are wonderful, I know that full well.
>
> Jeremiah 1:5 – before I formed you in the womb I knew you, before you were born I set you apart; I appointed you as a prophet to the nations.
>
> Ephesians 2:10 – for we are his workmanship, created in Christ Jesus for good works, which God prepared beforehand, that we should walk in them.

Sam's use of scriptural references reflects a postmodern, pick 'n' mix choice to current religious identifications, what Melissa Wilcox terms a 'biblical buffet' (2002: 501). Paul Heelas et al. discuss a detraditionalisation of religion which results in a 'subjective turn to self' (2005: 2). Their observations allow individuals to reconstruct religion or spirituality on their own terms, using intuition and experiences. Yip equally observes how the Christian tradition has become unstable because of individualisation:

> What is significant is that, in contemporary society, social processes such as detraditionalization and individualization increasingly empower the self over the institution as the basis of such self-directed hermeneutics that constitutes identity construction. Thus, the empirical 'what is' (based on personal experience) is prioritized over 'what ought to be'.
>
> (2005: 59)

Thus, recognising that theology is unstable too can be transformative for individuals who have experienced the trauma of their non-normative identifications, and/or who have experienced negativity from their church communities, as Sam narrates in their life story. Toft holds that 'bisexuality by its very nature and conceptualisation is full of uncertainty, flexibility and multifaceted meaning' (2009: 72). Toft's description of bisexuality is equally true of God. Revisioning Althaus-Reid's Bi/Christ thus means that God is unbound from traditional theology. A detraditionalisation of theology is akin to an undoing of theology, it is a dismantling of theological repetitions. The process of undoing theology allows for a release of God:

> contextual expectations about God are reshaped; God is creatively unbound. Queer theology can therefore move away from God as a fixed identity, and, what emerges is a truly queer God: unfixed, uncapturable and unpredictable.
>
> (Greenough, 2018: 175)

Concluding remarks

The Church of England's definition of bisexuality as 'ambiguous' has been a tool to explore ambiguity throughout Sam's narration of their living experiences within this chapter. The sharing of Sam's life story is theologically transformative when considering an epistemology of bisexuality in relation to theology. Sam's story is a powerful voice of being both insider and outsider to their church community – a community which has been neither affirming nor accepting of Sam's gender and sexuality.

The gender and sexual motifs of coming out activate authenticity, as Sam begins to live authentically. The narrative from Sam allows us to explore issues of authenticity – as bisexual, gender-fluid and Christian, as well as the actualisation of this authenticity, in terms of rendering each identification visible. My consideration of authenticity and actualisation leads to my contention is that the term 'identification' is a more appropriate lexicon than 'identity', as identification demarcates a process, whereas identity is a claim to a false crystallised concept. Simply put, identification allows temporality.

Of course, a Bi/Christ is essential to bisexual theology, and the story offered in this chapter offers a 'bottom-up' source for theology. Sam offers a significant example of detraditionalisation within their religious self, as their faith is negotiated on personal terms and based on individualised experiences.

Rather than exploring bisexuality as a tool to break the binary, this chapter sees a more appropriate metaphor of bisexuality as a cruising of the continuum: where identifications are plural, but together. This continuum allows God to dwell among us. A Bi/Christ reveals how God is unfixable, and this destabilises the Christian traditions. Sexual stories offer a glimpse into the messiness of life – birth, death, embodiment, sex, loss, trauma, joy – all of which reflect the lives of God's creations on earth.

Notes

1 A note on the use of verbs. When Sam's name is used as a pronoun, I follow with third person singular verbs, for example 'Sam says'. When used with the pronoun 'they', I use third person plural verbs, for example 'they say'. This usage reflects Sam's preferences at the time of writing.

2 Sam has been attending a Pentecostal church since the age of 15. They were 36 years of age at the time of the interview. The interview with Sam formed part of a wider study of Christians who identified as non-normative for my doctoral thesis. A monograph based on the thesis has been published as *Undoing Theology: Life Stories of Non-normative Christians* (SCM Press, 2018). Based on queer research, I adopt an 'undoing' approach to methodology, which allows for creative intuition and reflection as part of the process. Further details of the methods can be found in Greenough, 2017 and 2018.

3 See Robinson (2017) for discussion on the similarities between two-spirit and bisexual identities.

4 'Coming out' should not be idealised, and it is not desirable in all contexts. Jason Orne (2011) warns against researchers using the concept of coming out casually. Coming out is not a single act, it is strategically repeated and managed throughout an individual's life course. It is therefore multi-dimensional and multi-directional. Orne's work demonstrates how coming out is contentious, as he explores the concept of 'strategic outness – the contextual and continual management of identity – to emphasise the role of social context in sexual identity disclosure' (2011: 681). Also Emiel Maliepaard (2018) distinguishes between 'coming out' and 'disclosure' of bisexuality in the social and sexual lives of bisexuals: 'coming out is more than just communicating one's sexual identity or desire. Coming out is seen as a strategic process in which people decide to express or not express their sexuality in words to others' (2018: 148). Disclosures, on the other hand, may be spontaneous or reactive.

References

Althaus-Reid, M. 2000. *Indecent Theology*. London: Routledge.

Althaus-Reid, M. 2003. *The Queer God*. London: Routledge.

Bauman, Z. 2004. *Identity: Conversations with Benedetto Vecchi*. London: Wiley.

Brubaker, R. and Cooper, F. 2000. Beyond identity. *Theory and Society*, 29, 1–47.

Church of England House of Bishops. 1991. *Issues in Human Sexuality.* London: Church House Publishing.

Church of England House of Bishops. 2003. *Some Issues in Human Sexuality: A Guide to the Debate.* London: Church House Publishing.

Epstein, S. 1994. A queer encounter: Sociology and the study of sexuality. *Sociological Theory*, 12(2), 188–202.

Fielder, B. and Ezzy, D. 2018. *Lesbian, Gay, Bisexual and Transgender Christians.* London: Bloomsbury.

Gammon, M.A. and Isgro, K.L. 2006. Troubling the canon. *Journal of Homosexuality*, 52(1–2), 159–184.

Ganzevoort, R.R. 2008. Scars and stigmata: Trauma, identity, and theology. *Practical Theology*, 1(1), 19–31.

Garber, M. 1995. *Vice Versa: Bisexuality and the Eroticism of Everyday Life.* New York: Simon & Schuster.

Gooß, U. 2008. Concepts of bisexuality. *Journal of Bisexuality*, 8(1–2), 9–23.

Greenough, C. 2017. Queering fieldwork in religion: Exploring life-stories with non-normative Christians online. *Fieldwork in Religion*, 12(1), 8–26.

Greenough, C. 2018. *Undoing Theology. Life Stories from Non-normative Christians.* London: SCM Press.

Guest, D. 2005. *When Deborah Met Jael.* London: SCM Press.

Halperin, D. 2003. The normalization of queer theory, in *Queer Theory and Communication: From Disciplining Queers to Queering the Discipline*, edited by G.A. Yep, K.E. Lovaas and J.P. Elia. New York: Harrington Park Press, 339–343.

Hartman-Linck, J.E. 2014. Keeping bisexuality alive: maintaining bisexual visibility in monogamous relationships. *Journal of Bisexuality*, 14(2), 177–193.

Heelas, P. and Woodhead, L., with Seel, B., Szerszynski, B. and Tusting, K. 2005. *The Spiritual Revolution: Why Religion Is Giving Way to Spirituality.* Oxford: Blackwell.

Hunt, M. 2000. Foreword, in *Blessed Bi-Sprit: Bisexual People of Faith*, edited by D. R. Kolodny. New York: Continuum, xi–xvii.

Hunt, M.E. 2010. Surreal feminist liberation theology: Marcella Althaus-Reid, *Presente!* in *Dancing Theology in Fetish Boots*, edited by L. Isherwood and M. Jordan. London: Canterbury Press, 17–30.

Jowitt, K. 2017. The amazing invisible bisexual Christian, in *Our Witness: The Unheard Stories of LGBT+ Christians*, edited by B. Robertson. London: Darton, Longman & Todd, 115–120.

Klein, F. 1978. *The Bisexual Option.* Westminster: Arbor House.

Koch, T.R. 2001. Cruising as methodology: Homoeroticism and the scriptures, in *Queer Commentary and the Hebrew Bible*, edited by K. Stone. London: Sheffield Academic Press, 169–181.

Kolodny, D.R. (ed.) 2000. *Blessed Bi-Sprit: Bisexual People of Faith.* New York: Continuum.

Lawler, S. 2014. *Identity.* London: Wiley.

Layton, L.B. 2008. The psychopolitics of bisexuality. *Studies in Gender and Sexuality*, 1(1), 41–60.

Maliepaard, E. 2018. Disclosing bisexuality or coming out? two different realities for bisexual people in the Netherlands. *Journal of Bisexuality*, 18(2), 145–167.

Nelson, J. B. 1979. *Embodiment.* Minneapolis: Augsburg Publishing House.

Orne, J. 2011. 'You will always have to "out" yourself': Reconsidering coming out through strategic outness. *Sexualities*, 14(6), 681–703.

Robertson, B. (ed.) 2017. *Our Witness: The Unheard Stories of LGBT+ Christians*. London: Darton, Longman & Todd.

Robinson, M. 2010. Reading Althaus-Reid: As a bi feminist theo/methodological resource. *Journal of Bisexuality*, 10, 108–120.

Robinson, M. 2015. *Bisexual people, in The Oxford Handbook of Theology, Sexuality and Gender*, edited by A. Thatcher. Oxford: Oxford University Press, 640–656.

Robinson, M. 2017. Two-spirit and bisexual people: different umbrella, same rain. *Journal of Bisexuality*, 17(1), 7–29

Rust, P.C. 2000. Two many and not enough. *Journal of Bisexuality*, 1(1), 31–68.

Tigert, L. 1999. *Coming Out Through Fire: Surviving the Trauma of Homophobia*. Eugene: Wipf and Stock.

Toft, A. 2009. Bisexual Christians: The life-stories of a marginalised community, in *Contemporary Christianity and LGBT Sexualities*, edited by S. Hunt. Farnham: Ashgate, 67–85.

Toft, A. 2012. Bisexuality and Christianity: Negotiating disparate identities in church life, in *The Ashgate Research Companion to Contemporary Religion and Sexuality*, edited by S.J. Hunt and A.K.T. Yip. Farnham: Ashgate, 189–210.

Toft, A. 2014. Re-imagining bisexuality and Christianity: The negotiation of Christianity in the lives of bisexual women and men. *Sexualities*, 17(5–6), 546–564.

Whitney. E. 2001. Cyborgs among us. *Journal of Bisexuality*, 2(2–3), 109–128.

Wilcox, M.M. 2002. When Sheila's a lesbian: religious individualism among lesbian, gay, bisexual, and transgender Christians. *Sociology of Religion*, 63(4), 497–513.

Wilcox, M.M. 2009. *Queer Women and Religious Individualism*. Bloomington: Indiana University Press.

Yip, A.K.T. 2003a. The self as the basis of religious faith: Spirituality of gay, lesbian, and bisexual Christians, in *Predicting Religion: Mainstream and Margins in the West*, edited by G. Davie, L. Woodhead and P. Heelas. Farnham: Ashgate, 135–146.

Yip, A.K.T. 2003b. Spirituality and sexuality: The religious beliefs of non-heterosexual Christians in Great Britain. *Theology and Sexuality*, 9(2), 137–154.

Yip, A.K.T 2005. Queering religious texts: An exploration of British non-heterosexual Christians' and Muslims' strategy of constructing sexuality-affirming hermeneutics. *Sociology*, 39, 47–65.

Yip, A.K.T. 2010. Coming home from the wilderness: An overview of recent scholarly research on LGBTQI religiosity/spirituality, in *Queer Spiritual Spaces: Sexuality and Sacred Places*, edited by K. Browne, S.R. Munt and A.K.T. Yip. Farnham: Ashgate, 35–50.

8 'Sweet blasphemy'

Elif Shafak, bisexuality and Sufism

Cheryl Stobie

In 2017, acclaimed Turkish author Elif Shafak[1] publicly but briefly acknowledged her bisexuality in a TED talk in New York.[2] She reasoned, 'I have never had the courage to say in a public space that I was bisexual myself, because I so feared the slander and the stigma and the ridicule and the hatred that was sure to follow. But of course, one should never, ever, remain silent for fear of complexity.' As expected, her public affirmation of identity led to mixed reactions, often traditionalist, homophobic and misogynistic. The Turkish press and social media depicted her in overwhelmingly negative terms, with some exceptions. She was accused of 'ignoring Turkish traditions, codes of conduct, honor and family values – of exhibitionism and even of perversity', according to Itir Bagdadi, who noted sympathetically, 'It is no easy thing to admit that you are bisexual, which is a group that is the least understood and most ignored, even within the LGBT movement itself. Once such a declaration is made, it is irrevocable. No one has the right to question its sincerity – this in itself is patronizing and oppressive' (quoted in Ertan, 2017). Zehra Celenk commented wryly that although many Turkish people do not know what bisexuality is, they hate it regardless. She added, 'What has been written since her announcement precisely confirms what she has said – once you come out, you face disdain, insults and hatred' (quoted in Ertan, 2017). The courage of public figures such as Shafak in proclaiming their sexuality and in writing about LGBT issues is laudable. Although in the current global polarisation in attitudes and the provision of rights to LGBT individuals some countries are implementing positive changes, others are becoming increasingly draconian, often on religious grounds.[3] The authoritarian regime of Turkey's president Recep Tayyip Erdogan has diminished civil liberties and promoted Islamic zealotry, including a ban on LGBT events, making Shafak's public stand all the more meaningful.

More interesting for my purposes is an earlier occasion when Shafak came out as bisexual, during an email interview with Myriam J.A. Chancy in an academic journal, *Meridians: Feminism, Race, Transnationalism* in 2003. During the extensive interview Shafak offers some illuminating comments about her own positionality and creative work. She depicts her acceptance of the multiple vectors of her identity non-hierarchically as '*woman, writer, exile, bisexual, agnostic, leftist, mystic, a non-Western in the West*' (Shafak and Chancy, 2003: 63; italics in original) as a necessary core feminist insight. She sees her subjectivity and creativity as intimately connected: 'I adore and respect fluidity in both writing and being' (Shafak and Chancy, 2003: 68). 'Fluidity', of course, is frequently used as an adjective to describe bisexuality and its propensity to disrupt either/or conceptualisations of sexuality. Bisexuality occupies a liminal space between heterosexuality and homosexuality, embracing yet potentially destabilising binarist understandings of the erotic life. The editorial statement of the bisexual magazine *Anything that Moves* claims:

> Bisexuality is a whole, fluid identity. Do not assume that bisexuality is binary or duogamous in nature: that we must have 'two' sides or that we MUST be involved simultaneously with both genders to be fulfilled human beings. In fact, don't assume that there are only two genders. Do not mistake our fluidity for confusion, irresponsibility, or an inability to commit. [...] Nothing should be assumed about anyone's sexuality – including your own.
>
> (Quoted in Garber, 1995: 56)

Marjorie Garber notes that 'sexual fluidity, the capacity to attract and be attracted by' members of more than one sex is a 'genuinely dangerous attribute' (1995: 473). Bisexuality, she observes, is 'an identity that is also *not* an identity, a sign of the certainty of ambiguity, the stability of instability, a category that defies and defeats categorization' (1995: 70). Shafak similarly conceives of art as having the potential to rupture stasis, binaries and elitism and liberate new possibilities. Her bisexuality is part of a *Weltanschauung* that provides bridges, crossings and alliances between geographical locations, genders, sexualities, political affiliations and spiritual inclinations. Although she identifies as agnostic, she is deeply interested in religious histories, various branches of Islam and particularly the mystical tradition in religion which allows a voice to the marginalised, the heterodox and the 'heretical'.

In response to a question about how bisexuality operates as a trope in her work, Shafak links her life experiences with her creative practice. She notes that although she was aware of and comfortable with her bisexuality from an early age, her associates in society, and in the leftist intelligentsia in particular, saw her sexuality as wrong, a perception which she had to overcome. Later she confronted the question of whether to leave her readers to infer her bisexuality from her novels, or to come out. She mentions that in her novels there are 'homosexual and transsexual characters, themes, bisexual stories', and that these works are valued by Muslim women, including conservative ones, although there is more resistance from conservative Muslim men, for whom 'Homosexuality is ... *sapiklik*, which means perversion. And in the minds of these people sexual perversion goes hand in hand with religious deviation' (Shafak and Chancy, 2003: 80). For Shafak, bisexuality is both natural and political. It presents a challenge to ingrained habits of binarist thinking 'upon which many discriminatory practices and discourses are fostered' (81). In addition to this, writing about bisexuality is an aesthetic choice and an interpretive mode.

As bisexuals are marginalised in contemporary society, so too have Sufis been marginalised historically. Although the interview was conducted prior to the appearance of *The Forty Rules of Love* (2010), interesting comments about Sufism are offered. Shafak observes that in the seventeenth century orthodoxy was solidified in the Ottoman Empire, with the concomitant suppression of heterodoxies, including dervishes because they were heretics who promoted 'the oldest tradition of blasphemy in Islam: The tradition of *En-el Hak*. Which is to say I am God or I embody God in me' (Shafak and Chancy, 2003: 83). Various mystical traditions interpret religious transcendence in erotic terms, and I interpret Rumi's ecstatic poetry and Shafak's depiction of the bond between Rumi and Shams as being political and erotic.

Before I engage in textual analysis of *The Forty Rules of Love*, it is necessary to explain my choice of interpretive mode to employ in this chapter. I have chosen a mode which is in keeping with the focus of this edited volume's theme, namely bisexuality and spirituality, and the novel under scrutiny. This critical style is a take on that termed 'reparative reading' by Eve Kosofsky Sedgwick (following Melanie Klein) in various publications (1996, 1997, 2003, 2007). Sedgwick proposes this reading mode as an alternative to the dominant critical practice of a hermeneutic of suspicion, or what she calls 'paranoid reading' (1997: 1), exemplified for her by Judith Butler's *Gender Trouble* (1990). The history of Sedgwick's developing ideas is impressively charted by Robyn Wiegman (2014). Wiegman argues that reparative reading has been hailed as a critical 'turn' in contemporary times for queer feminist critics, who deploy an examination of the everyday, affect and queer temporalities in a mutually sustaining way. As Wiegman reveals:

> In the name of 'reparative reading', 'weak theory', or compassionate redescription, they seek new environments of sensation for the objects they study by displacing critical attachments once forged by correction, rejection, and anger with those crafted by affection, gratitude, solidarity, and love. Under these affective terms, the critical act is reconfigured to value, sustain, and privilege the object's worldly inhabitations and needs. (2014: 7)

Sedgwick and later proponents of reparative reading do not quail from using the auratic but loaded word 'love' to describe the intimate act of reading and interpreting works authored by individuals disavowed by their own cultures. As Sedgwick poignantly observes:

> Love of a book, even a sinister book, love that generates out of concentrated meditation on its pieces a different and needed book; the

> transformative, frankly instrumental love of the artifacts of a culture, threatening though that culture itself may be: perhaps no impulse has less warrant than such love in the climate of a hermeneutic of suspicion.
>
> (1996: 278)

A queer feminist reading, in such a climate, strives to acknowledge and ameliorate impediments to flourishing by engaging lovingly with textual representations of affect and time. This is an apposite interpretive mode to interpret Elif Shafak's *The Forty Rules of Love* (2010), which is concerned with love and other forms of affect, temporalities, writing and interpretation. While Wiegman reveals the co-constitutive strains between the paranoid and reparative modes, and further calls into question the effectiveness of interpretation, for my purposes interpretation remains a useful scholarly tool, and I argue that foregrounding the reparative (while not totally discounting the hermeneutic of suspicion) is crucial to my task.

In the same issue of *Feminist Theory* that features Wiegman's article, bisexual theorist Clare Hemmings responds to the piece, and muses about Wiegman's use of the term 'queer feminist':

> Is 'feminist' on its own in danger of either heterosexual myopia or lesbian essentialism? Can 'feminist' only remain relevant – critically or politically – when dragged out of anachronism through 'queer' re-description? Certainly this is one way of reading the field as Robyn [Wiegman] accounts for it here: as working to displace dull and confining structural (or poststructural) feminist accounts too attached to marginality within pervasive power relations, with generative queer ways of thinking history and subjectivity that allow for multiplicities we do not already have in mind.
>
> (2014: 28)

Hemmings's provocative questions offer a springboard for me to further define my own practice as a critic in responding to *The Forty Rules of Love* and Shafak as the novel's author and public figure. Hemmings tartly epitomises popular academic myths of feminism as staid and trapped in binarisms, while queer theory is portrayed as more 'radical and freeing' (2014: 29). Similarly, I might add, bisexual theory is often misrepresented and dismissed in intellectual circles as binarist and based on old-fashioned, essentialist identity politics[4] – a portrayal I would repudiate. I argue that 'queer' can be used in a flattening, regulatory and imperialist mode, and that pairing its terminology with the specificity of a named identity such as bisexuality (a marginal concept in most queer discourse and in society) can offset these unacknowledged reactionary effects. My lens in this textual analysis is that of bisexual feminist reparative criticism, examining representations of sexuality and Sufism from both emic and etic perspectives, in a spirit of generosity and affirmation. I am also implicitly building upon my previous work in which I limn the connections between sexuality and spirituality (e.g. Stobie, 2010, 2011, 2014).

Sufism and love

Love is the central theme within both time-settings of *The Forty Rules of Love*. In the contemporary period, 2008 to 2009, 40-year-old Jewish American Ella Rubinstein discovers that she is cynical about love in view of her husband's affairs and her stultifying feminine roles as wife, mother and home-maker. After she becomes a reader for a literary agency her first assignment is to assess a manuscript titled *Sweet Blasphemy*, set between 1242 and 1252 and recounting the love between Rumi and Shams of Tabriz through the eyes of some 17 characters. Ella becomes intrigued by the author of *Sweet Blasphemy*, a Scottish nomadic Sufi convert, Aziz Z. Zahara, and initiates an email correspondence which develops into love, and culminates in her leaving her husband and living with Aziz until his death, after which she plans to seek a new life in Amsterdam.

Sufism[5] is the spiritual interface between these mirrored tales. Aziz portrays the powerful bond between Rumi and Shams as the long-lasting blossoming of an influential strand of Sufism. Shams is shown to be 'a wandering dervish with unconventional ways and heretical proclamations' (Shafak 2015 [2010]: 19) who catalyses the transformation of Rumi from a respected, traditional Islamic scholar and cleric

> to a committed mystic, passionate poet, advocate of love, and originator of the ecstatic dance of the whirling dervishes, daring to break free of all conventional rules. In an age of deeply embedded bigotries and clashes, he stood for a universal spirituality, opening his doors to people of all backgrounds. Instead of an outer-oriented jihad – defined as 'the war against infidels' and carried out by many in those days just as in the present – Rumi stood up for an inner-oriented jihad where the aim was to struggle against and ultimately prevail over one's ego, *nafs*.
>
> (Shafak 2015 [2010]: 19–20)

This representation of Sufism accords with that provided by various scholars of religion. Reza Aslan, for instance, notes that Sufism differs from conventional Islam in its anti-intellectualism and focus on esoteric devotionalism; in addition, Sufism considers orthodox teachings and theology as inadequate for enlightenment, as enlightenment relies on a concern for all – especially the marginal – in society, and relies most especially on an acceptance of the primacy of the principle of love:

> Love is the foundation of Sufism. It is the language through which Sufism is most perfectly expressed and the sole avenue through which its ideals can be understood. The experience of love represents the most universal station on the Sufi Way, for it is love – not theology and certainly not the Law – that engenders knowledge of God.
>
> (2006: 210)

Aslan goes further in commenting that the love for and embedded in God conceptualised in Sufism does not accord with the Christian mystical notion of *agape* or spiritual love. By contrast, it is passionate and all-consuming, requiring self-annihilation and surrender to the will of the beloved; the desired union is often expressed in erotic terms, and it is a longing that is unfulfilled (2006: 211–212). A further dimension of the search for God in Sufism is that it is customarily undertaken 'under the direction of a master' (Green, 2012: 8). Nile Green also notes that Rumi, who is renowned as Sufism's finest poet, laid emphasis on human love (79), and affirmed that the divinity of God shone from the face of his beloved Shams (107).

Throughout *Sweet Blasphemy* the love-bond between the characters Rumi and Shams is represented as intense and erotically charged, although not overtly sexual in nature. This is shown early in *The Forty Rules of Love*. Despite the reciprocal yearning both characters have for a spiritually fulfilling companion, the transformative journey undertaken by Rumi is represented as arduous and painful, particularly as jealous and resentful people succeed in killing Rumi's beloved Shams. Even before they meet, Shams has a vision in which he anticipates his death and Rumi's anxious reaction to the portentous absence of his '*"Shams, dearest"*' (27; italics in original), leading to his discovery of Shams's body in a well and his anguished cry, '"*They killed my Shams!*"' (28; italics in original). Rumi's endearments and the mutuality with which Shams channels Rumi and screams in his voice testify to the strength of the mystical love-bond between the two.

In *The Forty Rules of Love* Shams is portrayed as a legendary figure with a heightened sensitivity and supernatural powers. His visions are evidence of this, as are his prophecies that Rumi will be renowned not as a scholar but as a poet known as the inspirational 'Voice of Love' both in the 'East and West' (208). For this to occur, however, once Shams arrives in the presence of Rumi he has to act as a gadfly by questioning his authority, challenging him in public, testing his certitudes and destroying his *nafs*. Shams calls upon Rumi to go to the tavern and order bottles of wine, in contravention of the Islamic prohibition against drinking alcohol, and orders him to throw his precious books into water. In these cases, however, they are tests to break with rules and tradition, trusting his love for his guide to lead him into a new path, and both have numinous conclusions. Shams opens Rumi's eyes to the travails of ordinary people, and fosters new thinking, feeling and creativity in him.

The bond of opposites between the unruly Shams and the rule-bound Rumi is seen as symbiotic and forging a powerful unity which counters the hidebound strictures imposed by zealots, and imagines new forms of aesthetic and spiritual expression. The two discuss the Forty Rules of Love, which combine the seeming binaries of the regulated and the passionate using a number with mystical associations. They employ the *ney*, a musical instrument which makes 'the sound of the lover for the beloved' (269) in the dance of the whirling dervishes they devise, the *sema*, in which one hand is raised to receive God's love, and the other gestures earthwards to symbolise sharing it with the people. Most significantly, love for Shams indeed inspires Rumi to create poetry. Rumi's wife Kerra recites one of these love poems which unites love for another human with spiritual devotion:

> *I have seen the king with a face of Glory*
> *He who is the eye and the sun of heaven*
> (286; italics in original)

Shams pays tribute to Rumi's gift in quoting his poetry expressing negative capability:

> *Not Christian or Jew or Muslim, not Hindu, Buddhist, Sufi or zen. Not any religion or cultural system. I am not of the East, nor of the West….*
> *My place is placeless, a trace of the traceless.*
> (183; italics in original)

This is a powerful refutation of sectarianism and chauvinism, which result in binarism, othering and violence. The novel's Shams glosses this meditation as reflecting Rumi's home as being on another plane than the earthly, in 'the Kingdom of Love', with 'the Beloved' (183). This chimes with Shafak's emphasis on multiplicity and boundlessness in the novel, in keeping with Sufism portrayed as evolving practice rather than ossified creed, and in line with Shafak's grateful acknowledgement to Sufis of her acquaintance for their 'amazing ability to see things from two points of view, their own and that of another' (351). This simultaneous double vision is also consonant with the inflection of bisexuality in the text.

Bisexuality

The Forty Rules of Love can be seen as a queer text in a number of ways, and an outline of some of these features will provide a springboard for applying a specifically bisexual optic to the text. Susan S. Lanser offers three academic meanings of the verb 'to queer': '(1) to make a claim for the non-heteronormative sex, gender, or sexuality of someone or something; (2) to disrupt or deconstruct binary categories of sex, gender, and/or sexuality; and (3) to disrupt or deconstruct any entity by rejecting its categories, binaries, or norms' (2018: 924). *The Forty Rules of Love* includes a number of queer representations which act to disrupt 'binary categories of sex, gender and sexuality'. Non-heteronormative sex is portrayed in the thirteenth-century time-setting through a 'hermaphrodite' character who is a brothel-keeper. Binarist conventions of gender are also queried in the novel. When Shams sets out to meet Rumi, he shaves his hair and his eyebrows, achieving a denuded, ageless, genderless appearance. Shams also tells Kimya (who later marries him) that an esoteric rather than a literal reading of the Nisa[6] interprets a particular verse as alluding to abstract states of womanhood and manhood rather than women and men, and he avers that everyone 'has both femininity and masculinity in us, in varying degrees and shades. Only when we learn to embrace both can we attain harmonious Oneness' (Shafak, 2015 [2010]: 198). Regarding sexuality, in the twenty-first-century setting mention is made of a deceased lover of Aziz whose complex identity comprised 'a bohemian, an idealist, a radical, a bisexual, a leftist, an individualist anarchist, a multiculturalist, a human-rights advocate, a counterculture activist, an ecofeminist' (213), and whom he regarded as 'a pendulum woman' (213) because of her mercurial temperament. Neither intersex nor bisexuality is idealised in the novel, but they are portrayed as vectors of identity with complicated interconnections, and conventional hierarchies of masculinity and femininity leading to oppression of women by men are called into question in both temporalities. For the reader, negotiating between the first-person voices of 17 characters in the novel-within-a novel *Sweet Blasphemy*, interspersed with the contemporary third-person narrative of Ella and Aziz, all placed within a tightly constructed framework, including the sections consisting of the elements of Earth, Water, Wind, Fire and the Void, and with some characters narrating from beyond the vale of death, offers a profoundly anti-binarist, disruptive, deconstructive and spiritually expansive experience which fulfils the parameters of Lanser's third and broadest category of queering.

The heart of the queer mystery in the book is the nature of the relationship between Rumi and Shams, and how the twenty-first-century characters and the reader are to interpret this. This reparative interpretive act can best be achieved, I argue, by employing a bisexual lens from the perspective of the present day, using a strategic double vision that refutes binarism and correlates representations of past and present behaviours without essentialising or de-historicising complex identity categories.

Two traditional stories are referenced in *The Forty Rules of Love* to depict the nature of the bond between Rumi and Shams. One is recounted by Rumi when he is explaining his passion for Shams, whom he perceives in terms of spiritual worship: his 'Sea of Mercy and Grace', his 'Sun of Truth and Faith', his 'King of Kings of Spirit' (193). Rumi compares his love for Shams to the famous heterosexual love story of Layla and the emperor Harun ar-Rashid, who was so deeply obsessed with his beloved that he lost his mind and was thereafter known as Majnun, the madman. The unifying, transformative bond between Rumi and Shams is illustrated in the novel by the magical blossoming of a red rose, traditional symbol of love. Rumi's connection to his wife Kerra is shown to suffer from his deep romantic connection to Shams, but their marriage persists, and after Shams's death they have a daughter, as he prophesied. Shafak is therefore representing a relationship that today would be termed bisexual, along the lines defined by Robyn Ochs: 'the potential to be attracted, romantically and/or sexually, to people of more than one sex, not necessarily at the same time, not necessarily in the same way, and not necessarily to the same degree' (2009: 9).

The second story is touched on by the character called the Zealot, that of Sodom and Gomorrah, and is intended to remind readers of the usual interpretations of Lut in the *Qur'an* and Lot in the Bible. In *The Forty Rules of Love* the Zealot casts aspersions on Sufism by connecting its heresies to fears of the unleashing of God's wrath, and noting in particular the hazards posed by wandering dervishes who fail to conform to social expectations of settling down, and therefore fall victim to *Sheitan* (Satan). The veiled reference is to the sin of sodomy. Significantly, however, in another chapter Shams refutes fear-mongering by zealots, who give selective weight to certain verses. Instead of a binarist view of the delights and rewards of heaven or the torments and punishment of hell, Shams offers a different, holistic vision embedded in one of the Rules of Love: '*Quit worrying about hell or dreaming about heaven, as they are both present inside this very moment. Every time we fall in love, we ascend to heaven. Every time we hate, envy, or fight someone, we tumble straight into the fires of hell*' (Shafak 2015 [2010]: 182; italics in original). When these two stories, that of Layla and Majnun and that of Lut, are juxtaposed, it is clear that Shafak is implicitly criticising zealous, punitive views about the sinfulness of same-sex love, and endorsing an acceptance of different forms of love, in particular bisexuality. However, she also raises the issue of the power of malicious homophobic gossip, as Rumi's son Sultan Walad informs Shams that people are saying '"for two men to be so fond of each other there has to be an unspeakable bond between them"' (211). Shams responds that such prejudices only harm those who hold them, and advises Sultan Walad: '"If you hear of anyone who cannot comprehend the depth of the bond between your father and me, tell him to wash his mind!"' This leads the reader to infer that the relationship between Rumi and Shams is not a carnal one, despite its erotic framing.

Historically, as Aisha Geissinger notes, while anal intercourse between males was condemned by Islamic jurists, there was also an idealised tradition of erotic poetry used to convey mystical concepts: 'Poetry that uses homoerotic themes to express Sufi teaching was authored by medieval Muslims in all of the major Islamic languages. Such a well-known theme is the story of the love between Sultan Mahmud of Ghazna (d. 1030) and his slave Ayaz' (2012: 76).

The account by Scott Siraj al-Haqq Kugle similarly refers to evidence of widespread male same-sex connections: 'when one looks through the historical and literary records of Islamic civilization, one finds a rich archive of same-sex sexual desires and expressions, written by or reported about respected members of society: literati, educated elites, and religious scholars' (2003: 198). Kugle gives one example to illustrate his point, that of the medieval writer Ibn Dawud al-Zahiri, who formed a romantic love with a male friend, and maintained that such a love was noble if it remained 'chaste' (230 n. 25). This allusion to chastity chimes with the representation of the love between Rumi and Shams in *The Forty Rules of Love*. Kugle also offers an interpretation of the story of Lut from a thematic perspective, arguing that it is about the dangers of greed, a lack of hospitality and the misuse of sexual power rather than an indictment of sex between men. He claims that binarist definitions of natural and unnatural forms of sex derive from Western Cartesian dualism. Ironically, however, Kugle also falls into the trap of binarist discourse in his book *Homosexuality in Islam: Critical Reflection on Gay, Lesbian, and Transgender Muslims* (2010), in which he summarily dismisses bisexuality as a suitable topic for analysis. In the first place, he implies that since it was behaviourally bisexual men who were the guilty parties in the story of Lut, the extension of analysis of Qur'anic prohibitions against male same-sex sexual relations is the fault of bisexuals. He also claims that examining bisexuality 'would call into question the definitiveness of gender difference and also the discreteness of gender difference which are assumed by gay men, lesbian women, and transgender people', as 'dispositional bisexuality challenges the idea that [gender and sexuality] categories are psychologically firm and socially forceful' (11). Kugle's focus in his book reveals that even in the group of Muslims who term themselves progressive there is a poor understanding of, and antipathy towards, bisexuality. This absolutist and binarist view is the antithesis of Shafak's openness to fluidity in sex, gender and sexuality.

Bisexual Sufi shaykh Ibrahim Farajajé points out the fearful cultural mindset that creates such 'fictions of purity' (the title of an experimental essay of his) as can be seen in the viewpoints of commentators such as Kugle:

> In cultures that prioritize either/or thinking, either/or monolithic/oppositional definitions of sexualities/genders, in an either/or world, anything that occupies a liminal, an intersectional, an interstitial location is seen as a threat. Whether it be in terms of racial/ethnic mixities, religious mixities, etc. those who inhabit interstitial spaces, those who move between worlds, those who are literally fringe-dwellers, are seen as the ultimate threat.
> (2014: 147)

The prevalence of reactionary response to the openness embraced by Sufism is noted by Jennifer Rycenga: 'No matter how Queer the tradition of the Sufis, or perhaps because of how Queer the traditions of the Sufis are, religious dualists suppress direct experience' (2004: 268). In the same roundtable discussion, Farajajé observes the dynamism of religion with particular reference to Sufism: 'I look just in the history of Sufism and see how much it has changed and evolved from the Middle Ages until now, and how it continues to evolve' (280). Recent accounts of direct experience by queer Muslims elicited in interviews conducted by Andrew Kam-Tuck Yip with Amna Khalid reveal that 'a significant number' of the participants in the study

> noted that their spirituality was informed by Sufism: a more tolerant and less hierarchical mystical tradition within Islam. It privileges the direct

> personal experience of God instead of institutionalised ways of accessing the divine; and emphasises the non-dualism of nature and existence as well as fluidity.
>
> (2010: 99)

The queer respondents note in particular elements of Sufism that are meaningful to them, such as the pre-eminence placed on love, spirit and joy, as opposed to prohibitions. They refer to uplifting experiences such as chanting and listening to devotional music, the kinds of practices Shafak illustrates as Rumi and Shams develop a new kind of Sufism together.

Despite the dualistic viewpoint of some Islamic scholars, there are radical Sufis, queer people (including bisexuals) and novelists who offer a rooted and interconnected theology and politics of liberation, such as that visualised by Farajajé-Jones (an earlier name of Farajajé):

> An in-the-life theology of liberation would be one that grows out of the experiences, lives and struggles against oppression and dehumanization of those in-the-life. It understands our struggle for liberation as being inextricably bound with those of oppressed people around the world, as we all struggle against racism, classism, imperialism, sexism, ableism, and all other forms of oppression. Such a theology also offers other theologies a liberation from the strictures of homophobia/biphobia, as well as a liberation from heterosexism.
>
> (1993: 140–141)

Returning to Shafak's representation of the intimate relationship between Rumi and Shams in terms of a present-day understanding of bisexuality and Sufism, in addition to the luminous, inspirational side of their connection, Shafak portrays a destructive element with regard to women in their lives, which can be connected to other instances of patriarchal power that she critiques in the novel. Rumi treats Shams with more affection and courtesy than he affords his wife, Kerra; Rumi bars her from his study and prohibits her from touching his books, but closets himself in the study with Shams, and follows Shams's test of casting his books into water. Shams is shown to be deeply flawed in his treatment of the young woman he marries, Rumi's ward Kimya. The marriage is seen as a means of curbing his nomadic tendencies and giving him social respectability. The reader is privy to Kimya's anguish when Shams refuses to consummate their marriage, despite his response to her body. However, he spares her reputation by cutting his hand and dropping blood on the wedding sheet to provide evidence suggesting that she was a virgin. After repeated rebuffs, including after a determined attempt at seduction on her part, she dwindles into heartbroken death, convinced that he does not love her. The reason for Shams's refusal to engage sexually with her is not given, and the only comment he makes is that he has made a dreadful mistake, as he is not a type to settle:

> I felt a strong urge to run away from everything, not only from this house, this marriage, this town, but also from this body I had been given. Yet the thought of seeing Rumi the next morning held me anchored here. … I was trapped.
>
> (Shafak 2015 [2010]: 307)

This oblique comment reveals a celibate temperament in line with the chaste relationship Shams notes between him and Rumi. However, the only tie Shams feels is that to Rumi, and Kimya is represented as collateral damage. Through the callous treatment accorded to both Kerra and Kimya, to varying degrees, Shafak is refuting an idealised vision of a love relationship that involves heterosexual partners of men who share a deep spiritual connection, as well as illustrating masculine privilege and sexism in action, despite the male characters being portrayed as sensitive and sympathetic.

Other instances of portrayed gender oppression in the earlier time-setting include the fetishisation of virginity, the presumption that educating girls is a waste of time, the implication that marriage represents death for a woman, and the harrowing treatment of the prostitute Desert Rose. However, the possibility of social change is illustrated by an older Rumi's recognition that girls are worthy and excellent students, and his decision to have *sema* training for women, a practice which he hopes will continue.

Shafak avoids an attitude of superciliousness of the present towards the past by also revealing and critiquing patriarchy in the contemporary setting, seen in Ella's subservience as a wife, her role as homemaker while her husband is the breadwinner, and her acceptance of her husband's affairs, although it is expected that she will remain faithful.

Openness to different religious/spiritual affiliations

The effect of the parallels between the insistently juxtaposed and mutually illuminating temporalities is to urge the reader to respond to both simultaneously in a doubled reading which parallels the theme of bisexuality. The relationship between Ella and Aziz is seen as a contemporary variant on the spiritually and socially liberating bond between Rumi and Shams. This heterosexual relationship functions to emphasise that transformative love – physical or spiritual – is open to people of all sexual orientations and religious affiliations. It is given a queer twist as Aziz is seen to act as a kind of reincarnation of Shams, while he urges Ella to be an equivalent of Rumi and embrace love, change and creativity: '"[Y]ou can be Rumi. If you let love take hold of you and change you, at first through its presence, and then through its absence—"' (326–327). The fact that Ella demurs that she is not a Sufi (as she is Jewish), but she is being tasked by her Sufi master to adopt the mantle of Rumi, suggests that the exterior form of religion is insignificant in the quest for spiritual transcendence. This openness to various forms of religion is also seen in the novel's thirteenth-century setting, when

Rumi is portrayed as possessing the rare scholarly attribute of being able to 'dig deep below the husk of religion and pull out from its core the gem that is universal and eternal' (68). Rumi is also shown to be open-minded in marrying a Christian woman, Kimya, who despite her conversion to Islam misses the comfort of the Virgin Mary; Shams displays his syncretic belief system as he counsels Kimya to continue worshipping her: '"Religions are like rivers: they all flow to the same sea. Mother Mary stands for compassion, mercy, affection, and unconditional love. She is both personal and universal. As a Muslim woman, you can keep liking her and even name your daughter Mary"' (299). Instead of adopting a righteous attitude of promoting one religion at the expense of others deemed wrong or sinful, Shafak offers a relativistic view of religion infused with spiritual generosity represented although not idealised in the form of Sufism.

The title used by Aziz for his novel *Sweet Blasphemy* is a further means by which the reader is invited to entertain a perspective which accords significance to two elements simultaneously. The term is an oxymoron, which provokes cognitive dissonance in a reader as it contains a paradoxical blending of opposites. The phrase is explained through a parable recounted by Shams, concerning Moses and a shepherd. Moses scolds the shepherd for his 'sheer blasphemy' when he prays to God, offering if called upon to kill his fattest sheep for God to eat, and to wash God's feet, clean his ears and pick off his lice. Moses teaches the shepherd appropriate formulaic prayers to offer instead. However, God rebukes Moses for his effrontery, saying that he was well pleased with the shepherd's sincerity, purity of heart and good intentions, which represented to him 'sweet blasphemy' (51). Doris Lessing interprets a similar story told by her Sufi master Idries Shah as illustrating that 'one religion is not better than another: each is an expression of local needs', and that '[b]eyond religion, most of whose practices are the ethics of the society in which it operates codified, is a range where experience becomes more complex than the rigidities of good/bad, black/white' (2004: 266).

Conclusion

As Shafak reveals in *The Forty Rules of Love*, blasphemy or impiety or behaving ethically are relative, not absolute, concepts. They need to be interpreted according to the emotional context rather than according to calcified rules. In the thirteenth-century temporality, Rumi and Kimya, who love Shams, recognise that according to the juristic popular opinion he is flouting sharia law and is blasphemous; however, they view his transgressions as offering deeper spiritual insights: sweet blasphemy. Similarly in the contemporary time-period of the novel Ella initially views her email conversations with Aziz as blasphemy, although she rationalises that they are 'sweet blasphemy' because of the 'platonic nature of their relationship' (Shafak 2015 [2010]: 143). As she gradually acknowledges that she loves Aziz, and that he is deepening her spiritual awareness, she decides to follow her heart, leave her husband and accompany Aziz for the time he has left before dying in Konya. Contrary to the popular view that her behaviour is unethical and impractical in utilitarian terms: 'Ella had come to understand that if there was anything worse in the eyes of society than a woman abandoning her husband for another man, it was a woman abandoning her future for the present moment' (346). Love – of self, other, the suffering, and God – is seen as the paramount goal in the novel, even though love entails heartbreak. In responding to the oxymoron of 'sweet blasphemy', to the intertwined dual narratives set seven and a half centuries apart, to the representation of Sufism as perceiving all antinomies such as good and evil as being internal to the human psyche, and to the textual inflection of bisexuality, the reader embraces unity with variation.

An article by Elena Furlanetto which examines *The Forty Rules of Love* from the position of a hermeneutic of suspicion, contrary to my reparative reading, and from a binarist frame, contrary to my unifying one, accuses Shafak of 'domestication of the figure of Rumi', succumbing to 'over-simplification and decontextualization' of his work, employing 'Orientalist strategies in the ways in which she positions the East as being instrumental to the West', and displaying 'a problematic notion of cosmopolitanism … inextricably bound to the logics of empire' (2013: 202). Ironically, Furlanetto's article itself is hypnotised by the concept of American imperialism, as she constantly refers to American readership and publishing markets to bolster her insinuations that Shafak is opportunistic, acting in bad faith and Orientalist by using Coleman Barks's volume of translations that tones down the Islamicism of the original Rumi. The article devotes little attention to the texture of the novel itself, but makes misleading claims based on selective quotation, suggesting that Shafak idealises thirteenth-century Anatolia in order to consolidate American hegemony. However, Shafak certainly does not idealise either thirteenth-century Anatolia, revealed to be the site of intolerance, violence against women and murder, or twenty-first-century America, shown to be materialistic, sexist and hypocritical. She has constructed a novel using Rumi and Shams as characters, and has incorporated Islamic and Sufist concepts appropriately. Contrary to Furlanetto's concentration on the USA, the character Ella decides to leave the country and move to the Netherlands. Furlanetto charges Shafak with failing 'to challenge American hegemony in world literature' (2013: 208). This is an unreasonable, absolutist demand to place on the shoulders of a novelist whose purpose is quite different. The novel is read globally, not merely in America, and if Turkish readers respond to it so positively, as Furlanetto admits, then it obviously resonates in an Islamic setting too, as well as elsewhere in the world.

Both of the last two sections of *The Forty Rules of Love* emphasise the continuity of love as a central precept of Sufism. The novel ends with Ella quoting the last of the Rules:

> *'A life without love is of no account. Don't ask yourself what kind of love you should seek, spiritual or material, divine or mundane, Eastern or Western…. Divisions only lead to more divisions. Love has no labels, no definitions. It is what it is, pure and simple.'*
>
> (Shafak, 2015 [2010]: 350; italics in original)

Shafak's life experiences as expressed in her reflections on the significance of her bisexual identity and her interest in Sufism have provided the background to this study. My critical stance of bisexual feminist reparative criticism has enabled me to trace the connections between Sufism and bisexuality in *The Forty Rules of Love*. In examining the novel I have demonstrated that the representation of Sufism as unorthodox, emancipatory and fluid accords with scholars' explications and queer Muslims' experiences. Analysing the novel through a queer and specifically bisexual lens I have shown that bisexuality is depicted as a fluid, anti-binarist sexuality, although it is not idealised. The novel offers a queer-friendly, mystical, liberatory version of Islam that offers love and solace to all, including the socially marginalised.

Notes

1 Shafak is an award-winning author who writes in English and Turkish; her works include ten novels. She is also a public intellectual and speaker who champions rights for women, minorities and LGBT individuals. See http://www.elifsafak.com.tr/home.

2 https://www.ted.com/talks/elif_shafak_the_revolutionary_power_of_diverse_thought.

3 Recent progressive moves include the decriminalisation of same-sex sexual acts by the world's second-largest country, India. However, homosexuality remains illegal in 71 countries, including 33 of Africa's 54 countries: British colonial-era laws and current American evangelicals promote homophobia, while Islamic countries in Africa and the Middle East have become increasingly hostile to homosexuality since the rise of Islamic fundamentalism in the 1980s (Villareal, 2018).

4 For instance, Susan Pell complains: 'Neither does bisexuality escape the traps of essentialist rhetoric. As a distinct community and movement bisexuals require an "ethnic" identity in which to trace out their borders and territories. As an inclusive movement or theoretical perspective bisexuality suffers two problems of language. Either the term is so inclusive that it loses all signs of comprehension and recognition, or it subsumes, or to use Ault's term, "cloaks" everyone into a universal sexuality. I think sexuality has to be reconceptualized altogether with new words to accompany it' (2002).

5 Sufism is a dimension of the Islamic tradition that has evolved since the ninth century. Sufism is characterised by mysticism, but unlike the Christian conception of individualistic mysticism, this is nurtured within a master–disciple relationship (see Green, 2012). Sufism is open-minded and questioning and is opposed to casuistry. Sa'diyya Shaikh summarises: 'Sufis focus on the inner processes of spiritual cultivation and experiential knowledge, both of which culminate in virtue and may be seen to be located in the heart' (2013: 10).

6 This refers to the fourth chapter in the *Qur'an*, which deals with women. The verse in question differs in translations, one of which suggests that women are inferior to men and that husbands have the right to beat their wives, while the second translation portrays men as the support of women and urges forbearance towards them.

References

Aslan, R. 2006. *No God but God: The Origins, Evolution, and Future of Islam*. New York: Random House.

Butler, J. 1990. *Gender Trouble: Feminism and the Subversion of Identity*. New York: Routledge.

Ertan, N. 2017. Prominent writer unleashes controversy around sexuality in Turkey, *Al-Monitor*. [Online]. Available at: https://www.al-monitor.com/pulse/originals/2017/10/elif-shafaks-bisexuality-gets-homophobic-reflex.html [accessed 1 March 2019].

Farajajé, I.A. 2014. Fictions of purity, in *Recognize: The Voices of Bisexual Men*, edited by R. Ochs and H. Williams. Boston: Bisexual Resource Center, 146–151.

Farajajé-Jones, E. 1993. Breaking silence: Toward an in-the-life theology, in *Black Theology: A Documented History, Volume 2: 1980–1992*, edited by J.H. Cone and G.S. Wilmore. Maryknoll: Orbis Books, 139–159.

Furlanetto, E. 2013. The 'Rumi phenomenon' between Orientalism and Cosmopolitanism: The case of Elif Shafak's *The Forty Rules of Love*. *European Journal of English Studies*, 17(2), 201–213.

Garber, M. 1995. *Vice Versa: Bisexuality and the Eroticism of Everyday Life*. New York: Touchstone.

Geissinger, A. 2012. Islam and discourses of same-sex desire, in *Queer Religion, Volume 1: Homosexuality in Modern Religious History*, edited by D.L. Boisvert and J.E. Johnson. Santa Barbara: Praeger, 69–90.

Green, N. 2012. *Sufism: A Global History*. Chichester: Wiley-Blackwell.

Hemmings, C. 2014. The materials of reparation. *Feminist Theory*, 15(1), 27–30.

Kugle, S.S.a-H. 2003. Sexuality, diversity, and ethics in the agenda of progressive Muslims, in *Progressive Muslims: On Justice, Gender, and Pluralism*, edited by O. Safi. Oxford: Oneworld, 190–234.

Kugle, S.S.a-H. 2010. *Homosexuality in Islam: Critical Reflection on Gay, Lesbian, and Transgender Muslims*. Oxford: Oneworld.

Lanser, S.S. 2018. Queering narrative voice. *Textual Practice*, 2(6), 923–937.

Lessing, D. 2004. The Sufis, in *Time Bites: Views and Reviews*, edited by D. Lessing. London: Fourth Estate, 254–268.

Ochs, R. 2009. What is bisexuality?, in *Getting Bi: Voices of Bisexuals Around the World*, edited by R. Ochs and S.E. Rowley. Boston: Bisexual Resource Center, 7–9.

Pell, S. 2002. Inescapable essentialism: Bisexually-identified women's strategies in the late 80s and early 90s. *Thirdspace* 2(1). [Online]. Available at: http://journals.sfu.ca/thirdspace/index.php/journal/article/view/pell/64#5back [accessed 3 March 2019].

Rycenga, J. 2004. Roundtable discussion: What is the future of lesbian, gay, bisexual, transgender, and queer studies in religion? *Culture and Religion*, 5(2), 267–281.

Sedgwick, E.K. 1996. Introduction: Queerer than fiction. *Studies in the Novel*, 28(3), 277–280.

Sedgwick, E.K. 1997. Paranoid reading and reparative reading; or, You're so paranoid, you probably think this introduction is about you, in *Novel Gazing: Queer Readings in Fiction*, edited by E.K. Sedgwick. Durham: Duke University Press, 1–37.

Sedgwick, E.K. 2003. Paranoid reading and reparative reading, or You're so paranoid, you probably think this essay is about you, in *Touching Feeling: Affect, Pedagogy, Performativity*, edited by E.K. Sedgwick. Durham: Duke University Press, 123–151.

Sedgwick, E.K. 2007. Melanie Klein and the difference affect makes. *South Atlantic Quarterly*, 106(3), 625–642.

Sedgwick, E.K. and Frank, A. 1995. Shame in the cybernetic fold: Reading Silvan Tomkins. *Critical Inquiry*, 21(1), 496–522.

Shafak, E. 2015 [2010]. *The Forty Rules of Love.* London: Penguin.

Shafak, E. 2017. The revolutionary power of diverse thought, TED Talk. [Online]. Available at: https://www.ted.com/talks/elif_shafak_the_revolutionary_power_of_diverse_thought [accessed 28 November 2017].

Shafak, E. and Chancy, M.J.A. 2003. Migrations: A Meridians interview with Elif Shafak. *Meridians: Feminism, Race, Transnationalism*, 4(1), 55–85.

Shaikh, S. 2013. *Sufi Narratives of Intimacy: Ibn 'Arabi, Gender, and Sexuality.* Claremont: UCT Press.

Stobie, C. 2010. Dethroning the infallible father: Religion, patriarchy and politics in Chimamanda Ngozi Adichie's *Purple Hibiscus. Literature and Theology*, 24(4), 421–435.

Stobie, C. 2011. Indecent theology, trans-theology and the transgendered Madonna in Chris Abani's *The Virgin of Flames. Research in African Literatures* 42(2), 170–183.

Stobie, C. 2014. 'The devil slapped on the genitals': Religion and spirituality in queer South Africans' lives. *Journal of Literary Studies*, 30(1), 1–19.

Villarreal, D. 2018. Where gay is criminal: The definitive guide to countries where homosexuality is illegal, *Hornet*. [Online]. Available at: https://hornet.com/stories/countries-where-homosexuality-is-illegal-anti-sodomy-laws/ [accessed 2 March 2019].

Wiegman, R. 2014. The times we're in: Queer feminist criticism and the reparative 'turn'. *Feminist Theory*, 15(1), 4–25.

Yip, A.K.T. with Khalid, A. 2010. Looking for Allah: Spiritual quests of queer Muslims, in *Queer Spiritual Spaces: Sexuality and Sacred Places*, edited by K. Browne, S.R. Munt and A.K.T. Yip. Aldershot: Ashgate, 81–109.

9 Religion, male bisexuality and sexual risk in Lebanon

Ismaël Maatouk and Rusi Jaspal

Introduction

In most Western industrialised societies, there has been a shift towards greater acceptance of lesbian, gay and bisexual (LGB) identities. Countries like the UK and the US and political institutions like the European Union have now enshrined LGB rights in law, to varying degrees, protecting the interests, identities and wellbeing of these diverse communities. Yet, there are societies in the world in which LGB identities are not recognised and in which LGB people face social stigma, ostracism and criminalisation. Furthermore, while gay men and lesbian women have won increased recognition and acceptance, the identities of bisexual men and women remain largely invisible, poorly understood and stigmatised for being 'indecisive' or 'uncertain' (Monro, 2015; Mulick and Wright, 2002).

The social position of bisexual men in Lebanon and indeed in other Arab Middle Eastern societies is complex – on the one hand, bisexuality *as a practice* has been silently tolerated in Arab societies for many centuries but, on the other hand, bisexuality *as an identity* is rejected as a cultural anomaly. Put simply, one can 'do' bisexuality but cannot 'be' bisexual (Murray and Roscoe, 1997). This is further complicated by the strong position of religion in Lebanese society, which often rejects bisexual and other sexual minority identities, potentially causing internalised stigma in bisexual men. The deleterious consequences of internalised stigma are manifold – including poor psychological health, increased suicide risk and poor sexual health (Igartua, Gill and Montoro 2003; Ross et al., 2013).

In this chapter, the interface of religion and bisexuality and its implications for sexual health are explored in relation to Lebanese men. First, theoretical issues concerning bisexuality as an orientation or identity are outlined, and social representations theory and identity process theory from social psychology are suggested as useful frameworks for understanding identity among bisexual men in Lebanon. Second, the social, theological and psychological aspects of bisexuality and religion in Arab Middle Eastern societies are presented. Third, the chapter provides an overview of key religious, cultural and political aspects of Lebanese society, its stance on LGB rights, and cultural, religious and sexuality issues. These sections contextualise identity construction and maintenance among bisexual men in Lebanon. Fourth, drawing on social representations theory and identity process theory, identity and well-being issues are discussed in relation to bisexual men in Lebanon. There is a particular focus on mental health and sexual health issues, in view of the small body of research into gay and bisexual men in Lebanon which has focused largely on the sexual health inequalities they face compared to heterosexual people. Some tentative hypotheses are offered in relation to bisexual men in Lebanon.

The social psychology of representation, identity and action

This section focuses on research into the social psychological aspects of bisexuality and its social representations in distinct societal contexts, and the distinction between sexual orientation and sexual identity. Social representations theory and identity process theory from social psychology, and their relevance to exploring bisexuality in Lebanon are outlined.

Bisexuality: orientation vs identity

Although the focus of this chapter is on the social psychological aspects of religion and bisexuality in Lebanon, it is worthwhile to describe briefly research into the definition and prevalence of male bisexual orientation. Some of this research has made its transition into public consciousness in the form of social representations of bisexuality and is, thus, relevant to the present discussion.

The American Psychological Association (2015) defines sexual orientation as 'one's enduring sexual attraction to male partners, female partners, or both. Sexual orientation may be heterosexual, same sex (gay or lesbian), or bisexual.' Research shows that the vast majority of men are heterosexual, that a small minority are gay, and that a much smaller minority report sexual attraction to both sexes (bisexual). The most recent census in the UK revealed a 0.6% prevalence of bisexuality in men (Office for National Statistics, 2017). Yet, even among those men who describe themselves as bisexual (bearing in mind that most studies of sexual orientation rely on self-reported sexual orientation), there are many who are in fact not attracted to both sexes but believe, or perhaps hope, that they are (e.g. Rieger, Chivers and Bailey, 2005).

In a psychophysiological study using plethysmography, Rieger, Chivers and Bailey (2005) measured 101 male participants' genital arousal in response to erotic videos of males and females. Predictably, they found that heterosexual and gay men were aroused by videos of women and men, respectively. However, their more interesting finding was that the bisexual men who reported sexual attraction to both sexes were actually more aroused by videos of men than by those of women. This suggests that these men are not actually bisexual (in terms of sexual orientation) but rather that they self-identify as bisexual. Therefore, non-sexual reasons may underlie self-definition as bisexual in this cohort of men.

In many cases, this is a question of sexual identification (rather than actual sexual orientation) because it concerns how people wish to view themselves and how they wish to be viewed by others. For many gay men, initial self-identification as bisexual is a preliminary step towards embracing a gay identity, because by self-identifying as bisexual the individual is not yet 'committing' to a full gay identity which he may still perceive to be stigmatised (Guittar, 2013). At this stage of his sexual identity development, he is not really part of the gay community and thus would not be exposed to bisexual erasure or stigma from other gay men. Of course, many men in this situation do permanently self-identify as bisexual.

However, it must be stressed that there is also empirical evidence that bisexual men do manifest sexual attraction to both sexes but that the level of attraction to both sexes may not necessarily be the same (Ebsworth and Lalumière, 2012). Indeed, Kinsey and his colleagues' seminal studies of sexual orientation showed that human sexual orientation is best measured on a continuum (as a continuous variable) rather than as a dichotomy between gay and straight (Kinsey, Pomeroy and Martin, 1948). In their research into the perceptions and experiences of bisexuals, Flanders et al. (2017) found that some of their respondents concealed their bisexuality from others in order to avoid stigma or invasive questions about their sexuality. In a study of bisexual men in the US, McCormack, Anderson and Adams (2014) found a 'cohort effect' on the coming out experiences of bisexual men in that older men were exposed to more negative stereotypes and prejudice on the basis of their bisexuality than younger men. Moreover, older bisexual men appear to hold more heteronormative attitudes about sexuality and relationships than younger bisexual men (Anderson, Scoats and McCormack, 2015). Furthermore, in their qualitative study of bisexual male youths at sixth form colleges in the UK, Morris, McCormack and Anderson (2014) state that almost all of their participants reported positive experiences of coming out as bisexual, which were not characterised by stigma or prejudice. The authors attributed this effect to the gradual decline of cultural homophobia and biphobia.

The uncertainties that often surround bisexuality perhaps stem from the coping strategies that have come to be associated with sexual minority groups facing stigma (Jaspal, 2019). As same-sex attracted individuals began to campaign for their rights and to protest against discrimination, there was a need to self-label – people came to identify, and to present themselves, dichotomously as 'gay' or 'lesbian', often in opposition to 'straight'. This has led to the perception that people are either gay or straight and, in some cases, to suspicion and scepticism about the existence of more fluid sexual orientations like bisexuality.

It is noteworthy that sexual orientation does not always lead to a sexual identity that is consistent with that orientation. The construction of a LGB identity can be challenging given that it entails the assimilation and accommodation of a non-traditional, stigmatised identity which may not always meet with acceptance from valued others. This can mean that 'coming out' occurs on three levels: the extent to which one (1) accepts one's LGB identity, (2) discloses this information to other people, and (3) views their LGB identity as a social group membership, that is sharing common traits with other LGB people.

There has been impactful research into 'coming out' models focusing on gay and lesbian people (e.g. Cass, 1979; Sophie, 1986), which has been critiqued for being unilinear and unidirectional and for failing to explain how and why some 'stages' are embraced and others are not (Jaspal, 2019). However, there is relatively little work on the construction and manifestation of bisexual identity. Weinberg, Williams and Pryor (1994) developed a four-stage model of bisexual identity formation focusing on initial confusion, the search for a self-label, self-acceptance in the new identity and continued uncertainty. Yet, this model implicitly views bisexual identity as one characterised by uncertainty in spite of identity acceptance. In this chapter, it is shown how culture, religion and politics impinge on the construction of sexual identity in Lebanon – principally in the form of social representations.

Social representations

Social representations theory (Moscovici, 1988) provides a useful framework for understanding perceptions of bisexuality and the social backdrop against which bisexual men in Lebanon construct their sexual identities. The theory was designed to examine how science becomes 'common-sense' knowledge; that is, how it enters public consciousness and becomes a topic that can be debated. At a basic level, a social representation can be defined as a collective 'elaboration' of a given social object which in turn enables individuals to think and talk about it. This elaboration consists of emerging beliefs, values, ideas, images and metaphors in relation to any given phenomenon. Social representations provide a cultural group with a shared social reality or 'common consciousness'. Two principal social psychological processes converge in the creation of social representations:

1 Anchoring refers to the process whereby a novel, unfamiliar phenomenon is integrated into existing ways of thinking;
2 Objectification refers to the process whereby an abstract phenomenon is rendered concrete and tangible, often through the use of metaphors.

Anchoring and objectification occur in a wide range of social contexts, including the media, film and literature, political discourse, patient–practitioner interactions and in everyday conversation. Interactions in these contexts all contribute to the genesis and development of social representations of bisexuality. Social, political and religious factors play a prominent role in Lebanese society and are, thus, also central to the formation of social representations. They will inform the ways in which bisexuality is anchored to, or objectified in terms of, particular social phenomena. Moreover, these factors inform the social context in which sexual identity is constructed among bisexual men in Lebanon.

Identity process theory

The chapter focuses principally on religion and sexuality, and the intersection of these identities. Identity process theory (Jaspal and Breakwell, 2014) provides an integrative model of how these identities are constructed and defended in the face of potential 'threats'. The theory postulates that individuals construct their identity by engaging in two social psychological processes:

1. Assimilation-accommodation refers to the absorption of new information (such as new identity characteristics or social representations) into identity and the creation of space for it within the identity structure. For instance, 'coming out' as bisexual requires the absorption of new information about oneself; that is, referring to oneself as bisexual and seeing this as an aspect of who one is (assimilation). The assimilation of this novel information may lead some bisexual men to re-think their relationship with other aspects of identity, such as their religion (accommodation). Crucially, bisexuality must first exist as a social representation in order for it to be available as an identity aspect (see Philogene, 1994). It has to exist as something that can be thought about, discussed and identified with.
2. Evaluation refers to the process of attributing meaning and value to the components of identity. Social representations are also central to this process. For example, while there is stigma associated with bisexuality in Western societies, bisexuality may be viewed more positively for the active[1] sexual partner in Lebanese society because this does not necessarily challenge gender norms in the way that being sexually passive might (Roscoe and Murray, 1997).

The two identity processes are in turn guided by various motivational principles, which essentially specify the desirable end-states for identity:

1. Self-esteem refers to personal and social worth. For instance, the social representation that homosexual behaviour is a sin can lead to internalised stigma and the inability to derive a positive self-conception (Super and Jacobson, 2011).
2. Self-efficacy can be defined as the belief in one's competence and control. Some bisexual men report their inability to 'resist' the temptation of homosexuality, which can undermine self-efficacy (Jaspal and Cinnirella, 2010).
3. Continuity is essentially the psychological thread between past, present and future. It is easy to see how 'coming out' as bisexual, that is

acquiring an identity based on one's sexual orientation, could disrupt this psychological thread (Weinberg, Williams and Pryor, 1994).

4 Coherence refers to the perception that relevant aspects of identity are coherent and compatible. As indicated in this chapter, some bisexual men perceive their sexual orientation to be incompatible and irreconcilable with their religious identity (Jaspal and Cinnirella, 2010).

When these principles are compromised, for instance, by changes in one's social context, identity is said to be threatened (Breakwell, 1986; Jaspal and Breakwell, 2014). Individuals differ in the extent to which they value each of the principles – when a principle that is valued by the individual is abrogated, identity will be threatened (Bardi et al., 2014). Identity threat is generally aversive for psychological wellbeing. However, the degree to which one's wellbeing is compromised is determined by the importance appended to each of the principles, the nature of the threat, the number of valued principles curtailed by the threat and one's ability to cope effectively. People attempt to cope with threats to identity at three distinct levels:

1 Intrapsychic strategies function at a psychological level. Some can be regarded as deflection strategies in that they enable the individual to deny or re-conceptualise the threat or the reasons for occupying the threatening position. Others are acceptance strategies that facilitate some form of cognitive re-structuring in anticipation of the threat. For instance, it is possible that a bisexual man living in Lebanon where same-sex sexual behaviour is stigmatised may refuse to accept that he is bisexual and self-define as heterosexual, although this sexual identity is inconsistent with his actual sexual behaviour.
2 Interpersonal strategies aim to change the nature of relationships with others. Most interpersonal strategies are maladaptive given that they may isolate themselves from others or feign membership of a group or network of which they are not really a member, in order to avoid exposure to stigma, for instance. Although a bisexual man is aware of his bisexual orientation, he may present himself as heterosexual in heteronormative contexts in order to avoid homophobic and biphobic stigma. An example of a proactive interpersonal strategy is that of self-disclosure, given that this can facilitate the acquisition of support from others. This can include 'coming out' as bisexual to a trusted significant other.
3 Intergroup strategies aim to change the nature of our relationships with groups. Most strategies are adaptive. Individuals may join groups of like-minded others who share their predicament in order to derive social support. They may create a new social group to derive support or a pressure group to influence social representations. It was in the 1990s that bisexual people in the US began to form a community and to advocate for the rights of bisexual people (Udis-Kessler, 1995). Similarly, the emergence of LGB support groups in Lebanon like *Helem* [2] have created

a social and political space in which LGB Lebanese people can advocate for their rights and create better conditions in which sexual minorities can live their lives (Makarem, 2012).

The chapter has hitherto focused on the theoretical aspects of religion and bisexuality through the lens of social representations theory and identity process theory. It is an opportune moment to turn to the social, theological and psychological aspects of bisexuality and homosexuality in Middle Eastern societies. The next section sheds lights on the social representations that will inform the construction of identity among Lebanese bisexual men.

Religion and bisexuality

Religious representations of homosexuality are generally negative. They are substantiated principally on the basis of Holy Scripture – the Qur'an and the Ahadith in the case of Islam and the Bible in the case of Christianity. Both Islam and Christianity – two major religions in Lebanon[3] – are heterogeneous traditions with many distinct denominations, cultural norms and practices. It is therefore difficult to generalise about their respective 'stances' on homosexuality. However, in general, it is reasonable to state that mainstream Islamic and Christian theologies in Lebanon generally append hegemonic status to heterosexuality and are largely opposed to homosexuality.

In Islam, this stance is ingrained in the major ideological channels of communication, such as Islamic holy scripture (the Qur'an), Islamic law (Shariah) and the verbal teachings of the Prophet Mohammed (Ahadith), all of which appear to outlaw homosexuality (Bouhdiba, 1998). Theological opposition to homosexuality is based on what is regarded by most Islamic scholars as the Qur'an's explicit prohibition of same-sex sexual relations. In both Islam and Christianity, the story of Lot in the Qur'an has been widely cited as evidence of God's condemnation of homosexuality. The Qur'an makes seven explicit references to the people of Lot, whose destruction by God is often attributed to their engagement in homosexual practices.

Although there has been some discussion of the authenticity and accuracy of the Ahadith (records of the sayings and traditions attributed to the Prophet Mohammed), they are frequently invoked by traditional Islamic scholars like Al Shafii, Malik and Ibn Hanbal in order to substantiate the dominant Islamic condemnation of homosexuality (Lange, 2009). However, some Islamic scholars have offered a more tolerant approach towards this topic. For instance, Scott Kugle argues that the divine punishment of Lot's people is a condemnation of assault and rape rather than homosexuality (Kugle, 2010).

Similarly, mainstream Christianity has always promoted heterosexuality and has not generally provided a space for the acceptance of homosexuality or bisexuality (Gnuse, 2015). Christian theologians who argue that the practice of homosexuality is condemned rely on texts from the Old and the New Testament. Beside the classic Book of Genesis that describes the men of

Sodom who wanted to rape the two male visitors to the city, the Book of Leviticus in the Old Testament – thought to be given to Moses by God on biblical Mount Sinai – is often employed to substantiate the claim that homosexuality is inconsistent with Christianity.

Liberal scholars in Christianity like Gnuse and Goss have provided alternative interpretations of biblical references to homosexuality, referring, for instance, to linguistic nuances in the Greek language that call into question mainstream understandings of the term 'homosexuality'. They also argue that Jesus, who espoused the message of love and acceptance, would never punish a monogamous homosexual relationship that has Christ at its centre (Gnuse, 2015; Goss, 2002).

In spite of these passages in Holy Scripture, homosexual relationships, especially those involving men with boys (known as pederasty), were generally tolerated in pre-modern Islamic societies. Homoerotic themes existed in poetry of the Muslim world as early as the eighth century and resemble the traditions of Graeco-Roman antiquity. Although Islam explicitly forbade all forms of homosexuality and pederasty, same-sex sexual practices persisted and, in some cases, were silently tolerated. During the Arab medieval era, many Muslim men belonging to the upper classes had wives, concubines and, sometimes, young male lovers. These relationships between adult men and their younger male partners were based on social and sexual inequality characterised by 'patriarchal sexuality' (Dialmy, 2010). Pederasty was tolerated and accepted but not openly discussed. The paradox is that, despite its prohibition in Islam and the religious conviction of the men who practised it, pederasty persisted during this era.

In his chapter on the precursors to Islamic male homosexuality, Murray (1997) outlines the apparent tolerance of homosexuality in Islamic societies provided that it is collectively denied and never publicly acknowledged. In line with hierarchical patriarchy, the sexually passive homosexual male (*moukhannath*, literally 'effeminate man' in Arabic) was socially devalued and de-masculinised. Conversely, the active partner was not regarded as homosexual but rather as a *louti* – in reference to people of Lot in the monotheistic religions. Men were expected to perform only an active role in homosexual intercourse once they reached adulthood. Those men who performed the active sexual role were perceived as having a double-faceted virility because they penetrate both males and females. Thus, culturally, there was actually a blurring of boundaries between homosexuality and bisexuality in the case of those men who perform the active sexual role. Social representations position them as socially superior – they get married, have children, and perform their religious and cultural duties.

Against this social representational backdrop, it could be hypothesised that bisexuals are unlikely to experience the threats to identity associated with exclusive homosexuality. In Lebanon, they clearly enjoy a higher social status than homosexual men who are implicitly understood to be sexually passive (Murray and Roscoe, 1997) and thus unlikely to face the threats to self-esteem to which homosexual men are susceptible. The lack of a bisexual identity in many societies means that few will contemplate 'coming out' as bisexual, which enables their sense of continuity to remain intact. In short, they never have to assimilate or accommodate bisexuality in their identity. Yet, given the strong and coercive social representation that homosexual behaviour is inconsistent with religious teachings, there is certainly potential for threats to the psychological coherence principle of identity. Bisexual men may come to question the legitimacy of their sexual behaviour in view of their religious identity, which is generally important and valued. They may struggle to reconcile their homosexual behaviour with their religious identity.

Although they engage in same-sex sexual practices, many Middle Eastern men simply do not identify as being gay or bisexual (Murray and Roscoe, 1997; Siraj, 2006). A hegemonic social representation promulgated mainly by mainstream religious scholars in Arab Middle Eastern societies is that homosexuality is a sinful and immoral behavioural choice. According to this social representation, God creates human beings perfectly and, thus, homosexuality is viewed not as an inherent human characteristic but rather as a choice that human beings themselves make and for which they are therefore responsible.

Conversely, there is an emerging, competing social representation – championed mainly by LGB organisations and pressure groups in Middle Eastern countries and beyond – that advocates, and creates space for, LGB identities. This social representation shifts the focus from sexual behaviour to sexual identity and emphasises the emotional, affective components of homosexuality *as a sexual identity*. LGB affirmative charities and pressure groups have emerged in several Arab Middle Eastern countries. As a largely secular organisation, the Lebanese organisation *Helem* has had a limited impact on religious social representations – it has not possessed the societal credibility necessary to shape religious representations. Moreover, its focus has not been on the reconciliation of religious and sexual identities among Lebanese LGB people.

In the next section, the cultural, religious and political aspects of Lebanon – as a state and society – are explored, as these factors shape the construction and management of bisexuality as a potential sexual identity in Lebanon.

Lebanon: religion, politics and sexuality

Having been a French protectorate, Lebanon gained its independence from the French Republic in 1943 with Beirut as its capital city. Between 1943 and 1975, Lebanon was one of a small minority of truly democratic states in the Middle East. It was renowned for its tolerant state ideological approach to different religious communities, including Christian Maronites, Greek Catholics and Greek Orthodox, Sunni and Shia Muslims, and the Druze. The diverse religious communities adhere to a set of national, public values, while retaining and nurturing their respective religious and cultural norms.

However, in 1975 a long and protracted sectarian conflict began, which brought about the collapse of the Lebanese government and, by 1990, over a million Lebanese people had been uprooted from their homes and ninety thousand people lost their lives (Labaki, 1994). The long and bloody conflict radically changed the demographic profile of Lebanon, and the subsequent fragility of the Lebanese state and the fragmentation of Lebanese national identity led to the strengthening of another competing social identity, namely religion. The primacy of religious identities has culminated in a range of sanctions aimed at curtailing homosexuality in Lebanon.

Lebanon has a problematic track record on LGB rights. According to Article 534 of the Lebanese Penal Code of 1943, sexual relations which 'contradict the law of nature' are prohibited by law, and those found guilty of this offence (which can include homosexual relations) can face up to a year in prison (Human Rights Watch, 2018; Makarem, 2012). Although this law has occasionally been used to harass, persecute and sometimes arrest LGB people, it is not widely enforced and several senior Lebanese lawmakers have disputed the law and the investigative practices (e.g. anal examinations) that it has encouraged. Thus, on balance, Lebanon can be viewed as more accepting and accommodating of LGB people than other countries in the Middle East – other than Israel.

Indeed, since 2006, LGB groups in Lebanon have organised LGB awareness and visibility-raising events – often on the International Day Against Homophobia, Transphobia, and Biphobia (IDAHOT). However, both Muslim and Christian religious leaders in Lebanon have repeatedly opposed LGB pride events through campaigns against these events or through the 'prior censorship approval' cover. For instance, Lebanon's Pride Week commemorating the IDAHOT 2017 was cancelled by the government on the grounds that the programme might lead to unrest and violence. Government agencies did not issue a public statement regarding cancellation of the events but rather resorted to coercion and threatening language. For instance, the protection of organisers and of venue owners was not guaranteed in the event of unrest and violence.

Opposition to the Pride events was prevalent across all faith groups in Lebanon. While Sunni groups were threatening to disrupt the Beirut Pride event in Beirut, a Christian Orthodox church in Tripoli, North of Lebanon, discussed in an open conference how to convert LGB communities to 'normative sexual behaviour'. Meanwhile, a Shia political and religious leader made a statement criticising Western countries for exporting LGB ideas to Lebanon: "Homosexual relations defy logic, human nature and the human mind."[4] In this context, it is important to note that bisexuality is never brought up in public discussion in Lebanon. Though there are clearly bisexuals in Lebanon (e.g. Wagner et al., 2013), bisexuality is simply not acknowledged as an identity. Therefore, there is an erasure of bisexual identity amid acknowledgement, but condemnation, of homosexuality.

Social representations of non-heterosexual identities in Lebanon are generally negative. A 2013 study revealed that 80 per cent of the Lebanese respondents did not believe that homosexuality is acceptable (Pew Research Centre, 2013). This social representation is grounded in representations disseminated by both religious and political institutions which generally stigmatise homosexuality. Yet, despite the social, religious and political constraints on open expressions of LGB identities, Lebanese LGB people do 'live out' their sexual identities. Its capital city, Beirut, is one of the most socially progressive cities in the Middle East and North Africa (MENA), with a vibrant gay community and gay bars, clubs and community centres. Moreover, online gay social networking sites and applications are pervasively used among gay and bisexual men to socialise, seek support and arrange casual sexual encounters. Many LGB young people do seek support with their relationships, sexual health issues, and claim their rights. Yet, it must be noted that Beirut is by no means representative of the whole of Lebanon, which is generally intolerant of homosexuality and devoid of a 'gay culture'.[5]

One of the most prominent LGB organisations in Lebanon is *Helem*, which is a significant non-governmental organisation established in 2004 to advocate for the visibility and right of LGB people in the region, and against discrimination on social, cultural and legal grounds. The organisation has made a significant contribution to positive social change in Lebanon. For instance, it helped secure the release of many individuals following unreasonable arrest and has proactively challenged homophobic stigma from the media by delivering continuous workshops and roundtable events with the Lebanese media community (Makarem, 2012). Another organisation, Mosaic,[6] offers a holistic programme committed to improve the health and wellbeing of LGB groups in Lebanon and in the MENA region. Through its national presence in Lebanon and its regional networks in the MENA region, *Mosaic*'s strategic goal is to achieve the coexistence of people in friendly communities and national systems. Unfortunately, Helem and Mosaic and other organisations have not yet succeeded in securing political and religious support to overturn Article 534 of the Lebanese Penal Code, which can be used to criminalise same-sex sexual behaviour.

In view of societal stigma towards sexual minorities in Lebanon, LGB people may face social and psychological challenges in relation to their sexual orientation. There have been some empirical studies of gay and bisexual men in Lebanon, which provide important insight into the lived experiences of non-heterosexual men but little specific focus on those of bisexual men. Yet, in view of the discussion earlier in this chapter, it is possible to offer some tentative hypotheses regarding the specific social and psychological experiences of bisexual men in Lebanon.

In a qualitative study of gay and bisexual men in Beirut, Wagner et al. (2012) found that most participants experienced discomfort in relation to their sexual orientation due to stigma from others and, especially, to the social representation that homosexuality is incompatible with their religion, and many anticipated or actually experienced rejection when disclosing their sexual orientation to significant others. In another qualitative interview study of gay and bisexual men in Beirut (Wagner et al., 2013), interviewees reported experiences of stigma and discrimination on the basis of their sexual orientation, and guilt and shame due to its perceived incompatibility with their religion. In accordance with identity process theory, it could be hypothesised that the stigma that bisexual men encounter on the basis of their sexual behaviour and identity could undermine the self-esteem principle of identity and that the anticipation of rejection could challenge the continuity principle of identity. After all, rejection from significant others represents a rupture in the psychological thread linking past, present and future. The adverse emotional experiences of guilt and shame may be responses to threats to self-esteem and continuity (Jaspal, 2012).

In a survey study of 210 Lebanese LGB people, it was found that legal discrimination, religiosity and negative parental attitudes (either real or anticipated) were significant predictors of internalised homophobia (Michli, 2016). Crucially, self-compassion was not found to be associated with internalised homophobia, suggesting a more powerful effect of the aforementioned social variables. These studies converge in showing that gay and bisexual men in Lebanon face and anticipate stigma towards their sexual orientation and that religion plays a significant role in their own cognitive appraisal of their sexual orientation. These studies suggest that bisexual men also experience self-stigma on the basis of their sexual orientation, which could be referred to as internalised biphobia.

Religiosity and negative social representations of same-sex desire (disseminated by significant others, such as parents, and embedded in legislation) clearly contribute to this self-stigma among bisexual men. Although the studies did not use identity process theory, it can be deduced from these data that dominant social representations in Lebanon lead to identity threat among sexual minority men. However, as noted above, there is no empirical research into the attitudes and experiences of bisexual Lebanon men, in particular, and existing research appears to conflate the attitudes and experiences of gay and bisexual men.

In view of the negative social representations of LGB people, Lebanese men who actually self-identify as bisexual may feel compelled to re-examine their identities – especially in view of religious influences. Yet, it is important to avoid the assumption that religious influences are invariably negative, given that some bisexual men do also utilise religion as a source of social psychological support (Jeffries, Dodge and Sandfort, 2008). Religious identification may provide feelings of self-esteem through the pride and positive self-conception that membership in this group can often facilitate. They may feel empowered by religion despite the stigma of their sexual attraction. Religious identification often provides a sense of continuity which can connect the past, present and future. Thus, those identity principles that might be threatened as a result of one's sexual orientation might conversely be enhanced by religious affiliation.

Furthermore, some of the coping strategies outlined earlier in this chapter can facilitate a robust connection with religion despite its perceived incompatibility with one's sexual orientation. For instance, it has been shown that some Muslim gay and bisexual men may 'postpone' sexual activity with their same-sex partner during the holy fasting period of Ramadan as a means of retaining a connection with their religious identity (Jaspal and Cinnirella, 2014). Yet, it must also be noted that a bisexual orientation may also enable some Lebanese men to deny their true sexual orientation (bisexuality) and to construct a heterosexual identity which is deemed to be more consistent with their religious identity.

In view of the discussion earlier in this chapter, this may be especially feasible for a bisexual male who takes the active (insertive) sexual role. The active sexual role is socially represented as indicating masculinity and male virility, and may therefore 'shield' the individual from the stigma of homosexuality, which conversely is associated with femininity and passivity in Middle Eastern cultures (Tolino, 2014). The male who penetrates both men and women is able to lay claim to the category 'bisexual' and therefore to benefit from the social capital that this generates (vis-à-vis homosexuality). It is important to note that bisexuality is by no means a publicly acknowledged or celebrated identity in Lebanon and that many men in Lebanon do not think of themselves in those terms. However, it is certainly preferable to homosexuality in cultural consciousness and therefore may be claimed even by those who do not actually feel any attraction to women.

The impact of sexual identity on psychological wellbeing and sexual health

A growing number of empirical studies conducted in the MENA region, and especially in Lebanon, have addressed wellbeing and sexual health issues in gay men (Wagner et al., 2013; Wagner et al., 2015). As indicated earlier, most studies have either excluded bisexual men or treated gay and bisexual men as a single group – there are no studies fully devoted to bisexual men, in particular. However, on the basis of the observations in this chapter, some tentative hypotheses regarding bisexual men in Lebanon can be offered.

Studies of sexual minority individuals in Lebanon have generally revealed an association between the experience of stigma/discrimination and poor mental health characterised by depression, psychological distress, substance use and social isolation. For instance, in Wagner et al.'s (2013) study of sexual identity development among gay and bisexual men in Lebanon, it was found that the experience of stigma adversely impacted both psychological wellbeing and engagement in social relationships in the participant sample. Almost 66 per cent of their study participants reported experiencing some discomfort with their sexual orientation, which could be attributed to societal stigma towards sexual minorities, on the one hand, and to participants' own religious beliefs, on the other hand. This demonstrates that individuals may internalise the stigma associated with their sexual identity. Acceptance of sexual orientation was related to sexual identity disclosure to family and parents.

Concealment of one's sexual identity is often coupled with the strategy of passing, that is feigning heterosexuality, which can have negative consequences for self-esteem and continuity. The key point is that some Lebanese bisexual men may not accept their sexual orientation and, thus, refrain from assimilating and accommodating their sexual orientation in their identity and from disclosing this information to other people. It could be hypothesised therefore that behaviourally bisexual Lebanese men will not readily assimilate and accommodate a bisexual identity but instead continue to view themselves as heterosexual, especially if they perform an active sexual role, which reinforces their self-image as masculine and virile.

There is also research that shows that the experience of discrimination is associated with engagement in sexual risk practices. For instance, exposure to gay-related discrimination has been shown to be associated with engagement in sexual risk behaviour among gay and bisexual men (Wagner et al., 2015). This can include an increased rate of unprotected anal intercourse in the past three months, decreased knowledge of one's sexual partners' HIV status, and withdrawal from social networks that normally provide HIV knowledge. All of these factors can increase an individual's HIV risk.

It is easy to see how exposure to stigma on the basis of sexual orientation can compromise an individual's self-esteem, potentially leading to decreased self-care behaviours which might promote good mental and sexual health outcomes. Focussing specifically on bisexual Lebanese men, it could be hypothesised that bisexual men will be exposed to less discrimination on the basis of sexual orientation given the greater social acceptance of bisexuality in Lebanese society. However, it could also be predicted that bisexual Lebanese men are just as likely to engage in sexual risk practices, possibly because of decreased exposure to HIV and sexual health knowledge that they might encounter through engagement with gay social contexts, such as clubs, bars and social support groups.

In their study of sexual stigma, psychological wellbeing and social engagement among same-sex attracted men, Wagner et al.'s (2013) research shows that individuals may engage in the maladaptive coping strategy of passing by adopting a heterosexual public identity while engaging in same-sex sexual practices in private. Given the absence of public acknowledgement and discussion of bisexuality in Lebanon, it could be hypothesised that behaviourally bisexual men are more likely than gay men to adopt a heterosexual public identity despite engaging in both heterosexual and same-sex sexual practices. In other words, bisexuality is not a social representation in Lebanese society and, thus, is not readily available as a social category with which Lebanese men can identify.

Passing itself is a strategy that can compromise the individual's mental health by increasing feelings of anxiety due to fear of involuntary disclosure of their sexual orientation and by compromising their sense of authenticity. In the case of Lebanese bisexual men, it could be predicted that 'passing' as heterosexual might not be construed as a threat to identity authenticity since various factors (e.g. performing an active sexual role) may reinforce their sense of heterosexuality – in their minds at least.

Yet, other factors may compromise wellbeing. For instance, it has long been known that internalised homophobia/biphobia can increase the risk of depression, suicidal ideation, substance misuse and sexual risk-taking (Doll and Beeker, 1996; Peterson et al., 1992). In his discussion of the relationship between mental and sexual health outcomes, Jaspal (2018) has argued that chronic exposure to identity threat, due to biphobia and other psychosocial stressors, can lead to maladaptive strategies, especially in social contexts in which social support is not readily available. In Lebanese society in which LGB identities are stigmatised, such social support may not be forthcoming for bisexual men.

Concluding remarks

This chapter has focused on the interface of bisexuality and religion and its implications for mental and sexual health in Lebanese men. Lebanon is a diverse society in which many religious groups coexist and for whom religious identity tends to be stronger than other identities. The norms, values and social representations associated with religious identity appear to stigmatise LGB identities. Even if the Lebanese state develops more accepting policies towards gay and bisexual men, it is hard to see how this alone would decrease the stigma associated with powerful religious representations that many value and prioritise in Lebanon.

Despite the prohibition of non-heterosexuality in Lebanon, bisexuality does appear to be tolerated as a practice but not as an identity. This is especially the case for those bisexual men who perform the active sexual role, rather than those who are sexually passive. There is a social representation of double-faceted masculinity for active bisexuals and one of femininity for those who are sexually passive. In view of the importance appended to religion in Lebanon, social representations that are grounded in theology may be drawn upon by members of society and bisexual men themselves in order to make sense of bisexuality. It is against the backdrop of these social representations that bisexual men construct and manage their identity. It is therefore important to intervene at the level of religion in order to promote more positive identities among bisexual men in Lebanon.

In a society characterised by overt homophobia, bisexual men may be susceptible to chronic threats to identity and to maladaptive strategies for coping with threat. There is an emerging culture of social support in Lebanon, such as local non-governmental organisations, but there are challenges – especially in view of the pervasive homophobia and criminalisation of homosexuality in the country. Social support for bisexual men is still in its infancy. It is easy to see how self-esteem, continuity and other identity principles might be threatened by the assimilation and accommodation of a bisexual identity. Put simply, bisexual men may be less willing to construct a bisexual identity despite continuing to engage in same-sex sexual practices. Identity is central to the behaviours that people adopt. If behaviourally bisexual men do not view themselves as bisexual, they may refuse, or be unable to access, social support aimed at bisexual men. In the absence of social support, bisexual men may adopt maladaptive coping strategies with negative outcomes for mental and sexual health.

This chapter has shown that there is a dearth of empirical research into bisexuality in Lebanon, but the available evidence suggests that the construction of bisexual identity appears to be challenging in this religious and cultural context. There is a pressing need for more empirical research into bisexual men in particular. There is a need for greater visibility and acknowledgement of male bisexuality in Lebanon. It is clear that negative social representations of bisexuality will need to be challenged at a religious level. In a country where religious identities are stronger than the superordinate Lebanese identity, this will clearly be a challenge but one that should be undertaken.

Notes

1 The term 'active' is used to refer to the insertive sexual partner, while 'passive' refers to the receptive sexual partner. Stigma appears to be appended to the passive role, given that the active male may be more able to lay claim to a 'masculine' identity (Murray and Roscoe, 1997). The terms 'active' and 'passive' often imply a power dynamic whereby the active partner as the penetrator is more powerful than the passive partner. However, it is acknowledged that 'power' can be shaped by several factors – not least the economic capital possessed by a sex worker's client who wishes to be penetrated for pleasure. Indeed, in this case, being 'passive' would not equate to the loss of power.

2 Helem is a Lebanese charity dedicated to the improvement of the legal and social status of lesbian, gay, bisexual and transgender people. http://www.helem.net

3 Lebanon has a specific profile of different religious communities, including Christian Maronites, Greek Catholics and Greek Orthodox, Sunni and Shia Muslims, and the Druze.

4 Beirut PRIDE: An analysis from the inside [available: https://dayagainsthomophobia.org/beirut-pride-an-analysis-from-the-inside/]

5 Beirut PRIDE: An analysis from the inside [available: https://dayagainsthomophobia.org/beirut-pride-an-analysis-from-the-inside/]

6 MOSAIC is an organisation dedicated to the improvement of health and wellbeing in marginalised gender and sexual minorities in Lebanon: https://www.mosaicmena.org

References

Anderson, E., Scoats, R., and McCormack, M. 2015. Metropolitan bisexual men's relationships: Evidence of a cohort effect. *Journal of Bisexuality*, 15(1), 21–39.

Bardi, A., Jaspal, R., Polek, E. and Schwartz, S. 2014. Values and identity process theory: Theoretical integration and empirical interactions. In *Identity Process Theory: Identity, Social Action and Social Change*, edited by R. Jaspal and G.M. Breakwell. Cambridge: Cambridge University Press, 175–200.

Bouhdiba, A. 1998. *Sexuality in Islam*. London: Saqi Books.

Breakwell, G.M. 1986. *Coping with Threatened Identities*. London: Methuen.

Cass, V. 1979. Homosexual identity formation: A theoretical model. *Journal of Homosexuality*, 4(3), 219–235.

Dialmy, A. 2010. Sexuality and Islam. *The European Journal of Contraception and Reproductive Health Care*, 15(3), 160–168

Doll, L.S. and Beeker, C. 1996. Male bisexual behavior and HIV risk in the United States: Synthesis of research with implications for behavioral interventions. *AIDS Education and Prevention*, 5, 205–225.

Ebsworth, M. and Lalumière, M.L. 2012. Viewing time as a measure of bisexual sexual interest. *Archives of Sexual Behavior*, 41(1), 161–167.

Flanders, C.E., LeBreton, M.E., Robinson, M., Bian, J. and Caravaca-Morera, J.A. 2017. Defining bisexuality: Young bisexual and pansexual people's voices. *Journal of Bisexuality*, 17(1), 39–57.

Gnuse, R.K. 2015. Seven gay texts: Biblical passages used to condemn homosexuality. *Biblical Theology Bulletin*, 45(2), 68–87.

Goss, R. 2002. *Queering Christ*. Cleveland: The Pilgrim Press.

Guittar, N.A. 2013. The queer apologetic: Explaining the use of bisexuality as a transitional identity. *Journal of Bisexuality*, 13(2), 166–190.

Human Rights Watch. 2018. World report, country: Lebanon 2018, *Human Rights Watch* [Online]. Available at: https://www.hrw.org/world-report/2018/country-chapters/lebanon [accessed 13 August 2018]

Igartua, K.J., Gill, K. and Montoro, R. 2003. Internalized homophobia: A factor in depression, anxiety, and suicide in the gay and lesbian population. *Canadian Journal of Community Mental Health*, 22(2), 15–30.

Jaspal, R. 2012. Coping with religious and cultural homophobia: Emotion and narratives of identity threat from British Muslim gay men. In *Religion, Gender and Sexuality in Everyday Life*, edited by P. Nynäs and A.K.T. Yip, Farnham: Ashgate, 71–90.

Jaspal, R. 2018. *Enhancing Sexual Health, Self-Identity and Wellbeing among Men Who Have Sex with Men: A Guide for Practitioners*. London: Jessica Kingsley.

Jaspal, R. 2019. *The Social Psychology of Gay Men*. Basingstoke: Palgrave.

Jaspal, R. and Breakwell, G. M. (eds) 2014. *Identity Process Theory: Identity, Social Action and Social Change*. Cambridge: Cambridge University Press.

Jaspal, R. and Cinnirella, M. 2010. Coping with potentially incompatible identities: accounts of religious, ethnic and sexual identities from British Pakistani men who identify as Muslim and gay. *British Journal of Social Psychology*, 49(4), 849–870.

Jaspal, R. and Cinnirella, M. 2014. Hyper-affiliation to the religious in-group among British Pakistani Muslim gay men. *Journal of Community & Applied Social Psychology*, 24(4), 265–277.

Jeffries, W.L., Dodge, D. and Sandfort, T.G.M. 2008. Religion and spirituality among bisexual Black men in the USA. *Culture, Health and Sexuality: An International Journal for Research, Intervention and Care*, 10(5), 463–477.

Kinsey, A.C., Pomeroy, W.R., and Martin, C.E. 1948. *Sexual Behavior in the Human Male*. Bloomington: Indiana University Press.

Kugle, S. 2010. *Homosexuality in Islam: Critical Reflection on Gay, Lesbian, and Transgender Muslims*. Oxford: Oneworld Publications.

Labaki, B. and Abou Rjeili, K. (eds) 1994. *Bilan des guerres du Liban: 1975–1990*. Paris: L'Harmattan.

Lange, C.R. 2009. Homosexuality in Islamic law, in *Oxford International Encyclopedia of Legal History*, edited by S.N. Katz. Oxford: Oxford University Press, 181–182.

Makarem, G. 2012. Lebanon and LGBT: The story of Helem. *Europe Solidaire sans Frontières.* [Online]. Available at: http://www.europe-solidaire.org/ [accessed 16 October 2018]

McCormack, M., Anderson, E. and Adams, A. 2014. Cohort effect on the coming out experiences of bisexual men. *Sociology*, 48(6), 1207–1223.

Michli, S. 2016. *Exploring the Risk and Protective Factors against Internalized Homonegativity in a Sample of Lebanese Individuals with Same-Sex Desires.* Unpublished MA thesis, Department of Psychology, American University of Beirut. [Online]. Available at: https://scholarworks.aub.edu.lb/handle/10938/10988 [accessed 16 October 2018]

Monro, S. (ed.) 2015. *Bisexuality: Identities, Politics, and Theories.* Basingstoke: Palgrave.

Morris, M., McCormack, M. and Anderson, E. 2014. The changing experiences of bisexual male adolescents. *Gender and Education*, 26(4), 397–413.

Moscovici, S. 1988. Notes towards a description of social representations. *European Journal of Social Psychology*, 18, 211–250.

Mulick, P.S. and Wright, L.W. 2002. Examining the existence of biphobia in the heterosexual and homosexual populations. *Journal of Bisexuality*, 2(4), 45–64.

Murray, S.O. 1997. The will not to know: Islamic accommodations of male homosexuality, in *Islamic Homosexualities*, edited by S.O. Murray and W. Roscoe. New York: New York University Press, 14–54.

Murray, S.O. and Roscoe, W. (eds) 1997. *Islamic Homosexualities: Culture, History and Literature.* New York: New York University Press.

Office for National Statistics. 2017. Sexual identity, UK: 2016. [Online]. Available at: https://www.ons.gov.uk/peoplepopulationandcommunity/culturalidentity/sexuality/bulletins/sexualidentityuk/2016 [accessed 2 April 2019]

Ouzgane L. 2006. *Islamic Masculinities.* London: Zed Books.

Peterson, J.L., Coates, T.J., Catania, J.A., Middleton, L., Hilliard, B. and Hearst, N. 1992. High risk sexual behavior and condom use among gay and bisexual African American men. *American Journal of Public Health*, 82, 1490–1494.

Pew Research Center. 2013. The Pew Global Project Attitudes, 4 October [Online]. Available at: https://www.pewglobal.org/2013/06/04/the-global-divide-on-homosexuality/ [accessed 13 March 2019]

Philogène, G. 1994. 'African American' as a new social representation. *Journal for the Theory of Social Behaviour*, 24(2), 89–109.

Rieger, G., Chivers, M. and Bailey, J. 2005. Sexual arousal patterns of bisexual men. *Psychological Science*, 16, 579–584.

Ross, M.W., Berg, R.C., Schmidt, A.J., Hospers, H.J.Breveglieri, M., Furegato, M. and Weatherburn, P. 2013. Internalised homonegativity predicts HIV-associated risk behavior in European men who have sex with men in a 38-country cross-sectional study: Some public health implications of homophobia. *British Medical Journal Open*, 3(2). [Online]. Available at: https://bmjopen.bmj.com/content/3/2/e001928 [accessed 2 April 2019]

Schmitt, A., Sofer, J. 1992. *Sexuality and Eroticism Among Males in Moslem Societies.* New York: Harrington Park Press.

Siraj, A. 2006. On being homosexual and Muslim: Conflicts and challenges. In *Islamic Masculinities*, edited by L. Ouzgane, London: Zed Books, 202–216.

Sophie, J. 1986. A critical examination of stage theories of lesbian identity development. *Journal of Homosexuality*, 12(2), 39–51.

Super, J.T. and Jacobson, L. 2011. Religious abuse: Implications for counselling lesbian, gay, bisexual and transgender individuals. *Journal of LGBT Issues in Counseling*, 5(3–4), 180–196.

Tolino, S. 2014. Homosexuality in the Middle East: An analysis of dominant and competitive discourses. *Deportate, Esuli, Profughe*, 25, 72–91.

Udis-Kessler, A. 1995. Identity/politics: A history of the bisexual movement, in *Bisexual Politics: Theories, Queries and Visions*, edited by N. Tucker, L. Highleyman and R. Kaplan. New York: Harrington Park Press, 17–30.

Wagner, G.J., Aunon, F.M., Kaplan, R.L., Rana, Y., Khoury, D., Tohme, J. and Mokhbat, J. 2012. A qualitative exploration of sexual risk and HIV testing behaviors among men who have sex with men in Beirut, Lebanon. *PloS one*, 7(9). [Online] Available at: https://www.ncbi.nlm.nih.gov/pubmed/23029103 [accessed 2 April 2019]

Wagner, G.J., Aunon, F.M., Kaplan, R.L., Karam, R., Khouri, D., Tohme, J. and Mokhbat J. 2013. Sexual stigma, psychological wellbeing and social engagement among men who have sex with men in Beirut, Lebanon. *Culture Health and Sexuality*, 15(5), 570–582.

Wagner, G.J., Hoover, M., Green, H., Tohme, J. and Mokhbat, J. 2015. Social, relational and network determinants of unprotected anal sex and HIV testing among men who have sex with men in Beirut, Lebanon. *International Journal of Sexual Health*, 27(3), 264–275.

Weinberg, T.S., Williams, C.J. and Pryor, D.W. 1994. *Dual Attraction: Understanding Bisexuality*. New York: Oxford University Press.

10 Depression and suicidality among bisexual Christians

Carol A. Shepherd

Introduction

This chapter looks specifically at the mental health of those who identify as bisexual and Christian in the Western Christian Church, based on my empirical research with this community. Given the pace of change in secular society over LGBT rights, it is somewhat surprising that an observation made by Klein forty years ago still largely holds sway in churches today:

> We tend to categorise people, to put them into the most readily available group … That this mistaken practice is also adopted by the individual in his or her search for self-identity – and held onto at all costs for lack of a suitable alternative – is tragic.
>
> (1993: 5)

As this quote suggests, bisexual erasure, and its corollary, poor mental health in bisexual people, is both a systemic and individual process. The tendency of society and social institutions to organise themselves within binary systems (e.g. man or woman, gay or straight), in the interests of maintaining existing power bases and out of sheer convenience and intellectual laziness, shoehorns vulnerable individuals into definitive categories, which may or may not prove a good fit. In the case of the bisexual Christian, they almost never fit these binary systems. As the observation from Klein reveals, often the bisexual person, in the desperate search for belonging, pre-empts the inevitable process by diving voluntarily into the relentless social flow towards binary normality. The bisexual person then aligns themselves within the peer group that appears to offer the closest source of sanctity, be that the 'straight camp' or the 'gay camp'. In the case of the bisexual Christian, this is usually the former, for the fear of reprisals in adopting the latter option in a Western Christian Church still riven with prejudice over so-called 'gay lifestyles'. As Venn-Brown (2018) notes, straight people have 'lives' but LGBT people have 'lifestyles', as if LGBT people do not engage in the same prosaic daily chores as their heterosexual peers.

Oppression of bisexual people within the Christian LGBT community is potentially as damaging to the bisexual individual as the Church's silence on the subject. Arguably more so, as in so doing LGBT faith organisations are failing in their bespoke mission to offer support to the whole LGBT community. The bisexual person of faith has already been damaged by the heteronormative environment of the mainstream Church, so faces a 'double dip' repression.

As with society as a whole, the Church has an issue with the messiness of non-binary categories. As Stuart and Thatcher comment:

> bisexuals undermine the whole sexual system, the neat classification of people into homosexual and heterosexual, the pathologizing of homosexuality as a heterosexual disorder and so on. Bisexuality represents desire unfettered, and perhaps that is why those who experience it are so studiously unacknowledged in church documents, and on the odd occasion where they are acknowledged, they are pathetically misrepresented as sexually indiscriminate and promiscuous.
>
> (1997: 190)

Bisexual people (similar to transgendered and intersex people of faith) are flies in the ointment of a (patriarchal) authoritarian system. Such a system seeks to impose behavioural boundaries on its subjects, where theological certainty, clarity of procedure and the maintenance of existing power relations (often masquerading particularly in Church life as the cuddlier term *family values*), take precedence over the realities of human experience and any form of compassionate quest for knowledge or understanding. This is the moralism defined by Heyward as 'an ideology of rightness and a posturing of certitude that absolutizes ideas and abstractions rather than actual relationships that are loving and just' (1999: 17).

This moralism is totally inflexible and cannot encompass actual human realities, as it is 'unchanging, unbending, and therefore not open to honest questioning even by conscientious, responsible people' (1999: 19). As Heyward notes: 'When we are moralistic, we do not wish to have our ideas disrupted by questions or information pertaining to actual human need, feelings, or desire' (1999: 117). The lived reality of individual experience is therefore ignored in favour of prescriptive ideologies of human romantic and sexual love. This pharisaic prioritising of theory over practice would seem juxtaposed to Christ's notion of love as the fulfilment of the law (see Galatians 5:14).

This quest for certainty organically results in a 'them and us' situation, a simplistic organisation of subjects into more manageable binary categories. Such dichotomies are convenient as they reinforce the group identity – in this scenario, as in Western capitalist society, male white heterosexual supremacy – and greatly facilitate identity politics, for gay and straight people alike.

The dualistic paradigm is contradicted by bisexual people, who are, according to Hunt (in Kolodny, 2000) 'living proof that it is an inadequate way to think'. Such binary thinking 'excludes their reality entirely' (2000: xi). Rohr speaks of the 'seven Cs of delusion' and describes the sequencing of the dualistic mind that 'compares, competes, conflicts, conspires, condemns, cancels out any contrary evidence … then crucifies with impunity' (2011: 147).

Certainty cannot by definition encompass any trace of ambiguity, which may partially account for the relative paucity of dialogue on the bisexual experience. In this way, there appears to be a conspiracy of silence of sorts on bisexuality within the Church. This silence is profoundly damaging to the mental health of bisexual Christians, who are squeezed out by such binary thinking.

It is no coincidence that my monograph on the subject of bisexual Christians (Shepherd, 2018) devotes more lineage to the issue of mental health than to any other issue (two chapters). Indeed, it was practically impossible in my empirical research to separate psychological distress from the experience of being bisexual and Christian. As Smith (2010) directly notes in the preface to her doctoral thesis, 'being bisexual is a head-fuck'. Barker elaborates:

> the very clear main finding of overviews of the research literature is the higher rates of mental health problems (such as self-harm, suicide, and depression) among bisexual people than among heterosexual, or lesbian and gay, people. Virtually all studies on this, whether quantitative or qualitative, and across a range of countries and contexts, replicate this finding.
>
> (2015: 374)

Depressive illness appears to be the recurring thread running throughout any discussion of bisexual people's lives and especially when it comes to the taboo subject of non-binary sexualities within the Christian faith.

Until my study, only Levy and Harr (2018), Charron (2014), Toft (2009, 2014), M. Robinson (2014), Alford-Harkey and Haffner (2014), Hutchins and Williams (2014), Kolodny (2000) and Sommers (2016) have, to the best of my knowledge, looked exclusively into the specific bisexual Christian intersection. Of these scholars, Alford-Harkey and Haffner (2014) have written a general church resource for those who pastor bisexual Christians in the United States, whereas others focus on empirical studies. The project discussed in this chapter, which was undertaken as part of my doctoral research (Shepherd, 2017) and which is also referenced in Shepherd (2018), *Bisexuality and the Western Christian Church: The Damage of Silence*, is the only work to encompass qualitative research with both church practitioners and their bisexual congregants. Sommers's work *119: My Life as a Bisexual Christian* (2016) covers both, but is autobiographical and, by its own admission, a trade publication.

Specific studies of bisexual mental health are either secular (Barker, 2015; et al., 2015) – which, of course, is not to assume interviewees did not have a religious faith, but this was not deemed to be an influential factor – or subsume bisexual data within LGBT Christian statistics (Gibbs and Goldbach, 2015; Jorm et al., 2002). This makes assessing findings regarding bisexual mental health in specific more challenging.

Whilst I am aware of the further complexities posed by the additional intersections of race, gender and disability, the scope of this specific chapter necessitates limiting the discussion to the mental health of bisexual Christians in the generic sense. As Crenshaw (1990) and Meyer (2003) indicate, the more intersectional the identity, the greater the erasure and propensity towards oppression. That said, we are currently witnessing an increased focus on intersectionality as a sociological buzzword, both within academia and within fundraising arms of the charity sector. This research might lead to an emerging recognition of the phenomenon of intersectionality, and with it an increased desire by individuals to own and express their specific intersectional identity.

My research sought to discover whether, in line with existing studies, bisexual Christians were also affected by a systematic and internalised erasure of their identity, and whether this erasure was embedded in participants' minds through belonging to a faith community. To what degree, if any, did they take pride in their intersectionality? Or, to return to Klein, are bisexual Christians still, out of convenience or fear, miscategorising themselves as homosexual or heterosexual? To this end, in 2016, I undertook qualitative interviews with self-identified bisexual Christians in the UK and USA, the methodology for which is outlined below.

Methodology and operationalisation

The optimal methodology for uncovering the lived experience of bisexual Christians was grounded theory. Given my role as both an applied theologian and a LGBT faith activist, it was not possible to approach my participants without prior knowledge of the presenting issues. I therefore adopted Charmaz's constructivist grounded theory approach (Charmaz, 2006), engaging in frequent self-reflection to avoid researcher bias where possible, yet acknowledging my participatory role in the interview process.

The vast majority of participants engaged in semi-structured interviews either in person or by video call, to ensure good rapport and more elaborate responses. All participants were asked about their mental health within the context of their faith and worship communities using the interview protocol questions: Do you have health issues – depression, anxiety, etc. – related to your sexuality and/or faith? Have you had suicidal thoughts or attempted suicide? If so, was this related to your faith and/or sexuality? Have you ever taken part in any gay aversion therapy or healing ministry for your sexuality? If so, how did this make you feel? What would make church better for you?

Interviews typically lasted 45–60 minutes. I also documented other psychological conditions revealed during interviews, as well as Autistic Spectrum Disorders and learning disabilities, as potential indicators of other root causes of anxiety beyond the spirituality/sexuality intersection.

Bisexual Christians in the UK and USA

From February to November 2016, I interviewed 54 British and American bisexual Christians for my study *Bisexual Christians and Mental Health: Why the Church Needs to be More Welcoming*. Participants were recruited via my social networks, and via popular social media channels. Given the sensitive and contentious nature of identifying as bisexual and Christian, I exceeded the anticipated number of individuals willing to speak at length, largely due to some advantageous snowball effects, particularly at one Christian college campus in Tennessee and within an affirming church in the north west of England. The vast majority elected for anonymity, particularly those from non-affirming Church denominations.

I interviewed 28 bisexual Christians in the UK and 26 in the USA. Within the UK subsample, whilst all participants resided in England at the point of interview, there were representatives of Scottish (n = 3), Welsh (n = 1) and Northern Irish (n = 1) descent, as well as dual nationalities from continental Europe (n = 3) and India (n = 1). One interviewee had dual US/Italian nationality but had married and resided in the UK for some time. All participants had identified as bisexual within a church environment in the UK, in line with project criteria. All but one participant was white, with one participant of Anglo-Indian descent. Attempts were made to recruit black, Asian and minority ethnic (BAME) interviewees by contacting organisations such as Bis of Colour, but without success (whether the enhanced stigma surrounding bisexuality in the BAME community made BAME bisexual Christians more reluctant to come forward is speculative). All participants identified as bisexual, except one, who now identified as lesbian but had previously identified as bisexual in a church setting and therefore matched the person specification. Two participants also identified as transgender and one as gender queer and bisexual. In total, I interviewed seven cisgendered bisexual males, 17 cisgendered bisexual females, one cis-gendered lesbian, one female-to-male and one male-to-female bisexual transgender person and one gender queer (biologically male) participant. The youngest respondent was aged 21 years and the eldest 62 years, and the mean age was 38 years (SD = 12.2 years). Pseudonyms were used for all participants in this cohort.

Regarding employment, interviewees ranged from professionals and academics to administrators and semi-skilled workers. All self-identified as Christian except Susannah, who now identified as atheist, Demi, who practised Buddhism, and Corinne, who described herself as 'not Christian'. However, all three had previously engaged with Christianity and had attended mainstream denominations, thus fitting the person specification.

In the US subsample, 24 participants resided in the US at the time of interview, with two based in the UK, both on academic grounds. Concerning ethnic diversity, 21 whites, two Latinos, one Hispanic, one African-American and one Taiwanese-American were interviewed. Participants came from 14 states in total, with the most respondents coming from the southern states of Tennessee (n = 5) and Georgia (n = 4) and the eastern state of Massachusetts (n = 3). Both East and West Coasts were well covered, with the only significant absence being the Midwest, with just two states, Ohio and South Dakota, represented.

All participants identified as bisexual and cisgendered, except for one, who identified as both bisexual and gender queer. In total, 20 cisgendered females, five cisgendered males and one gender queer (biological male) were interviewed. The youngest participant was aged 18 years and the eldest 65 years, and the mean average age was 32 years (SD = 10.5 years), making this a younger research cell than its UK counterpart by six years. This can be explained by the larger number of college students interviewed owing to the snowball effect at a college in Tennessee (n = 5).

In terms of employment, interviewees ranged from clergy, professionals and academics to musicians, entertainers, activists and students. All self-identified as Christian at the point of interview except one, who no longer claimed a religious affiliation. All participants had experience of identifying as bisexual within a church environment in the USA, in line with project criteria.

Bi-affirming pastors and educators in the UK and USA

A further decision was made to interview pastors, LGBT support workers and educators in the UK and USA to see what attempts were made to support bisexual Christians. This was with a view to uncovering what, if any, pastoral resources or practices were available to congregants or visitors to the Church identifying as bisexual. Was it truly the case that bisexuality was erased in worship communities or were bisexual Christians simply not accessing sources of available support?

To this end, I interviewed a total of 32 pastors, support workers and experts in the field (UK n = 14; USA n = 18). Only one Conservative Evangelical was willing to be interviewed – Ron of The Narrow Way Ministry, a Seventh-day Adventist organisation from Arkansas. This reinforced the sense that bisexuality is 'the great unmentionable' in terms of sins among conservative Evangelicals, though in reality a suspicion of academics and the fear of negative press in an increasingly liberal climate could also lie behind the decision not to speak to me.

Reparative therapy organisations in both countries simply did not respond. Indeed, silence was the overwhelming response to my email and contact form requests to speak to conservative pastors about faith and sexuality – and silence, of course, cannot be tangibly documented.

A range of major denominations was covered, encompassing a broad churchmanship, from more conservative Anglican and Catholic traditions, to more progressive denominations (US Episcopal Church, UK Methodist Church), to liberal, fully LGBT affirming churches (Metropolitan Community Church, Liberty Church UK, United Church of Christ, Unitarian Universalists, Quakers). I also spoke to representatives of the Bisexual Resource Center in Boston and Believe Out Loud, an LGBT Christian campaigning group in New York. In the UK, I interviewed the President of the Lesbian and Gay Christian Movement (now known as One Body One Faith). In addition, two psychotherapists were interviewed in both the UK and USA on the subject of bisexuality, faith and mental health.

'They just can't handle it': voices of bisexual Christians

From a total of 54 bisexual Christians interviewed, 50 (93%) reported poor mental health, based on the questions asked in my semi-structured interviews around depression and anxiety, outlined earlier in this chapter. These health conditions ranged from periodic bouts of low mood (dysthymia), to sustained periods of depression and/or anxiety (both clinically and self-diagnosed), to suicide ideation and attempted suicide. The four participants who scored 'no' across the four categories of anxiety, depression, suicide ideation and suicide attempts reported only mild feelings of stress relating to work, the process of coming out and parental divorce.[1] An overall depressive behaviour rate of 93% does indeed confirm previous studies on adverse mental health among bisexual people (e.g. Brennan et al., 2010; Colledge et al., 2015).

Anxiety and depression among bisexual Christians

In both UK and US cohorts, some participants reported having anxiety but not depression. Others reported having depression but not anxiety, while a third group had comorbid diagnoses. In addition, those who reported only suffering from depression then revealed clear anxiety during interview and vice-versa. For this reason, it was impossible to separate findings for anxiety and depression without going far more in depth into the psychology of these individuals, which was deemed beyond the scope of this study. It was possible, however, to arrive at statistics for suicidality. Within the British cohort (n = *28*), all but four (86%) reported some form of depressive illness, with eight (29%) reporting suicide ideation or suicide attempts. All 26 (100%) of US bisexual Christians had experienced adverse mental health, with nine (35%) expressing suicidality of varying intensity.

It was clear that British participants were less fluent in mental health terminology, whereas American participants were able to articulate and differentiate between depressive conditions, citing dysthymia and generalised anxiety disorder (GAD), where British interviewees were more likely to speak generically of feeling stressed, or low. As most participants cited a number of factors behind low mood and anxiety, I chose to include all occurrences of each factor.

In terms of Figure 10.1, sexuality encompasses those socio-cultural experiences directly related to sexuality within a faith context, such as coming out, parental reaction, spiritual conflict and identity crises. Other health issues refer to anxiety or depression linked to existing physiological or psychological issues, but which have no direct link to sexuality. For example, some respondents reported experiencing seasonal affective disorder (SAD), side-effects from anti-depressants or obsessive compulsive disorders (OCD), but made no link between these conditions and their bisexuality. Social isolation as a cause of depression counted separately, where sexuality was not cited as the reason for loneliness.

Figure 10.1 shows a total of 12 reasons cited for anxiety and/or depression among the participants. Of these 12 reasons, sexuality-related conflict was cited on 26 occasions by the 54 participants, the most popular reason, followed by workplace stress (n = 5). However, 10 of those reporting adverse mental health (19%) believed their sexuality to be the sole or dominant contributory reason for their depression and anxiety. This calls into question more recent surveys on bisexuality, such as Jorm et al. (2002), Carr (2011), Taylor (2013) and Colledge et al. (2015), which pointed to the dual processes of stigmatisation and erasure of bisexual people and the outworking of this in daily life as being central to adverse mental health among this cohort, rather than bisexual stigma being just one of a range of external factors impacting on health.

Childhood sexual abuse, acknowledged by three participants (6%), was a reason given in the US cohort only. Other reasons were given similar prominence by US and UK participants: 43% of British and 42% of American bisexual Christians respectively cited sexuality/faith conflict as being a reason for their anxiety and depression.

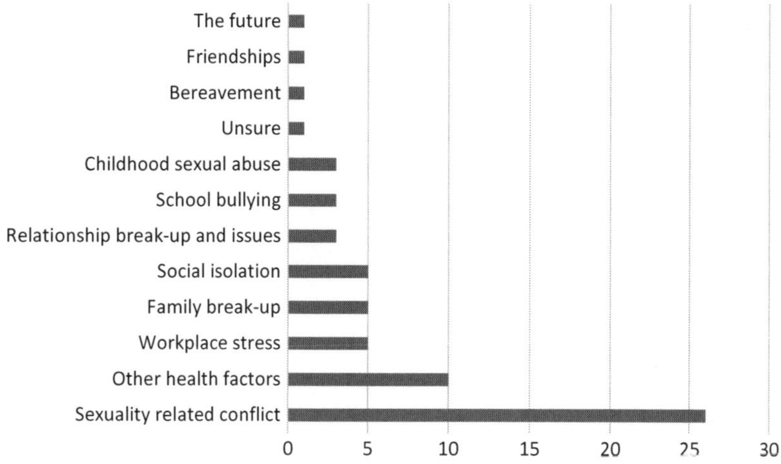

Figure 10.1 Reported causes of anxiety and depression among bisexual Christians

Suicide ideation and attempts among bisexual Christians

In total, 21 out of 54 participants (39%) reported suicide ideation and/or suicide attempts, though figures were higher in the USA than in the UK (35% versus 29%). Some participants distinguished between suicidal thoughts and suicide attempts; others conflated the two. Whilst it is acknowledged that both suicide ideation and attempted suicide may vary enormously in intent, I felt, nevertheless, that both were indicative of a serious depressive condition. Therefore, all statements (n = 30) of suicidality were included in the statistics show in Figure 10.2.

In total, nine reasons were stated for suicidality, though six were not entirely sure of the reason for their suicidal feelings. Sexuality was cited as a reason on twelve occasions, with other reasons cited 14 times. In other words, sexuality was given as a key reason for 40% of bisexual Christians' suicide attempts or instances of suicide ideation.

To conclude, of 54 participants, 50 (93%) reported depressive symptoms, ranging from anxiety and depression to suicide ideation or suicide attempts. Only four (7%) reported no depressive symptoms at all, and all of these participants were British. To place these figures in perspective, statistics published online by MIND[2] (2016) and Mental Health America (2015) suggest that one in four UK adults (25%) and one in five US adults (20%) suffer from mental health problems at any one time regardless of their sexual orientation.

'It's this huge conflict': in the words of bisexual Christians

In line with existing studies on bisexual mental health – for reviews, see Anderson and McCormack (2016) and Shepherd (2017, 2018) – it would appear that bisexual people do indeed experience vastly higher rates of

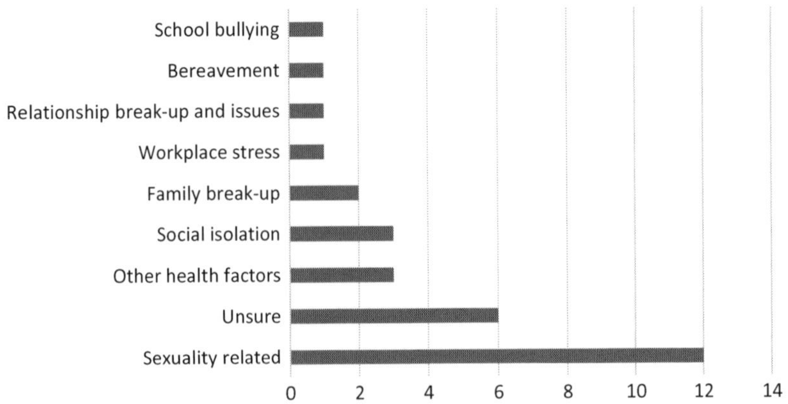

Figure 10.2 Reported causes of suicide ideation and attempts among bisexual Christians

depression, anxiety and suicidality, and that this is augmented within church communities, where their sexuality remains largely unaffirmed.

Melissa, an Evangelical student from Tennessee, gave this account of her teenage experiences identifying as bisexual and Christian:

> When I first recognised my feelings of a same-sex attraction to someone, my anxiety and depression began. I knew that I wasn't in control of my attraction and that scared me, especially when thinking about how God, the world, my family, and my friends would view me. I had the belief that I was a sinner because of my sexuality and that I would go to Hell. I tried so hard to hold back and deny myself of this attraction, but it made my anxiety and depression so much worse … I experienced self-hate, obsessive thoughts, constant worry and deep depression. My body physically changed as well. I often got nauseous and would throw up regularly when my anxiety got so bad. I developed an eating disorder in which I could not eat without throwing up and I lost 15 pounds. I became very weak and gloomy, feeling dread every day. I tried an anti-anxiety medication, Lexapro, and after taking it for three days, I had the worst anxiety attack I have ever experienced and voluntarily admitted myself to a psychiatric hospital for three days.

Freda, a Seventh-day Adventist also from Tennessee, but unemployed and living in York, UK, at the time of interview, stated:

> It's this huge conflict and I literally think about it every single day. [Crying] I just genuinely want to be genuine and be myself and not just me existing, be like this horrible thing. I don't want another kid to feel like me growing up.

While at face value, such experiences could arguably be true of all LGBT identities, it was the particular confusion, or 'head-fuck' (Smith, 2017), of being bisexual – and the apparently toxic combination with Christianity – that was cited by all participants as being central to their distress. It was clearly the case that bisexuality was a source of both internalised and external phobic reactions.

Des, an Episcopal church worker from Virginia, also highlighted erasure and stigmatisation of his bisexual orientation as a key stressor, leading to confusion and self-doubt:

> Part of my mental health struggles are … the not knowing where I fit, if I fit, not knowing if I'm normal in the experience of gay men or straight men, you know, because bisexuality is not talked about very much and there's not much publicity about it …. Surely I'll wake up one day and realise, you know, I'm either straight or gay and this kind of dancing in the middle is just my process of getting there.

While such statistics (93% of them with depressive disorders) clearly confirm existing research into bisexuality, which highlight significantly enhanced levels of depression and suicidality among bisexual people, the results of this study also challenge claims that cultural phenomena such as identity erasure and stigmatisation are the root cause of depressive behaviour amongst bisexuals (e.g. Flanders, Dobinson and Logie, 2015; Klein 1993). Whilst issues surrounding peer acceptance and identity formation were clearly expressed by a number of participants, they by no means dominated. Indeed, non-sexuality related grounds for poor mental health were also widely reported, as can be seen in Figures 10.1 and 10.2. These other reasons combined actually exceeded incidences of sexuality-related conflict, both in terms of depression, anxiety and suicidality rates.

Whilst we can draw speculative links between social isolation and bisexual identities, it cannot be presumed that bisexuality itself accounts for self-reported marginalisation. As Barker notes, 'human experience is complexly biopsychosocial' (Barker, 2015: 372). It would thus be disingenuous to claim from my modest and unrepresentative sample that biphobia and marginalisation alone accounted for these elevated mental health statistics. One US respondent, Gabriela, a freelancer from California and member of the LGBT-affirming United Church of Christ, perfectly encapsulated the complexities of untangling the root causes of her anxiety amid a vast array of cultural influences:

> I do have anxiety, but I don't blame my faith or sexuality as root causes. I think it's more accurate to say that my brain latches onto, for example, the impostor syndrome of being a bi woman who has never been in a relationship with another woman or the guilt complex that comes with being Catholic as more fodder for my anxiety. But then again, my job, my relationship, my friendships, my future, all of these things cause me equal amounts of anxiety, spiralizing negative thought cycles.

It should also be taken into account that many reported reasons for poor bisexual mental health were not specific to bisexuality. For example, the male shame relating to same-sex attraction discussed by psychosexual therapist Michael Salas from Vantage Point Counselling, Dallas, is common to homosexual men, too, while the lack of credibility afforded female sexualities applies equally to lesbian and heterosexual women (Blumstein and Schwartz, 1977). These distinctions are important, to avoid giving misleading information on bisexual mental health for political ends. I was particularly careful as a self-identified bisexual Christian researcher, not to 'sensationalise' the data for publicity's sake or personal academic gain.

Internalised biphobia in the context of self-erasure was also present – that is to say, self-loathing at being attracted to more than one gender leads to the individual's public denial of their bisexuality. This was mainly on the part of participants from less accepting church cultures. This was unsurprising, particularly in the United States, with the strong associations between bisexuality and immorality (and presumptions around polyamorous practices). For many participants, it was simply less stressful to stay in the closet or exercise their heterosexual privilege than contend with the 'revolving closet door'[3] (Johnson, 2008) or the disparaging remarks of others. It was certainly evident from this study that 'having to lie, to conceal and not be completely what one is – even with close friends' was 'a black cloud hanging over the heads of many bisexuals' (Klein, 1993: 125).

The cloud of bisexual erasure within the Church was perhaps best articulated by Gabriele from California:

> They said they were 'welcoming' but by no means were they affirming. I found that 'progressive' evangelical spaces pull the 'bait and switch' on many LGBT people. They are seemingly cool and accepting, but when it comes to matters of leadership, theology or full membership, they are just as closed minded and bigoted as the fundamentalists they so often distance themselves from. I would like to see bisexuality said in the same breath as gay, lesbian and trans. I think most affirming churches and LGBT organisations/programmes are actually only affirming of gay men and lesbian women. There's been some great work done with trans visibility as of late and that's great to see. I wish bi erasure wasn't so prevalent in these spaces.

'A squeamishness around sexuality': interviews with pastors and support workers in the UK and USA

As indicated in the methodology, I also interviewed pastors and LGBT support workers in the UK and USA, as a check against allegations of bisexual erasure in Church life on the part of bisexual congregants. Some participants wished to remain anonymous and therefore names and geographical locations were anonymised; others expressly wished to be quoted under their own name with details of the organisations they represented made transparent.

Here it emerged that a distinct lack of attention was indeed paid to bisexuality across the board, from verbal and printed media to pastoral support. This had a detrimental effect on pastors' and educators' ability to support bisexual Christians who approached their organisation, either through a lack of knowledge or a lack of pastoral resources, or indeed both. The woeful absence of bisexuality as a subject matter in clergy training materials was noted by Reverend Shanon Ferguson, of the Metropolitan Community Church North London. Shanon made particular reference to the Church of England's *Issues in Human Sexuality* (Church of England, 1991), which dedicates just a single (derogatory) paragraph to bisexuality amid 17 pages on 'The Phenomenon of Homosexual Love' (1991: 31). In this paragraph, the bisexual Christian is advised to give in only to their heterosexual leanings and seek a counsellor for their potential personality disorder. No concessions are made to those attracted to more than one gender and there would appear to be neither consciousness nor acknowledgement that monosexist discourses are potentially damaging. This is key, as *Issues in Human Sexuality* is mandatory reading for all those taking up orders in the Church of England. Participants in both UK research cells – both pastors and lay people – pointed to this document as being particularly damaging, and direly in need to updating to reflect a more humane and accurate understanding of bisexuality. It should be noted that while a sequel to the document was published in 2003, *Some Issues in Human Sexuality* (Church of England, 2003), this discussion report did little to address the shortfall.

This does not bode well for the future in terms of improving provision for bisexual Christians. Jane (55), an Anglican charity worker from London, commented:

> The invisibility and the silence about it … it kind of drives me a bit crazy. It's kind of of like, if you're trying to be something that's so silent and not talked about, and you know the B in LGBT is so silent, there's something about asserting it at the same time that can lead me to feeling a bit mad.

In the US, pastors and educators painted a portrait of an erotophobic American church culture, where sex-negativity abounds and sexuality in general is barely discussed, let alone bisexuality. Reverend Marie Alford-Harkey of the Religious Institute in Connecticut, also co-author of *Bisexuality: Making the Invisible Visible in Faith Communities* (Alford-Harkey and Haffner, 2014), currently the world's only pastoral guide to bisexuality,[4] stated:

> I desperately want to be hopeful, but I have so much experience in mainline congregations and traditions and at least in this country, the squeamishness around sexuality and the very idea of sexual fluidity in any form is just so deeply ingrained that … I just don't know … I feel like these are only conversations I'm having among my academic and my progressive activist friends.

Another participant pointed out to me issues with the word bisexuality itself. The conservative American press is loath to print any word containing the root sex or sexual, which was why bisexual women and men are frequently mislabelled lesbian or gay instead, as it was deemed less offensive in print.

Though political developments such as marriage equality and the recent spate of bathroom bills relating to transgender rights are forcing churches to confront issues of gender and sexuality, bisexuality was still almost uniformly ignored or denied credibility. Neither nation offered a healthy pastoral environment for nurturing bisexual people of faith. Indeed, it was confirmed in interviews that neither churches nor LGBT faith organisations in the UK or USA had much idea of how to handle bisexuality, from a teaching or pastoral perspective, with the result that the B in LGBT was all but erased in documentation, sermons and other faith communications. Reverend Shanon

Ferguson of Metropolitan Community Church, North London, commented at interview:

> We use this acronym of LGBT, but the B is incredibly silent. It's almost like it's just there to fill a gap and most bisexuals are overlooked … people haven't really wanted to deal with bisexuality as an identity and as a construct in its own right, and that I find both distressing and it makes me angry, because it's just as important an identity as any other identity and consequently we should value it in exactly the same way.

Few saw the church addressing bisexuality in the short-term future. In this way, these findings confirmed the fears and suspicions of their pastors and leaders, that they had little to offer their bisexual congregants.

Bisexuality scholar Lisa Diamond of the University of Utah referred in her interview (March 2016) to the 'specific challenges' faced by bisexual Christians and commented on the 'unique and very damaging type of social pressure' that obedience to religious faith puts on vulnerable individuals. The specific challenges of bisexuality were clearly conveyed by those carrying that intersectional identity, and there had patently been inattention paid to these challenges on the part of pastors, churches and other faith organisations. This led to bisexual people of faith deliberately 'misidentifying' as straight or gay to simplify their Church experience. Christian Spiritual Director Jeremy commented:

> I'm quite sure that there are a great many bisexual people out there, but because of the difficult of talking about it at church, they would rather align themselves with gay or straight, preferably straight, because that's the simplest and less likely to cause them problems.

Confirming with the strictures of the faith as laid out in doctrinal statements, liturgies and biblical hermeneutics was rarely achievable in a way that supported the psychological wellbeing of participants. Not only were church leaders ignorant of bisexuality, but mandatory training materials for ordinands (those training for ministry) either refused to acknowledge bisexuality as a bona fide sexual orientation, or, in the case of the Church of England (1991, 2003), discounted it entirely as a valid moral choice. Little more justice was done to bisexuality in works of applied theology either in those churches that contained bookstores. Only the Cathedral of Hope in Dallas, the world's largest bespoke LGBT church, stocked books specifically related to bisexuality, though only two amid dozens of works on homosexuality and LGBT in general: Sheri Eisner's *Bi: Notes for a Bisexual Revolution* (2013) and Ochs and Rowley's (2005) *Getting Bi: Voices of Bisexuals Around the World.* The only church to stock a stand-alone leaflet on bisexuality was the Metropolitan Community Church in North London.

Concluding remarks

A sizeable number of people identify as bisexual and Christian. Research has shown elevated rates of depressive disorders among bisexual people (Carr, 2011; Colledge et al., 2015) and among LGBT Christians (Gibbs and Goldbach, 2015). My research aimed to look specifically at the bisexual Christian intersection. I anticipated poor mental health among this under-researched cohort but perhaps not to the extent uncovered. In fact, 86% of UK and 100% of US participants revealed a depressive condition of varying intensity in this study, though it was beyond the scope of this research to definitively link either a bisexual orientation, a Christian faith or indeed both to poor mental health. My interviews do, however, suggest that the processes underpinning an association between bisexuality and poor mental health are more nuanced than painted in extant research.

I sought to uncover whether it was possible for a bisexual Christian to bring their 'full selves', i.e. their integrated (or embodied) physiological and spiritual being to church with them, and have this embodied self affirmed and celebrated. It appeared from my interviews with participants either side of the Atlantic that this was rarely achieved. It was also clear that the issue was not ontological. It was not being bisexual that was the problem on the whole; as Fritz Klein (1978) suggests, it is how bisexual individuals are perceived by others and its subsequent impact on their sense of wellbeing that is problematic. In this respect, the influential *Issues in Human Sexuality* (Church of England, 1991) would appear to have had a large influence on perceptions of bisexuality as a valid sexual orientation (or not) within the Church in the UK. My interviews suggest that God was not the source of anxiety either. My participants gave little indication that they felt God had 'made a mistake' with their orientation and that inside a confused bisexual mind and body was a monosexual being screaming for liberation, as *Issues in Human Sexuality* (Church of England, 1991) would suggest. Instead, it would seem that, ignorant or misinformed clergy and society at large were the issue.

There was clear evidence of horizontal oppression from within the (lay) LGBT community, too, and this was felt by a number of participants to pose a major threat to their sense of wellbeing. This took place among peers and within pastoral resources, both of which focused on the monosexual categories of gay or straight.

There were clearly limits to this study. While it could be demonstrated that bisexual Christians were adversely affected by the twin stressors of stigmatisation and erasure, it was not possible to definitively link bisexuality to adverse mental health. The causes of poor mental health are manifold; indeed, in this study, a range of reasons led to participants disclosing depressive conditions which were by no means exclusive to sexual minorities. It should also be acknowledged that with qualitative research of this kind, those individuals who have something to say often put themselves forward for interview more readily than those who have reached a place of resolution. There were also cultural differences; I found American participants had a more clearly defined 'coming out' narrative and spoke with greater ease about distressing situations and medical conditions. Whilst this study confirmed that minority stress (Meyer 2003; Meyer and Frost, 2013) exists among bisexual Christians, and that elevated rates of depressive illness are seen among this cohort in line with recent studies on bisexuality, it was not clear-cut from the data that the typical stressors of bisexual erasure and biphobia alone were to account for depression and suicidality. In fact, it would be disingenuous to make such a claim.

Yet, while the reasons for the co-existence of poor mental health and bisexuality cannot be established from this study, it is evident from my interviews that bisexual Christians suffer acute minority stress, owing to their multi-intersectional identity. This was particularly evident, not only in the personal accounts provided by a large number of young American students, but also from several Anglicans in the UK interview cohort. If the current climate prevails, it would seem unlikely that bisexual Christians will achieve any degree of heightened visibility within the more fundamentalist branches of the Church, either side of the Atlantic, where bisexuality is largely overshadowed by gay, lesbian and, increasingly, transgender issues.

However, there is every chance that bisexual Christians may thrive in worship communities that are openly inclusive of existing and emerging sexual identities, where progressive readings of Scripture (or other sacred or seminal texts) are encouraged. A minority of participants demonstrated this to be the case in the UK and USA, from denominations such as the Quakers, The Metropolitan Community Church, Liberty Church (UK), The United Church of Christ and the Unitarian Universalists. Indeed, the latter organisation funded the publication of a 20-page resource entitled *The Bisexuality Curriculum* (Dwinell et al., 2007), aimed at educating congregants about bisexuality within small group workshops. It is interesting that the denomination which does not hold store by the Bible alone (the Unitarian Universalists) and includes other traditions within its body of teaching is the most proactively affirming of bisexual people. The United Church of Christ, as well as publishing Alford-Harkey and Haffner's bisexual pastoral guide *Bisexuality: Making the Invisible Visible in Faith Communities* (2014), also sells a video simply entitled 'Bisexual', featuring interviews with bisexual Christians and an accompanying study resource.

On the whole, my research revealed that clergy were challenged by bisexuality and that bisexual Christians were frustrated and, in some cases, angered by the present situation confronting them in church communities. This frustration and anger sat alongside poor mental health. While progress was tangible in terms of gay and lesbian affirmation, particularly through marriage equality, this appeared to be at the expense of the visibility of individuals attracted to more than one gender. The increased awareness of transgender rights, whilst simultaneously giving expression to some vicious prejudice, nevertheless raised the profile of the trans community too, once more leaving bisexuality as the invisible, invalid, silent partner within the LGBT acronym.

I witnessed ignorance about bisexuality from pastors, as well as accounts of institutionalised biphobia from participants. While heterosexist attitudes and exclusively heterosexual behaviours appear to be on the decline (Laughlin, 2016; IPSOS-MORI, 2018; YouGov, 2015), with increased affirmation in general of LGBT individuals, especially among Christians (Swales and Tayler, 2017), this has not been to the socio-cultural benefit of bisexual people. Those people I interviewed, several of whom were in tears, often found it simply easier and less mentally exhausting to remain in the closet than to publicly disclose their orientation. This was unfortunate, as it became apparent as interviews progressed that a unified bisexual voice might raise the profile and affirmation of bisexual people of faith, much in the manner that the trans community has mobilised itself online. Whilst the bisexual identity is incontestably 'complexly biopsychosocial' (Barker, 2015), complexity is not a reason to back away from self-identifying as bisexual. Should not bisexual Christians, insofar as they feel psychologically able, raise their heads above the parapet and 'take one for the team'?

Reports vary on what percentage of the LGBT population identifies as bisexual. A PEW Report of 2013 revealed that 40% of the LGBT community in the USA identifies as bisexual (Taylor, 2013), while the Williams Institute report of 2011 found that 52% of LGB Americans gave their orientation as bisexual (Gates, 2011). Bisexual people comprise the largest sector of the LGB community (Gates, 2011). Yet they receive by far the least coverage. A YouGov report in the UK in 2015 reported that 49% of 18–24-year-olds in the UK (and 33% in the USA) did not identify as 'exclusively straight'. It does not seem so far-fetched to propose that sometime in the not so distant future being attracted to more than one gender will be the norm. Significantly, this may also be the norm among young people in our worship communities, assuming, of course, that parents are somehow able to entice their children into church buildings in the first place. The 2014 suicide of teenager Lizzie Lowe in Manchester (Slater, 2014), who was struggling to reconcile her Christian faith with same-sex attraction, sent shockwaves around the Anglican community in the UK. Can the Church afford to be silent on the complex issue of human sexuality?

Notes

1 Incidentally, all four were from the UK sample; further analysis of this discrepancy was deemed beyond the scope of this chapter.
2 MIND is a UK-based mental health charity, https://www.mind.org.uk/
3 The 'revolving closet door' refers to the multiple coming-out experiences that bisexual people must endure, due to the perceived ambiguity of their sexual identity.
4 A guide to pastoring bisexual Christians in Europe by Carol Shepherd is forthcoming with Esuberanza Press, Netherlands, 2019 (Shepherd, forthcoming).

References

Alford-Harkey, M. and Haffner, D.W. 2014. *Bisexuality: Making the Invisible Visible in Faith Communities.* Westport: The Religious Institute.

Anderson, E. and McCormack, M. 2016. *The Changing Dynamics of Bisexual Men's Lives Social Research Perspectives.* New York: Springer Publishing.

Barker, M.J. 2015. Depression and/or oppression? Bisexuality and mental health. *Journal of Bisexuality*, 15(3), 369–384.

Blumstein, P.W. and Schwartz, P. 1977. Bisexuality: Some social psychological issues. *Journal of Social Issues*, 33(2), 30–45.

Brennan, D.J., Ross, L.E., Dobinson, C., Veldhuizen, S. and Steele, L.S. 2010. Men's sexual orientation and health in Canada. *Canadian Journal of Public Health/Revue Canadienne de Sante'e Publique*, 101(3), 255–258.

Carr, C.L. 2011. Women's bisexuality as a category in social research, revisited. *Journal of Bisexuality*, 11(4), 550–559.

Charmaz, K. 2006. *Constructing Grounded Theory: A Practical Guide through Qualitative Analysis.* London: Sage

Charron, N.A. 2014. *Bisexual Women in the Christian Faith: Composing with a Complex Identity.* Doctoral thesis, St Paul's University, Ottawa.

Church of England. 1991. *Issues in Human Sexuality.* London: Church House Publishing.

Church of England. 2003. *Some Issues in Human Sexuality.* London: Church House Publishing.

Colledge, L., Hickson, F., Reid, D. and Weatherburn, P. 2015. Poorer mental health in UK bisexual women than lesbians: evidence from the UK 2007 Stonewall Women's Health Survey. *Journal of Public Health*, 37(3), 427–437.

Crenshaw, K. 1990. Mapping the margins: Intersectionality, identity politics, and violence against women of color. *Stanford Law Review*, 43, 1241–1299.

Dwinell, J., Dwinell-Yardley, D., Hamm, A.D., McNeil, S., Morganstern, A.Z. and Schranz, A. 2007. *The Bisexuality Curriculum.* [Online] Available at: http://api.ning.com/files/0PKyB0rYTqrxxWfy5u2J2J6Qthzc4kjHCEsxA5OfqRrjHDHA8DPPi2w-SI5HtesZ2WAWgw4f5KmxGqyoF13y8aiLPxn1ZSK*/TheBisexualityCurriculum.pdf [accessed 28 May 2019].

Eisner, S. 2013. *Bi: Notes for a Bisexual Revolution.* New York: Seal Press.

Flanders, C.E., Dobinson, C. and Logie, C. 2015. "I'm never really my full self": Young bisexual women's perceptions of their mental health. *Journal of Bisexuality*, 15(4), 454–480.

Gates, G.J. 2011. How Many People are Lesbian, Gay, Bisexual and Transgender?Los Angeles: The Williams Institute. [Online]. Available at: https://williamsinstitute.law.ucla.edu/wp-content/uploads/Gates-How-Many-People-LGBT-Apr-2011.pdf [accessed 13 April 2019]

Gibbs, J.J. and Goldbach, J. 2015. Religious conflict, sexual identity, and suicidal behaviors among LGBT young adults. *Archives of Suicide Research*, 19(4), 472–488.

Heyward, C. 1999. *Saving Jesus from Those who Are Right: Rethinking What it Means to Be Christian.* Minneapolis: Fortress Press.

Hutchins, L., and Williams, H.S. 2014. *Sexuality, Religion and the Sacred.* Oxford: Routledge.

IPSOS-MORI. 2018. IPSOS-MORI Research Highlights, July 2018. [Online]. Available at: https://www.ipsos.com/ipsos-mori/en-uk/ipsos-mori-research-highlights-july-2018 [accessed 28 May 2019].

Johnson, S.M. 2008. My revolving closet door. *Journal of Lesbian Studies*, 12(1), 59–67.

Jorm, A.F., Korten, A.E., Rodgers, B., Jacomb, P.A. and Christensen, H. 2002. Sexual orientation and mental health: results from a community survey of young and middle–aged adults. *The British Journal of Psychiatry*, 180(5), 423–427.

Klein, F. 1993. *The Bisexual Option* (2nd edn). New York: Harrington Park Press.

Kolodny, D. ed. 2000. *Blessed Bi Spirit: Bisexual People of Faith*. New York: Bloomsbury Academic.

Laughlin, S. 2016. *Gen Z Goes Beyond Gender Binaries in New Innovation Group Data: J. Walter Thompson Intelligence Report*, 11 March 2016. [Online] Available at https://www.jwtintelligence.com/2016/03/gen-z-goes-beyond-gender-binaries-in-new-innovation-group-data/ [accessed 28 May 2019].

Levy, D.L. and Harr, J. 2018. 'I never felt like there was a place for me': Experiences of bisexual and pansexual individuals with a Christian upbringing. *Journal of Bisexuality*, 18(2), 186–205.

Mental Health America. 2015. *The State of Mental Health in America*. [Online] Available at: http://www.mentalhealthamerica.net/issues/state-mental-health-america [accessed 25 May 2019]

Meyer, I.H. 2003. Prejudice, social stress, and mental health in lesbian, gay and bisexual populations: conceptual issues and research evidence. *Psychological Bulletin*, 129(5), 674–697.

Meyer, I. H., and Frost, D.M. 2013. Minority stress and the health of sexual minorities, in *Handbook of Psychology and Sexual Orientation*, edited by C.J. Patterson and A.R. D'Augelli. New York: Oxford University Press, 252–266.

MIND. 2016. How common are mental health problems? [Online] Available at: https://www.mind.org.uk/information-support/types-of-mental-health-problems/statistics-and-facts-about-mental-health/how-common-are-mental-health-problems/#.XOj1YfZFzIU [accessed 25 May 2019]

Ochs, R. and Rowley, S.E., 2005. *Getting Bi: Voices of Bisexuals around the World*. Boston: Bisexual Resource Center.

Robinson, M. 2014. Bisexual people, in *The Oxford Handbook of Theology, Sexuality, and Gender*, edited by A. Thatcher. Oxford: Oxford University Press, 640–656.

Rohr, R. 2011. *Falling Upward: A Spirituality for the Two Halves of Life*. New York: John Wiley & Sons.

Shepherd, C.A. 2017. *Bisexual Christians and Mental Health: Why the Church Needs to be More Welcoming*. Unpublished doctoral thesis, University of Winchester, UK.

Shepherd, C.A. 2018. *Bisexuality and the Western Christian Church: The Damage of Silence*. London: Palgrave Macmillan

Shepherd, C.A. (forthcoming). *Bi The Way: Pastoring Bisexual Christians in Europe*. Utrecht: Esuberanza Press.

Slater, C. 2014. 'Teenager killed herself in Didsbury park over "misplaced" fears about telling devastated parents she might be gay' [Online]. Available at: https://www.manchestereveningnews.co.uk/news/teenager-found-hanged-after-fears-8299328 [accessed 14 April 2019]

Smith, K.E. 2010. *Towards a Critical Bisexual Theology*. Unpublished doctoral thesis, University of Winchester, UK.

Sommers, J. 2016. *119: My Life as a Bisexual Christian*. London: Darton Longman Todd.

Stuart, E. and Thatcher, A. 1997. *People of Passion: What the Churches Teach About Sex*. London: Mowbray.

Swales, K. and Tayler, E. 2017. *Moral Issues: Sex, Identity and Euthanasia. British Social Attitudes, 34*. [Online] Available at: http://bsa.natcen.ac.uk/media/39147/bsa34_moral_issues_final.pdf [accessed 28 May 2019]

Taylor, P. 2013. *A Survey of LGBT Americans: Attitudes, Experiences and Values in Changing Times*. Washington DC: Pew Research Center.

Thatcher, A. 1993. *Liberating Sex: A Christian Sexual Theology*. London: SPCK.

Thatcher, A. 2014. *The Oxford Handbook of Theology, Sexuality, and Gender*. Oxford: Oxford University Press.

Toft, A. 2009. Bisexual Christians: The life stories of a marginalized community, in *Contemporary Christianity and LGBT Sexualities*, edited by S. Hunt. Aldershot: Ashgate, 67–85.

Toft, A., 2014. Re-imagining bisexuality and Christianity: The negotiation of Christianity in the lives of bisexual women and men. *Sexualities*, 17(5–6), 546–564.

United Church of Christ. n.d. *A Position of Faith Bisexual Study Guide*. [Online]. Available at: http://d3n8a8pro7vhmx.cloudfront.net/unitedchurchofchrist/legacy_url/5978/A-Position-of-Faith-Bisexual-study-guide-COLOR.pdf?1418430242 [accessed 14 April 2019]

Venn-Brown, A. 2018. *Gay Lifestyle: What is the Gay Lifestyle*? [Online]. Available at: http://www.abbi.org.au/2017/09/gay-lifestyle/ [accessed 3 April 2019]

YouGov. 2015. *One in Two Young People Say They Are Not 100% Heterosexual*. [Online]. Available at: https://yougov.co.uk/topics/lifestyle/articles-reports/2015/08/16/half-young-not-heterosexual [accessed 13 April 2019]

11 Bisexual wellbeing

Impacts of current religion and childhood experiences

Margaret Robinson and Shayan Asadi

Introduction

Mental health is a broad concept, defined by the World Health Organization as 'a state of well-being in which the individual realizes his or her own abilities, can cope with the normal stresses of life, can work productively and fruitfully, and is able to make a contribution to his or her community' (2001: 1). The wellbeing of bisexual people is likewise shaped by their ability to navigate the stress they encounter in their daily lives and by their ability to participate in the communities to which they belong. Research has been mixed on whether religious affiliation promotes wellness. While religiosity among the general public is usually associated with low scores on measures of psychological distress (Hackney and Sanders, 2003), religiosity among sexual minority people had been associated with mixed or negative mental health conditions (Gibbs and Goldbach, 2015; Lassiter et al., 2017; Shilo, Yossef, and Savaya, 2016). However, the cultural context is changing rapidly as mainstream religious groups become more accepting of sexual diversity (Sherkat, 2016), opening the possibility that a welcoming religious environment may offer support and stability for sexual minority people.

While social acceptance of sexual minority people has increased in Canada, the United States and the United Kingdom (Kohut et al., 2013; Rayside, 2008), sexual minority people still report high rates of harassment and violence in comparison to their straight peers (Balsam, Rothblum, and Beauchaine, 2005; Berrill, 1990; Herek, Cogan, and Gillis, 2002; Katz-Wise and Hyde, 2012; Silverschanz et al., 2008). Psychiatric epidemiologist Ilan H. Meyer (2003) suggests that prejudice against sexual minority people, expressed through violence, harassment or social exclusion, can result in mental health problems such as anxiety, depression and suicidality. Meyer's Minority Stress Theory connects discrimination, hypervigilance (heightened sensitivity to threat) and the internalizing of negative attitudes with the high rates of mental health problems we see in bisexual populations. For example, bisexual people report high levels of psychological distress (Effrig et al., 2014; McAleavey, Castonguay and Locke, 2011) and internalized homophobia (Rosario et al., 2002) compared to their gay and lesbian peers. A study using nationally representative data from the Canadian Community Health Survey of 2003 and 2005 found that bisexual people had worse self-reported metal health compared to heterosexual and gay/lesbian Canadians, and were more likely to have been diagnosed with a mood disorder (e.g. depression) or an anxiety disorder (Tjepkema, 2008). Similar patterns have been observed elsewhere. A study of 64,271 participants from college counselling centres, primarily in the United States, found that bisexual people reported a higher rate of psychological distress compared to heterosexual, gay or lesbian participants (Lefevor, Park, and Pedersen, 2018). To gauge psychological distress, Lefevor, Park, and Pederson (2018) used the Counseling Center Assessment of Psychological Symptoms instrument, which assesses depression, general anxiety, social anxiety, academic distress, eating concerns, hostility and alcohol use. Results on 34 questions are combined to form a score called the Distress Index (Locke et al., 2011). Bisexual participants in that study had a mean Distress Index score of 2.05, indicating more psychological distress than was reported by participants who identified as lesbian (1.90), gay (1.84), or heterosexual (1.69), but less than those identified as questioning (2.10) or queer (2.11). Lefevor, Park, and Pederson (2018) speculate that bisexuals' higher rates of distress are due to their marginalized position in sexual minority communities relative to gay or lesbian people, and because bisexuals may experience biphobia from gay and lesbian peers.

Meyer's Minority Stress Theory (2003) also proposes that negative outcomes can be reduced by positive experiences, such as social support. For example, a study of 63 lesbian, gay and bisexual young adults in Montreal, Canada found that social support predicted lower depression scores and higher self-esteem scores for participants with high levels of internalized homophobia, while support from parents predicted lower depression and anxiety scores for those with low internalized homophobia (Benibgui, 2010). Benibgui's findings suggest that support from family and friends could increase the wellbeing of sexual minority youth. Looking at research on bisexual people specifically, the impact of positive support is mixed. A study conducted by Flanders (2015) found that micro-affirmations (small moments of support from others) were negatively associated with anxiety and stress (meaning participants with more support showed less anxiety and stress), suggesting that support may increase mental wellbeing, even in the face of multiple stressors. However, a subsequent study did not support the hypothesis that positive experiences related to bisexual identity would be associated with increased happiness or with lower depression and suicidality (Salim, Robinson and Flanders, 2019), suggesting that the relationship between negative stressors and positive social support is not clear or simple.

The availability of social support may differ depending on sexual identity, and researchers should be careful about assuming that access to sexual minority community space equates to support for bisexual identity. An Australian study of 4824 adults found that bisexual participants had less support from family, more negative interactions with friends and worse mental health compared to heterosexual, gay or lesbian participants (Jorm et al., 2002). Lack of support may occur at a structural level as well as an individual one. Balsam and Mohr note that while sexual minority organizations may include bisexuals in their name or mandate, they may not support bisexuality fully, suggesting that for bisexuals the benefits of community belonging 'may be outweighed by the potential for marginalization and rejection by gay men and lesbians' (2007: 314).

Failure to support bisexual peers may be related to how bisexuality is perceived by others. A study of 357 residents of the United Kingdom, by Hubbard and de Visser, examined whether beliefs about bisexuality were associated with negative attitudes toward bisexuality. Hubbard and de Visser (2015) examined three beliefs: 1) that bisexuality has a genetic basis (immutability); 2) that bisexuality occurs in all cultures and time periods (universality); and 3) that sexual orientations have clear boundaries (discreetness). The only predictor of a negative attitude to bisexuality was discreetness – the belief that bisexuality could be clearly distinguished from other sexual identity categories, suggesting that biphobia results from the idea that bisexuals are fundamentally different from people of other sexual identities. As Hubbard and de Visser explained, 'biphobia takes the form of othering that involves both the denial of existence and the exaggeration of differences' (2015: 270). When a group experiences high levels of stress that strain their coping resources – as postulated in Meyer's Minority Stress theory – then limiting social support to those perceived as insiders while denying it to those perceived as outsiders may be a coping strategy. Such a strategy may frame bisexuals as outsiders without a legitimate claim on social support. If sexual minority communities are not always supportive spaces for bisexuals then the support that might be obtained in other venues, such as through belonging to a religious community, may be important for maintaining mental health.

Most studies examining the impact of religious affiliation or spirituality on wellness have combined sexual minority people into a single group (e.g. LGB), and this practice has long been critiqued for the way it masks differences between bisexual and gay/lesbian populations on markers of mental wellness (MacDonald, 1983; Miller, André, Ebin and Bessonova, 2007; Rust, 2009). For example, a number of studies in Canada and the United States indicate that bisexuals report higher rates of anxiety and depression compared with their gay and lesbian peers, a difference that is lost if the group is combined into a single population (Bostwick, Boyd, Hughes and McCabe, 2010; Case et al., 2004; Kerr, Santurri and Peters, 2013; King et al., 2008; Koh and Ross, 2006; Steele et al., 2009; Tjepkema, 2008). The differences observed among sexual minority groups has prompted Jorm and colleagues (2002) to suggest that the mental health risk for gay men and lesbians may have been overstated, with results being skewed by combining them with bisexuals. Guidelines for conducting and reporting research involving bisexual participants recommend against amalgamating bisexual people with other sexual orientation groups, enabling differences among groups to be more clearly demonstrated (Barker et al., 2012).

The relative social power of one's faith community may also be a factor shaping how much support an individual can access. Work by Lefevor, Park and Pedersen (2018) found that identifying with a mainstream religious tradition may provide more support than identifying with a less dominant tradition. Those whose religious views and practices are socially normalized get spared the effort of explaining or translating that may be expected of more marginalized traditions. For example, obtaining a holiday at Christmas requires less explaining in spaces where Christianity is mainstream than would obtaining time off for the winter solstice, a holiday for those in Neo-pagan traditions.

However, mainstream traditions such as Christianity rarely address bisexuality and those that do tend to frame sexuality as binary and bisexuality as illegitimate (Robinson, 2009, 2014). The Church of England's House of Bishops, for example, describe bisexuality as 'ambiguous', conflate 'bisexual activity' with being unfaithful to a partner and advocate counselling to help bisexual people 'discover the truth of their personality' as if that truth is not bisexuality (2003: 42). Similarly, Catholic theologians have tended to subsume all same-sex attraction under the umbrella of 'homosexuality' (Robinson, 2009, 2014), describing bisexuals as 'indecisive between love of man and love of woman' (Harvey, 1987: 185), or viewing bisexual identity as an attempt to avoid 'being regarded as homosexual' (Zuanazzi, 1997: 9).

The Church of England's House of Bishops notes they do not reject gay and lesbian members who feel called to enter into a 'loving and faithful homophile partnership, in intention lifelong, where mutual self-giving includes the physical expression of their attachment' (Church of England, 1991: 41). However, they discourage bisexuals from pursuing same-sex relationships arguing those 'who are capable' of a relationship with an other-sex partner should pursue such an outlet (Church of England, 2003: 283). The Anglican Bishops seem ambivalent about this policy as they also suggest that a bisexual individual's marriage to an other-sex partner 'may lead to complications at some later date' (Church of England, 2003: 216; citing Thatcher, 1993: 156). Similarly, Catholic scholar John F. Harvey proposed bisexuals ought not to marry 'unless the apparent bisexual has given up his homosexual friends and milieu *definitively*' (Harvey, 1987: 185; emphasis in original).

In framing sexuality as binary and equating bisexuality with indecision, confusion or promiscuity, the Church of England and theologians within the Catholic Church reflect stereotypes within society more broadly. In an experimental study, 261 heterosexual residents of the United States recruited through Amazon's Mechanical Turk website, were asked to identify stereotypes associated with heterosexual, lesbian, and bisexual women, then to read a description of two people on a date and to answer questions about one of the characters. When that character was identified as bisexual participants evaluated her as more confused, more promiscuous, and more likely to be non-monogamous than when the character was identified as heterosexual or lesbian (Zivony and Saguy, 2018). An earlier study reported similar findings for men, with the bisexual male character being evaluated as more confused and promiscuous than heterosexual or gay characters (Zivony and Lobel, 2014). Participants whose responses indicated less awareness of stereotypes associated with bisexual women were more likely to engage such stereotypes, and Zivony and Saguy (2018) interpret this to mean that stereotypes are not learned directly (e.g. from television or social media), but deduced from general attitudes regarding sexuality. Such stereotypes have surprising longevity. Twenty years earlier a study of 229 heterosexual undergraduates in the United States found that 39% of them agreed that, compared to heterosexuals, 'bisexuals are more likely to have more than one sexual partner at a time', and 'bisexuals are more confused about their sexuality' (Eliason, 1997: 322). Given the longevity and pervasiveness of such stereotypes it is not unexpected to find them evoked in the few instances where mainstream religious organizations have addressed bisexuality.

Bisexuals in mainstream Christian faith communities may be exposed to the same homophobia and heteronormativity as their gay and lesbian peers while also facing issues such as bisexual erasure, biphobia, or monosexism – the privileging of heterosexual and gay/lesbian identity over other sexual orientations (Highleyman, 1995). As a result, bisexuals may experience faith communities as less welcoming than their gay and lesbian peers do. This possibility is supported by Andrew Yip's study of lesbian, gay and bisexual Christians in Great Britain, in which bisexuals were less likely to 'agree' or 'strongly agree' with statements such as 'God hears prayers and answers them', 'God's will is final and there is no questioning of his will', 'Jesus Christ is God made man' and 'Jesus Christ is coming again to judge all people and "rapture" those who are saved' (Yip, 2003: 144). The bisexuals in Yip's study may be more comfortable challenging the tenets of a religious group if that group has already misunderstood or denigrated their bisexual identity. Moreover, possessing a marginalized social identity, even within groups otherwise marked as mainstream, may make it easier to adhere to alternative theological views.

Our study aimed to explore the relationship between bisexual religiosity and health to examine how psychological, social and spiritual factors interact to shape wellness. Understanding this relationship in greater detail is important since religiosity and engagement with religious community has been correlated with positive health outcomes. Greater clarity in this area can help us understand how religious affiliation is associated with robust mental health for some people and diminished mental health for others.

Methodological account

Our analysis drew data from the Risk & Resilience Study of Bisexual Mental Health, a respondent driven sample of 405 bisexuals in Ontario, Canada, collected between 21 December 2011 and 27 November 2012. The online survey was designed by a team of bisexual, pansexual, fluid, queer, two-spirit and ally researchers, and informed and guided by an 11-person community advisory team made up of bisexuals from the province of Ontario. Participants were age 16 and older, living or receiving medical services in the province of Ontario, who were attracted to more than one sex or gender (hereafter, bisexual). The study's broad definition of bisexual reflected the way the term was used in bisexual communities in Ontario at the time. The entire sample met this definition, with 61.6% also naming 'bisexual' as their sexual identity. In addition to bisexual, other common identities reported by participants included 'queer' and 'pansexual'.

Our study measured depression using the Patient Health Questionnaire Depression Scale (PHQ-9) (Kroenke, Spitzer and Williams, 2001), which asked, 'Over the last two weeks, how often have you been bothered by any of the following problems?' and offered nine examples of depressive symptoms such as 'Feeling down, depressed, or hopeless' or 'Feeling tired or having little energy'. Participants entered responses on a four-point Likert scale, which asked the frequency of symptoms from 'not at all' (scored as 0) to 'nearly every day' (scored as 3). Total scores range from 0 to 27, ascending with severity of depressive symptoms. A score higher than 20 indicates major, severe depression. A previous analysis of the Risk and Resilience data determined that the prevalence of severe depression in Ontario's bisexual population was 4.7% (Ross et al., 2014: 1). Since Risk and Resilience only collected data from bisexual people, comparison figures for gay and heterosexual populations are not available. However, a Canadian national survey from 2008 found that 11.4% of bisexual men and 11.1% of gay men reported a diagnosed mood disorder (such as depression) compared to 4.0% of heterosexual men. For women, the rates of diagnosed mood disorder were 25.2% for bisexuals, 11.4% for lesbians and 7.5% for heterosexuals (Tjepkema, 2008: 58). The 2008 study did not distinguish between levels of depression (low, moderate, severe), which may account for the discrepancy in rates.

In the Risk and Resilience study, anxiety was measured using the Overall Anxiety Severity and Impairment Scale (OASIS), which had five questions such as 'In the past week, how often have you felt anxious?' (Norman et al., 2006; Campbell-Sills et al., 2009). Participants indicated how often they experienced symptoms in the past week on a five-point Likert scale ranging from 'no anxiety' (scored as 0) to 'constant anxiety' (scored as 4). Total scores range from 0 to 25, with scores over 8 suggesting an anxiety disorder (Campbell-Sills et al., 2009). A previous analysis of the data by Ross and colleagues (2014: 1) determined that the prevalence of a possible anxiety disorder among bisexuals in Ontario was 30.9%. By comparison, Canadian national data found that 17.7% of bisexual women and 10.1% of bisexual men had a diagnosed anxiety disorder, as did 8.7% of lesbians and 8.5% of gay men, compared to 8.7% of heterosexual women and 3.0% of heterosexual men (Tjepkema, 2008: 58). The lower national anxiety rates may be partially explained by the 24.2% of bisexual women and 26.2% of bisexual men who reported lacking a regular doctor, reducing the likelihood of receiving a diagnosis (Tjepkema, 2008: 57).

The Risk and Resilience study measured social support using the Medical Outcome Study Social Support Survey (MOS-SSS) (Sherbourne and Stewart, 1991), which asked participants whether they could access 19 types of support such as 'someone to help you if you were confined to bed' or 'someone to confide in or talk to about yourself or your problems'. Responses were given on a five-point Likert scale from 'none of the time' (scored as 1) to 'all of the time' (scored as 5). Scores were summed, with higher scores indicating greater social support.

For the current analysis, we prepared the data using a software package called Statistical Package for the Social Sciences, with geographic identifiers and demographic data stripped from the file. The Risk and Resilience data was collected using respondent driven sampling, a complex design that generates individual weights for dependent variables of interest. The sampling frame and design are specified in detail elsewhere (Robinson, Sanches and MacLeod, 2016; Ross et al., 2014). For the current analysis we interpreted the data without weights, as a convenience sample. Full, weighted demographics and prevalence of outcomes are reported by Ross and colleagues, but in general 64.2% of participants identified as women, 27.7% identified as men, 6.6% were genderqueer, 3.2% were two-spirited, 1.7% identified as trans man, and 0.5% identified as trans women. Participants could select more than one gender option. The sample was young and less racialized than Canada as a whole, with 79.4% under age 34 and 85.2% reporting their racial or ethnic identity as White (Ross et al., 2014: 4).

For the current analysis, data were cleaned and exported to R, a statistical computing software (Hornik, 2002). Our analysis focused on spiritual affiliation in childhood and at the time of the survey to explore the relation (if any) with depression (based on PHQ-9 scores), anxiety (based on OASIS scores) and social support (based on MOSS scores).

Results

To assess childhood religious affiliation participants were asked, 'When you were a child, what was the religious or faith practice of your family?' Participants could check multiple options from the following alphabetical list: Aboriginal Spirituality; Buddhism; Christianity; Hinduism; Islam; Jehovah's Witness; Judaism; No religion (e.g. atheism or agnosticism); Paganism or Neo-paganism (e.g. Wiccan); Sikhism; Unitarianism; and Other, please specify. Where participants wrote in a religious affiliation that could be considered to be a subset of a listed category their responses were re-coded; so those reporting 'Catholic', for example, were re-coded as 'Christian'. Current religious affiliation was assessed using the question 'What is your current religious or faith practice? Please check all that apply', and the same list of traditions was offered. Childhood and current religious affiliations are reported in Table 11.1.

The most common childhood religion was Christianity, reported by 67.16% of participants. The second most common response was 'No Religion', reported by 26.91% of participants. In regard to current faith, 56.30% endorsed no religious tradition while 11.36% reported being Christian. Aboriginal spirituality,

Table 11.1 Participants' childhood and current religious affiliation

	*Childhood affiliation**		*Current affiliation**	
Religious identification	Number of valid cases	Percentage of participants	Number of valid cases	Percentage of participants
Aboriginal	12	2.96	16	3.95
Buddhism	10	2.47	37	9.14
Christianity	272	67.16	46	11.36
Hinduism	0	0.00	5	1.23
Islam	5	1.23	0	0.00
Jehovah's Witness	0	0.00	0	0.00
Judaism	36	8.89	18	4.44
No religion	109	26.91	228	56.30
(Neo-) Paganism	10	2.47	56	13.83
Sikhism	1	0.25	0	0.00
Unitarianism	12	2.96	12	2.96
Other	37	9.13	63	15.55
Total	603	124.53*	481	118.76*

* Percentages do not total 100% as participants could select more than one option.

Buddhism, Hinduism and Neo-Paganism gained adherents between childhood and adulthood, but the largest shift was towards 'no religion'.

The degree to which participants' childhood religious tradition was affirming of lesbian, gay, bisexual, trans or queer (LGBTQ) identity or people was assessed by asking, 'How LGBTQ-friendly was the religion or faith tradition in which you were raised?' Response options included: 'Very LGBTQ-friendly' (e.g. visible LGBTQ leaders); 'Quite LGBTQ-friendly' (e.g. welcoming and affirming); 'Indifferent on LGBTQ issues' (e.g. never came up); 'Somewhat LGBTQ-negative' (e.g. love the sinner, hate the sin); 'Very LGBTQ-negative' (e.g. authorities spoke regularly against LGBTQ people); and 'This question does not apply to my upbringing'. The LGBTQ friendliness of participants' past religious tradition is reported in Table 11.2.

As Table 11.2 shows, 41.97% of participants describe their religion of childhood as somewhat or very LGBTQ-negative, and only 9.87% describe their childhood tradition as somewhat or very LGBTQ-friendly.

We assessed the degree of childhood religiosity by asking 'How religious or faith-based was your upbringing?' with response options presented on a scale from 1 to 6, and defined as: 'Not at all'; 'a bit'; 'somewhat'; 'fairly'; 'quite'; and 'extremely'. Results are reported in Table 11.3.

Table 11.2 LGBTQ-friendliness of childhood religious tradition

LGBTQ-friendliness of childhood religion	*Number of valid cases*	*Percentage of participants*
Very LGBTQ-friendly	9	2.22
Quite LGBTQ-friendly	31	7.65
Indifferent on LGBTQ issues	78	19.26
Somewhat LGBTQ-negative	97	23.95
Very LGBTQ-negative	73	18.02
Does not apply to me	84	20.74
Total	372	91.85

Table 11.3 Degree of childhood religiosity

Religious commitment	*Number of valid cases*	*Percentage of participants*
Not at all religious	84	20.74
A bit religious	88	21.73
Somewhat religious	72	17.78
Fairly religious	60	14.81
Quite religious	46	11.36
Extremely religious	24	5.93
Total	374	92.35

Participants reported low childhood religiosity, with 42.47% indicating that their upbringing was 'not at all' or only 'a bit' religious, and 17.29% describing their upbringing as 'quite religious' or 'extremely religious'.

The current relevance of spirituality was assessed by asking, 'Do spiritual values play an important role in your life?', with response options limited to 'yes' or 'no'. Table 11.4 shows the result.

Despite low childhood religiosity and the relatively high rate of participants reporting 'no religion', 51.60% of participants affirmed the importance of spiritual values. To assess current religious involvement we asked, 'Not counting events such as weddings or funerals, during the past 12 months, how often did you participate in religious activities or attend religious services or

Table 11.4 Importance of spiritual values

Do spiritual values play an important role in your life?	*Number of valid cases*	*Percentage of participants*
Yes	209	51.60
No	169	41.73
Total	372	91.85

meetings?' Response options included: 'Once a week or more'; 'Once a month'; '3 or 4 times a year'; 'Once a year'; and 'Not at all'. The relevance of spiritual values and the degree of religious involvement are reported in Table 11.5, with the most common response, 'not at all', reported by 53.09% of participants.

We examined differences in averaged scores for current and past religious characteristics in relation to measures of depression, anxiety and social support. We used two-way, independent-measures analysis of variance tests to analyse each outcome separately, to determine if there was a statistically significant difference between average scores for one group (e.g. religious importance) and another (e.g. religious involvement). Depression and anxiety variables were positively skewed, indicating low rates of chronic depression or severe anxiety. We expected this since participants were drawn from the general bisexual public rather than from people seeking treatment for a mental health problem. Depression and anxiety scores were transformed by a logarithmic function to normalize the distribution of scores and to avoid floor effects (where the majority of participants report lower scores). Our ability to detect differences between any one participant's score and the average score for the group as a whole (variance) is likely to be compromised if the majority of respondents are reporting low scores, making interpretation more challenging. Raw descriptive statistics for mean outcomes are reported in Table 11.6.

There was no statistically significant relation between depression, anxiety or social support scores and participants' perception of past religiosity (LGBTQ-friendliness and degree of religious upbringing) or to current religiosity (religious importance and involvement). We tested for significance at $p < .05$, and detailed results of those tests are discussed below. This suggests that past or current religiosity is not associated with mental wellness for the bisexuals in our sample, and that past or present religious affiliation is not associated with current access to social support.

Results for LGBTQ-friendliness of childhood tradition by childhood religiosity is reported in Table 11.7. A two-way analysis of variance found no interaction between how LGBTQ-friendly and how religious participants

Table 11.5 Current religious involvement

Involvement in religious activities	*Number of valid cases*	*Percentage of participants*
Once a week or more	27	6.67
Once a month	27	6.67
3 or 4 times a year	59	14.57
Once a year	46	11.36
Not at all	215	53.09
Total	374	92.35

Table 11.6 Descriptive statistics of outcome variables

Measures	*M*	*Median*	*SD*
PHQ-9 Depression	7.30	6.00	5.56
OASIS Anxiety	5.93	6.00	3.82
MOS-SSS Social Support	2.44	2.4	0.87

Table 11.7 LGBTQ-friendliness of childhood tradition by childhood religiosity

Characteristics	*Frequencies (n)*			
LGBTQ friendliness of faith	Religiosity of upbringing			Row totals
	None	Some	High	
Not friendly	9	71	90	170
Indifferent	10	50	18	78
Friendly	6	16	18	40
Does not apply	58	23	3	84
Column totals	83	160	129	372

considered their upbringing to be ($F(6, 354) = .80$, $p = .57$) and no main effect for LGBTQ-friendliness ($F(3, 354) = .34$, $p = .79$) or degree of religiosity ($F(2, 354) = .04$, $p = .96$) for depression scores. For anxiety, we likewise found no interaction between friendliness and degree of religiosity ($F(6, 360) = .91$, $p = .49$), and no main effect for friendliness ($F(3, 360) = .66$, $p = .58$) or degree of religiosity ($F(2, 360) = .06$, $p = .94$). The same was observed for social support, with no interaction between friendliness and degree of religiosity ($F(6, 359) = 1.29$, $p = .26$) and no main effect for friendliness ($F(3, 359) = 1.45$, $p = .23$), or degree of religiosity ($F(2, 359) = 1.39$, $p = .26$).

Results for current religious involvement by perceived importance of religion is reported in Table 11.8. A two-way analysis of variance found no interaction between religious involvement and importance $F(2, 361) = 2.66$, $p = .07$, and no main effect for importance $F(1, 361) = .48$, $p = .49$, or involvement $F(2, 361) = .26$, $p = .78$, for depression scores. For anxiety, our analysis found no interaction between religious involvement and importance, $F(2, 360) = 2.13$, $p = .12$ and no main effect for importance, $F(1, 360) = 1.05$, $p = .31$ or involvement, $F(2, 361) = .23$, $p = .80$. For social support, we found no interaction between religious involvement and importance, $F(2, 366) = 2.63$, $p = .07$ and no main effect for importance, $F(1, 366) = .91$, $p = .34$ or involvement, $F(2, 366) = 2.02$, $p = .13$.

Table 11.8 Current religious involvement by perceived importance

Characteristic	*Frequencies (n)*		
Religious involvement	Religious importance		Row totals
	Yes	No	
High involvement	51	3	54
Some involvement	66	39	105
No involvement	87	127	215
Column totals	204	169	374

Concluding remarks

Our analysis found no statistically significant relation between scores on measures of depression, anxiety or social support, and factors such as how LGBTQ-friendly participants rated their religion of upbringing, how LGBTQ-friendly participants rated their current faith, and how religious participants considered themselves to be in childhood and in the present. Religiosity was not a risk or a protective factor for bisexuals in our sample, and religion did not impact the relationship between bisexual identity and mental health. These findings go against conventional wisdom in a number of ways. Based on trends in minority stress literature, one would expect unsupportive religious experiences to expose bisexual people to greater stressors, taxing their coping mechanisms past their limits and resulting in mental health problems. One might also expect an LGBTQ-friendly religious or spiritual affiliation to be a source of support, promoting mental health. Yet neither of these expectations are reflected in our results.

This negative finding is not unique; Barnes and Meyer (2012) did not find support for their hypothesis that engagement with a non-affirming religion would predict increased depressive symptoms and worsened psychological wellbeing. Similarly, a study of sexual minority women found that depression scores did not differ by religiosity or spirituality (Drabble et al., 2018). Our own negative findings suggest that religious affiliation and involvement have no impact (positive or negative) on the mental health and social support of the bisexuals in our sample, or that the relationship could not be measured using the methods we chose. Why would an LGBTQ-negative religious upbringing not negatively impact one's mental health as a bisexual adult? Identity salience, particularly in an increasingly secular country, may be a relevant factor. Additionally, why would an active and involved religious life in the present not result in greater social support for bisexual people? These questions are worthy of further study using more sensitive measures, and qualitative interviews may identify relevant factors that were not included in our analysis.

Although the majority of participants in our study reported being raised Christian (67.16%), few maintained this affiliation as adults (11.36%). A large proportion were not raised in a faith tradition (26.91%) and did not report a current affiliation (56.30%). While our data set was not longitudinal, this increasing secularity may reflect broader social shifts. The number of religiously unaffiliated Canadians grew from 4% in 1971 to 24% in 2011 (Pew Research Center, 2013). A similar pattern is evident in the United States where the number of religiously unaffiliated Americans rose from 16.1% in 2007 to 22.8% in 2014 (Mohler, 2008), and in the United Kingdom where those with no religious affiliation rose from 15% in 2001 to 25% in 2011 (Office for National Statistics, 2013). Increasing secularity has generally been framed as a positive development for sexual minority people. American sociologist Darren E. Sherkat notes that public values of 'secular reasoning' have clashed with conservative religious movements that attempt to limit the rights of sexual minorities, sparking an 'ongoing, public, and heated' struggle (2016: 756). Future studies may wish to explore whether a robust secular, atheist, or anti-theist identity impacts wellness for people who identify as bisexual.

As 41.97% of participants reported their religion of upbringing as unaffirming of LGBTQ people, a lack of religiosity may represent an adaptive shift as bisexuals leave traditions they find unsupportive. If this is the case, increasing secularity among bisexuals may be an effect of gender intersecting with sexuality. Population based research conducted in Canada and the United States indicate that women comprise 62.6% of the bisexual population in Canada (Tjepkema, 2008: 54) and 63.2% of the bisexual population in the United States (Winter, 2012: 6). Given this high percentage of women, religious traditions may be unappealing to bisexuals to the degree that they are perceived as anti-woman. Generations of feminists have exposed mainstream religious misogyny (Daly, 1968, 1973; Manning, 1999; Radford Ruether, 1983; Schussler Fiorenza, 1992; Stanton, 1895; Trible, 1984). Some Christian denominations, for example, do not ordain women, and those that do still have a mostly male decision-making body and a mostly female laity. In addition, Christian moral discourse has focused on issues such as abortion and 'homosexuality' rather than the feminization of poverty, violence against women, institutionalized sexism, sustainable living, consumerism, food justice or the environment (Robinson, 2003, 2009). On many of these issues women may find communities of faith out of step with their concerns. Melissa Wilcox (2002) identified a number of strategies by which sexual and gender minority Christians within the Universal Fellowship of Metropolitan Community Churches reconciled their sexuality with their faith. Some participants in Wilcox's study used a 'biblical buffet' approach where they adopt only those beliefs and practices that resonate with them personally and leave what does not (Wilcox, 2002: 501). Strategies like this require effort that some may judge out of proportion to the comfort afforded by such 'spiritual bricolage'

(Wilcox, 2002: 498) or by the community belonging it enables, which may be deemed less valuable in an increasingly secular world.

While 53.09% of participants in our study had not attended a religious event in the past year, 51.60% considered spiritual values important. Yet given that 41.97% of participants considered their childhood religion to be LGBTQ-negative, bisexuals may feel alienated from communities of faith and may benefit less from such belonging. Sherkat's (2016) analysis of 23 years of nationally representative data from the United States found that bisexual people had the lowest rates of church attendance (2.9% for bisexual men and 3.1% for women) and were less likely than other sexual minority groups to identify with a religious community (Sherkat, 2016: 763). Sherkat's findings echo those of Alex Toft, whose study of 80 bisexual Christians in the United Kingdom found that 70% emphasized the importance of 'personal spiritual exploration' in their religious life over communal worship (2012: 194). Such studies suggest that bisexual people may attempt to obtain the benefits of religious or spiritual belief while reducing stressors associated with belonging to a biphobic religious community.

Work needs to be done to understand how intersecting identities influence the mental health impact of religious belonging or spiritual practices for sexual minority people. Such research should use nuanced measures of religious and spiritual experience and should also include individuals who are still developing a sexual identity or whose sexual identity is not gay, lesbian, or bisexual. As noted above, Lefevor, Park and Pederson (2018) found that the highest distress levels in their study were reported by those identifying as questioning or queer, and evidence indicates that people who identify as 'mostly heterosexual' have similarly elevated rates of mental distress (Ross et al., 2017) Since religious allegiance, doctrine and sexual identity may all change over time longitudinal work is needed to determine how changes in a tradition's LGBTQ-friendliness, long-term exposure to LGBTQ-negative traditions and ending or shifting allegiances might impact on wellbeing for sexual minority people across the lifespan.

Limitations

Since we used the Risk & Resilience data as a convenience sample our findings do not generalize to the entire population of networked bisexuals in Ontario. The statistical methods we used to analyse the data in our study may have limited our findings and our results may have been different had we analysed the data as a networked sample or used a convenience sample of bisexuals from the internet. Given the community-based nature of the original survey, in which measures were selected and questions designed by bisexual researchers in collaboration with a bisexual advisory committee, participant responses may be more accurate than similar data gathered by a source less embedded within bisexual communities.

A multivariate statistical design may be able to test religiosity variables, minority stress and health outcomes more effectively, but this is beyond the scope of our current, exploratory study. Sample averages between and within groups were similar, but elevated given that the majority of participants fell within the 'moderate' range for anxiety symptoms and 'mild' depression symptoms. Given the relative homogeneity of scores between groups, as shown by our analysis of variance, we can understand the depression and anxiety of bisexuals in this sample to be similar across domains of religion. Yet while similar they are also elevated, which is cause for concern. These elevated rates may be attributed to the complex and intersecting marginalization of bisexual people, which exacerbate forms of othering (Ross et al., 2014). Available research shows that poverty, low educational attainment and sexual orientation interact in ways that significantly impact mental health outcomes for bisexuals as well as other sexual and gender minority people (Ross and Khanna, 2018). The complicated othering of bisexual people may not be buffered by social support derived from religious group belonging. Other forms of social support may prove more meaningful for bisexuals and may act as stronger protective factors against minority stressors. Given the rarity with which mainstream religious organizations address bisexuality, it may be that bisexuals simply experience their religious lives as irrelevant to their sexuality.

References

Balsam, K.F., and Mohr, J.J. 2007. Adaptation to sexual orientation stigma: A comparison of bisexual and lesbian/gay adults. *Journal of Counseling Psychology*, 54(3), 306–319.

Balsam, K.F., Rothblum, E.D., and Beauchaine, T.P. 2005. Victimization over the life span: a comparison of lesbian, gay, bisexual, and heterosexual siblings. *Journal of Consulting and Clinical Psychology*, 73(3), 477–487.

Barker, M., Yockney, J., Richards, C., Jones, R., Bowes-Catton, H., and Plowman, T. 2012. Guidelines for researching and writing about bisexuality. *Journal of Bisexuality*, 12(3), 376–392.

Barnes, D.M. and Meyer, I.H. 2012. Religious affiliation, internalized homophobia, and mental health in lesbians, gay men, and bisexuals. *American Journal of Orthopsychiatry*, 82(4), 505–515.

Benibgui, M. 2010. *Mental Health Challenges and Resilience in Lesbian, Gay, and Bisexual Young Adults: Biological and Psychological Internalization of Minority Stress and Victimization*. Unpublished doctoral dissertation, Concordia University, Montreal.

Berrill, K.T., 1990. Anti-gay violence and victimization in the United States: An overview. *Journal of Interpersonal Violence*, 5(3), 274–294.

Bostwick, W.B., Boyd, C.J., Hughes, T.L., and McCabe, S.E. 2010. Dimensions of sexual orientation and the prevalence of mood and anxiety disorders in the United States. *American Journal of Public Health*, 100(3), 468–475.

Campbell-Sills, L., Norman, S.B., Craske, M.G., Sullivan, G., Lang, A.J., Chavira, D.A., Bystritsky, A., Sherbourne, C., Roy-Byrne, P., and Stein, M.B. 2009. Validation of a brief measure of anxiety-related severity and impairment: The Overall Anxiety Severity and Impairment Scale (OASIS). *Journal of Affective Disorders*, 112(1–3), 92–101.

Case, P., Bryn Austin, S., Hunter, D.J., Manson, J.E., Malspeis, S., Willett, W.C., and Spiegelman, D. 2004. Sexual orientation, health risk factors, and physical functioning in the Nurses' Health Study II. *Journal of Women's Health*, 13(9), 1033–1047.

Church of England House of Bishops. 1991. *Issues in Human Sexuality: A Statement by the House of Bishops.* London: Church House Publishing.

Church of England House of Bishops. 2003. *Some Issues in Human Sexuality: A Guide to the Debate.* London: Church House Publishing.

Daly, M. 1968. *The Church and the Second Sex*. New York: Harper & Row.

Daly, M. 1973. *Beyond God the Father: Toward a Philosophy of Women's Liberation*. Boston: Beacon Press.

Drabble, L., Veldhuis, C.B., Riley, B.B., Rostosky, S., and Hughes, T.L. 2018. Relationship of religiosity and spirituality to hazardous drinking, drug use, and depression among sexual minority women. *Journal of Homosexuality*, 65(13), 1734–1757.

Effrig, J.C., Maloch, J.K., McAleavey, A., Locke, B.D., and Bieschke, K.J. 2014. Change in depressive symptoms among treatment-seeking college students who are sexual minorities. *Journal of College Counseling*, 17(3), 271–285.

Eliason, M.J. 1997. The prevalence and nature of biphobia in heterosexual undergraduate students. *Archives of Sexual Behavior*, 26(3), 317–326.

Flanders, C.E. 2015. Bisexual health: A daily diary analysis of stress and anxiety. *Basic and Applied Social Psychology*, 37(6), 319–335.

Gibbs, J.J. and Goldbach, J. 2015. Religious conflict, sexual identity, and suicidal behaviors among LGBT young adults. *Archives of Suicide Research*, 19(4), 472–488.

Hackney, C.H. and Sanders, G.S. 2003. Religiosity and mental health: A meta–analysis of recent studies. *Journal for the Scientific Study of Religion*, 42(1), 43–55.

Harvey, J.F. 1987. *The Homosexual Person: New Thinking in Pastoral Care.* San Francisco: Ignatius Press.

Herek, G.M., Cogan, J.C., and Gillis, J.R. 2002. Victim experiences in hate crimes based on sexual orientation. *Journal of Social Issues*, 58(2), 319–339.

Highleyman, L. 1995. Identities and ideas: Strategies for bisexuals. [Online]. Available at: http://www.black-rose.com/articles-liz/bipol.html [accessed 8 April 2019].

Hornik, K., 2002. The r FAQ. [Online]. Available at: http://www.mlb.co.jp/linux/science//R/doc/manual/R-FAQ.html [accessed 8 April 2019].

Hubbard, K., and de Visser, R.O. 2015. Not just bi the bi: The relationship between essentialist beliefs and attitudes about bisexuality. *Psychology and Sexuality*, 6(3), 258–274.

Jorm, A., Korten, A., Rodgers, B., Jacomb, P., and Christensen, H. 2002. Sexual orientation and mental health: Results from a community survey of young and middle-aged adults. *British Journal of Psychiatry*, 180, 423–427.

Katz-Wise, S.L., and Hyde, J.S. 2012. Victimization experiences of lesbian, gay, and bisexual individuals: A meta-analysis. *Journal of Sex Research*, 49(2–3), 142–167.

Kerr, D.L., Santurri, L., and Peters, P. 2013. A comparison of lesbian, bisexual, and heterosexual college undergraduate women on selected mental health issues. *Journal of American College Health*, 61(4), 185–194.

King, M., Semlyen, J., Tai, S.S., Killaspy, H., Osborn, D., Popelyuk, D., and Nazareth, I. 2008. A systematic review of mental disorder, suicide, and deliberate self harm in lesbian, gay and bisexual people. *BioMed Central Psychiatry*, 8(70), 1–17.

Koh, A.S. and Ross, L.K. 2006. Mental health issues: A comparison of lesbian, bisexual and heterosexual women. *Journal of Homosexuality*, 51(1), 33–57.

Kohut, A., Wike, R., Bell, J., Horowitz, J.M., Simmons, K., Stokes, B., Poushter, J., Ponce, A., Gross, E.M., Barker, C., and Devlin, K. 2013. The Global Divide on Homosexuality. Pew Research Center. [Online]. Available at: http://www.pewglobal.org/2013/06/04/the-global-divide-on-homosexuality/ [accessed 8 April 2019].

Kroenke, K., Spitzer, R.L., and Williams, J.B. 2001. The PHQ-9: validity of a brief depression severity measure. *Journal of General Internal Medicine*, 16(9), 606–613.

Lassiter, J.M., Saleh, L., Grov, C., Starks, T., Ventuneac, A., and Parsons, J.T. 2017. Spirituality and Multiple Dimensions of Religion Are Associated With Mental Health in Gay and Bisexual Men: Results From the One Thousand Strong Cohort. Psychology of Religion and Spirituality. [Advanced online publication] Available at: http://dx.doi.org/10.1037/rel0000146 [accessed 8 April 2019].

Lefevor, G.T., Park, S.Y., and Pedersen, T.R. 2018. Psychological distress among sexual and religious minorities: An examination of power and privilege. *Journal of Gay and Lesbian Mental Health*, 22(2), 90–104.

Locke, B. D., Buzolitz, J.S., Lei, P.W., Boswell, J. F., McAleavey, A.A., Sevig, T.D., and Hayes, J.A. 2011. Development of the Counseling Center Assessment of Psychological Symptoms-62 (CCAPS-62). *Journal of Counseling Psychology*, 58, 97–109.

MacDonald Jr, A.P. 1983. A little bit of lavender goes a long way: A critique of research on sexual orientation. *Journal of Sex Research*, 19, 94–100.

Manning, J. 1999. *Is The Pope Catholic? A Woman Confronts Her Church*. Toronto: Malcolm Lester Books.

McAleavey, A.A., Castonguay, L.G., and Locke, B.D. 2011. Sexual orientation minorities in college counseling: Prevalence, distress, and symptom profiles. *Journal of College Counseling*, 14(2), 127–142.

Meyer, I.H. 2003. Prejudice, social stress and mental health in lesbian, gay, and bisexual populations: Conceptual issues and research evidence. *Psychological Bulletin*, 129(5), 674–697.

Miller, M., André, A., Ebin, J., and Bessonova, L. 2007. *Bisexual Health: An Introduction and Model Practices for HIV/STI Prevention Programming*. Washington, DC: National Gay and Lesbian Taskforce Policy Institute.

Mohler, R.A., 2008. America's changing religious landscape. [Online] Available at: http://www.pewforum.org/2015/05/12/americas-changing-religious-landscape/ [accessed 8 April 2019].

Norman, S.B., Cissell, S.H., Means-Christensen, A.J., and Stein, M.B. 2006. Development and validation of an Overall Anxiety Severity and Impairment Scale (OASIS). *Depression and Anxiety*, 23(4), 245–249.

Office for National Statistics. 2013. Full story: What does the census tell us about religion in 2011? Available at: https://www.ons.gov.uk/peoplepopulationandcommunity/culturalidentity/religion/articles/fullstorywhatdoesthecensustellusaboutreligionin2011/previousReleases [accessed 8 April 2019].

Pew Research Center. 2013. *Canada's Changing Religious Landscape. Religion and Public Life*. [Online] Available at: http://www.pewforum.org/2013/06/27/canadas-changing-religious-landscape/ [accessed 8 April 2019].

Radford Ruether, R. 1983. *Sexism and God-Talk: Toward a Feminist Theology*. Boston: Beacon Press.

Rayside, D.M. 2008. *Queer Inclusions, Continental Divisions: Public Recognition of Sexual Diversity in Canada and the United States*. Toronto: University of Toronto Press.

Robinson, M. 2003. Bisexual women and lesbians: What will keep us in our churches? *Making Waves: An Ecumenical Feminist Journal*, 3(2), 30–32.

Robinson, M., 2009. *Turning Points in Identity and Theology: Bisexual Women Choosing between Monogamous and Polyamorous Relationships.* Unpublished doctoral dissertation, University of St. Michael's College, Toronto.

Robinson, M. 2014. Bisexual people, in *The Oxford Handbook of Theology, Sexuality and Gender*, edited by A. Thatcher. London: Oxford University Press, 640–656.

Robinson, M., Sanches, M., and MacLeod, M.A. 2016. Prevalence and mental health correlates of illegal cannabis use among bisexual women. *Journal of Bisexuality*, 16 (2), 181–202.

Rosario, M., Schrimshaw, E.W., Hunter, J., and Gwadz, M. 2002. Gay-related stress and emotional distress among gay, lesbian and bisexual youths: A longitudinal examination. *Journal of Consulting and Clinical Psychology*, 70(4), 967–975.

Ross, L.E., Bauer, G.R., MacLeod, M.A., Robinson, M., MacKay, J., and Dobinson, C. 2014. Mental Health and Substance Use among Bisexual Youth and Non-youth in Ontario, Canada. *Public Library of Science One*, 9(8). Available at: https://doi.org/10.1371/journal.pone.0101604 [accessed 8 April 2019].

Ross, L.E. and Khanna, A. 2018. *What are the Needs of Lesbian, Gay, Bisexual, Trans, and Queer (LGBTQ+) People that Should be Addressed by Canada's Poverty Reduction Strategy?: A Joint Submission from the Canadian Coalition Against LGBTQ+ Poverty.* Available at: https://lgbtqhealth.ca/projects/docs/prsjointsubmission.pdf [accessed 8 April 2019].

Ross, L.E., Manley, M.H., Goldberg, A.E., Januwalla, A., Williams, K. and Flanders, C.E. 2017. Characterizing non-monosexual women at risk for poor mental health outcomes: A mixed methods study. *Canadian Journal of Public Health*, 108 (3), 296–305.

Rust, P.C.R. 2009. No more lip service: How to really include bisexuals in research on sexuality, in *Handbook of Research with Lesbian, Gay, Bisexual, and Transgender Populations*, edited by W. Meezan and J.I. Martin. York, NY: Taylor & Francis, 100–130.

Salim, S., Robinson, M. and Flanders, C. 2019. Bisexual women's experiences of microaggressions and microaffirmations and their relation to mental health. *Psychology of Sexual Orientation and Gender Diversity*, 6(3), 336–346. http://dx.doi.org/10.1037/sgd0000329.

Schussler Fiorenza, E. 1992. *But She Said: Feminist Practices of Biblical Interpretation*. Boston: Beacon Press.

Sherbourne, C.D. and Stewart, A.L. 1991. The MOS social support survey. *Social Science and Medicine*, 32(6), 705–714.

Sherkat, D.E. 2016. Sexuality and religious commitment revisited: Exploring the religious commitments of sexual minorities, 1991–2014. *Journal for the Scientific Study of Religion*, 55(4), 756–769.

Shilo, G., Yossef, I., and Savaya, R. 2016. Religious coping strategies and mental health among religious Jewish gay and bisexual men. *Archives of Sexual Behavior*, 45(6), 1551–1561.

Silverschanz, P., Cortina, L.M., Konik, J., and Magley, V.J. 2008. Slurs, snubs, and queer jokes: Incidence and impact of heterosexist harassment in academia. *Sex Roles*, 58(3–4), 179–191.

Stanton, E.C. 1895. *The Woman's Bible*. New York: European Publishing Company.

Steele, L.S., Ross, L.E., Dobinson, C., Veldhuizen, S., and Tinmouth, J.M. 2009. Women's sexual orientation and health: Results from a Canadian population-based survey. *Women and Health*, 49(5), 353–367.

Thatcher, A. 1993. *Liberating Sex: A Christian Sexual Theology. London: Society for Promoting Christian Knowledge.* London: SPCK.

Tjepkema, M. 2008. Health care use among gay, lesbian and bisexual Canadians. *Health Reports*, 19(1), 53–64.

Toft, A. 2012. Bisexuality and Christianity: Negotiating disparate identities in church life, in *Ashgate Research Companion to Contemporary Religion and Sexuality*, edited by S.J. Hunt and A.K.T. Yip. Farnham: Ashgate, 189–203.

Trible, P. 1984. *Texts of Terror*. Philadelphia: Fortress Press.

Wilcox, M.M. 2002. When Sheila's a lesbian: Religious individualism among lesbian, gay, bisexual, and transgender Christians. *Sociology of Religion*, 63(4), 497–513.

Winter, C. 2012. *Responding to LGBT Health Disparities. St. Louis, Missouri: Missouri Foundation for Health Promotion.* Available at: http://research.policyarchive.org/96557.pdf [accessed 8 April 2019].

World Health Organization. 2001. *Strengthening Mental Health Promotion (Factsheet No. 220)*. Geneva: World Health Organization.

Yip, A.K.T. 2003. Spirituality and sexuality: An exploration of the religious beliefs of non-heterosexual Christians in Great Britain. *Theology and Sexuality*, 9(1), 137–154.

Zivony, A. and Lobel, T. 2014. The invisible stereotypes of bisexual men. *Archives of Sexual Behavior*, 43(6), 1165–1176.

Zivony, A. and Saguy, T. 2018. Stereotype deduction about bisexual women. *The Journal of Sex Research*, 55(4–5), 666–678.

Zuanazzi, G. 1997. The homosexual condition I: Definition and causal factors. *L'Osservatore Romano*, 17 (23 April), 9.

Index